To Bobbie, thank you for your hospitality. God bless you and to God be the Glory!!!

George R Castillo

Feb. 01

My
Life
Between
The Cross
And
The Bars

by

Reverend George R. Castillo

Retired Federal Bureau Of Prisons

G & M
Publications
Shalimar, Florida
1996

ISBN No. 0-9649916-0-8

DISCLAIMER

The stories in this book are true. I have used actual names, but in some instances I have chosen to alter names to protect the individuals' privacy.

Second Printing

JACKET ART AND DESIGN
Robert and Brian Stegner

CONTENTS

DEDICATION

I dedicate this book to the four most important women in my life and to my late brother, Esteban Jimmy Castillo, who gave me the wherewithal to start a new life in America.

My loving mother..................Tolentina N. Castillo
My helpful mother-in-law.....Susan A. Jermain
My faithful helpmate............Muriel J. Castillo
My beloved daughter...........Marcelle A. Castillo
My committed brother..........Esteban Jimmy Castillo

ACKNOWLEDGEMENT

My heartfelt thanks go to my wonderful family for their understanding, support, and abiding love, which gave me the strength and support to do what was mine to do. I also thank all those other wonderful people who helped me. Special thanks go to Daniel J. Bayse, Executive Director of Prison Family Foundation and author of the best-selling book, "FREE AS AN EAGLE," for being my editor; Stanley Berg of Shalimar, Florida, for being such a meticulous proofreader; the artist Robert Stegner and his brother, Brian Stegner, who designed the book jacket; and to Cheryl Bliss, Ph.D. for her proficient computer skills. Their devotion, hours of labor, encouragement, and belief in me helped make this book a reality. I am eternally grateful to them. To God be the Glory!

Author's Note:

Women are very important in our lives, and I respect their contributions and do not intend to diminish their importance by writing only about male inmates and male Chaplains with whom I served. My 20 years of experience have been exclusively in male institutions. However, I recognize that female prisoners have had experiences similar to those of their male counterparts. When I began with the Bureau of Prisons in 1973, the first female Chaplain had not yet been hired. I am delighted that female Chaplains are now an integral part of the team.

PREFACE

MY LIFE BETWEEN THE CROSS AND THE BARS shows God's power to use people for His service and to bring about positive changes in their lives regardless of their humble or high circumstances.

My story begins in Belize where, as a young child, I decided to become a minister. Although school held no fascination for me, my kind mother encouraged me to go to school by saying, "George, if you don't go to school, you won't become a minister." That was enough motivation for me to grab my hat and catch up with my siblings and try to outrun them to the school door.

The road to becoming the second black chaplain for the U.S. Bureau of Prisons was fraught with hardship, tears, frustration, happiness and, finally, success. I tell about the lives that I touched, and the prisoners who touched mine in meaningful and life-changing ways. This book provides insight as to how chaplains work within the prison system.

It sheds light on the joys and disappointments experienced by prisoners during their incarceration and by their family members outside the walls. But it also shows God's power to "free" many inmates to become happy, productive, religious, worshippers within the confines of prison. God's power changed their lives so that many are now working in His service and helping others.

Readers will share my experiences as I tried to do God's will for "the least of these, my brethren...Inasmuch as you have done it to one of the least of these my brethren, you have done it to Me." Matthew 25:40.

FOREWORD

The appalling statistics of offenders who repeat after spending time in our country's prisons have raised many questions. Is prison a real deterrent? Does the individual come out a better person or a better trained criminal?

The job of the prison chaplain includes the task of motivating the prisoners toward a change of life style. But the chaplain very often is faced with an overwhelming fact — the ratio of prisoners to chaplains can range from 200-to-1 to as high as 1000-or more-to-1! How can you possibly have a one-on-one relationship that is meaningful with 500 to 1000 individuals?

My friend, George Castillo, has devoted his life to this seemingly impossible struggle. He relates for us the ups and downs of this work — and makes us wonder — are we placing our priorities in the right place. We spend millions on prisons and guns and walls and bars — but very little on trying to change a man's heart. George has found a way, but he is only one among thousands of prisoners. He has been very successful in using the volunteer as one way to multiply himself and he has demonstrated over his many years of service that the key to it all is the practice of "agape" love toward hurting souls. The simple but all-powerful word of the Gospel message works even behind the walls. George has proved it.

This account from one of God's servants, who works behind the walls and bars to reach out to the lonely and broken souls, will remind you again of the power of the Lord. It will remind you of the truth that He accepts us unconditionally right where we are in our life's experience. And one of the most heartwarming revelations is that He uses His servants, like George Castillo, to bring about absolutely miraculous changes in the lives of men.

Stanley J. Jarrett

Stanley J. Jarrett
Area Director
Prison Fellowship USA

INTRODUCTION

It was never my idea to write a book, especially about my life in the Federal Bureau of Prisons. However, sometimes life-threatening events motivate people into action. I am no exception. Mine came on August 19, 1983, after driving our daughter Marcelle to the University of South Florida. Returning home, on Interstate 75 North, Muriel came upon a huge piece of tire, maneuvered to avoid it, and lost control. Our car swerved, stopped, then straddled across the center line. Muriel and I faced impending death. Shaken, I began to wonder if part of the reason that I was spared was that I had a unique story to tell about how God changed this immigrant, labeled "untrainable" by authorities, and gave him the ability to minister to the outcasts of society and the strength to face the trials along the way.

I thought about the six years I served in parish ministry and the ten as a Chaplain and said, *Lord, I have been in full-time service for you. What else can I do for You and my fellowmen?* The answer to my question came less than 24 hours later when inmate Lloyd Williams, a middle-aged former Pastor of Macedonia Baptist Church in New Orleans, walked into my office. The Reverend Williams was active in the Christian community at Eglin Federal Prison Camp and rarely missed a sermon. He reminded me of a sermon that I had recently preached about Jonah being in the belly of the whale and how I, like Jonah, had originally refused the call to the Chaplaincy. After we had talked awhile, he added, "Chaplain, you have such a peculiar and interesting background and so much to offer and say, why don't you write a book?"

In prison, distractions are a way of life and this day was no different as the shrill ring of my telephone brought me back to reality. "Chaplain, this is Control Center. There's an inmate's wife with five children here. We can't do anything with her. Will you please come and talk to her?"

"I'll be right there," I responded, wondering what I was going to face. As I reached the Control Center, a distraught, unkempt woman, carrying one child and with another walking and tugging at her skirt, looked at me as if I were an alien from outer space. I introduced myself. She shouted at me, "But you're black!" The staff member, who overheard, blushed. Years of prejudicial treatment had taught me how to overcome, and her statement amused rather than angered me.

"How can I help you?" I asked. Still staring, she introduced herself as inmate Robert Smith's wife. It was obvious that she was emotionally disturbed as she shouted to her three playing children and started following me to the officers' lounge. Starting from the time we left Control Center and throughout the interview, she jumped from one topic to another without giving me a chance to answer her rapidly fired questions. Finally I was able to ask, "Mrs. Smith, why do you want to see me?"

"Chaplain, as you know my husband is in this prison, and I want to be with him tonight just like other wives are going to be with their husbands making out in the woods. It's my turn to get some relief. Can you help me?"

"Mrs. Smith, I'm not aware of the information you're giving me. Inmates are not meeting with their wives tonight or at any time except when they go home on furlough. I can't help you. What you heard is not true. Inmates are not meeting their wives at night in the woods."

"As a man of God, you were my last hope since the Bible tells ministers to keep families together. But it seems you're not a man of God. Will you tell my husband that I'll be in the woods tonight?"

"Mrs. Smith, I'm sorry. I won't give your husband your message."

"What kind of Chaplain are you? Aren't you here to help people?"

"Yes, I am," I replied, "but I'm not here to get anyone in trouble. I suggest that you don't go into the woods, Mrs. Smith, but stay at home."

Angrily, she glared at me and screamed: "Chaplain, it seems that you are not listening to me. I have to go now." She grabbed her children, flung open the door and stomped out, shouting: "I am going to write my Senator about you."

Later, a very embarrassed inmate Smith visited my office. "I'm sorry," he said. "I heard about my wife's wild outburst. Please excuse her. She's emotionally ill. If she doesn't take her medicine, she's liable to say or do anything."

"It has been rough, hasn't it?" He nodded in the affirmative as tears filled his eyes. Expressing my concern for his family, I inquired about the children's welfare when his wife was not on medication. Smith told about his wife's years of mental illness and how lucky he was that his sister-in-law checks on them regularly. A few days later, as I greeted the visitors, Mrs. Smith looked at me as if she had never seen me before.

Lloyd's words rang in my head. I do have some stories to tell about my years as prison Chaplain. As I pondered whether I should put my life story in print, another incident happened.

My concentration during a counseling session was suddenly disturbed by someone pounding on my door. Startled, and somewhat annoyed because the DO NOT DISTURB SIGN was up, I opened the door to hear a frantic inmate say, "Chaplain, you have to come immediately. Jim and John Copley are at it again. The father is asking for a thick belt to whip his son."

I dismissed the counselee and hurried toward the loud voices at the end of the Chapel. Before I could say a word, red-faced Jim Copley exclaimed, "My son doesn't believe the Bible because he won't listen to me. The Bible says to honor your father and mother. Am I right, Chaplain?"

Before I could answer, John shouted at his father, "I'm not going to listen to you. Listening to you got me here. I'm going to use my common sense which God gave me." Saying a prayer, I stepped between them and invited them into my office so we could talk privately. While I held them apart, the father screamed: "I'm not going, Chaplain, except if you have a strap in your office for me to beat the crap out of him." Obviously relieved that I was there, John said, "Chaplain, I'll go with you. My father is crazy." Some of those listening on the sidelines asked the senior Copley to join them while John walked with me to my office.

After about 40 minutes of reality therapy, I was able to get through to John and calm him down. Thanking me, he shook his head and said, "Chaplain, I came to the realization that as long as I'm here, I'll have to keep away from my father. I can respect him, but only from a distance." It worked, and the distance kept the feuding Copleys from exploding.

Chapter 1

My Beginnings

"Before I formed you in the womb I knew you,
and before you were born I
consecrated you." (Jeremiah 1:5)

The fifth of seven children, I was born to Philip and Tolentina (nee Velasquez) Castillo, on Sunday, February 28, 1931, in Dangriga, British Honduras, now Belize. My mother was Methodist and my father Roman Catholic. I followed Ernesta, Jimmy, Roberto, and Simeona. The other two children, Alexandrina and Charles, came later. All of us were baptized in the Roman Catholic Church. Growing up, five attended the Methodist school; Simeona and I attended Roman Catholic school.

From the age of five I can remember telling my mother that someday I was going to be a minister. Every time I didn't want to go to school she would remind me in Garifuna, the native tongue of our Carib Indian people, "George, you will never become a minister if you don't go to school." Those words always sent me scurrying to catch up with the other children. Once I got to school, I was happy. In fact, my early childhood years were happy ones. I vividly remember my siblings, neighbors, and me jumping rope, playing soccer and cricket, and enjoying tops and toys we made ourselves.

I didn't realize that we were poor, although I remember eating bread made with only flour and water. In good times, mother substituted coconut milk for water. We didn't see much of father. His time was spent fishing, stevedoring, cutting mahogany, farming, and doing any other honest work he could find to keep food on the table for his family. Father was very loving. I still remember the day he saved me from one of mother's spankings by quickly handing me five cents and sending me to the store to get him some tobacco. In gratitude, I ran as fast as I could. I always felt proud whenever I sat in church with him, and even more so when he passed the long-handled collection container.

Tolentina N. Castillo
1902 — 1957

My mother, 1955

Unfortunately, he died when I was seven. His funeral is vague in my memory. But I recall the loud crying and my younger siblings and I being passed over his casket. This ancient Carib custom still stands to this day.

My father's death left my 36-year old mother to rear seven children without money. Ernesta, the oldest child, was 16 and Charles, the youngest, eight months old. Added to her pain was the refusal of Father Marin, a Carib Roman Catholic Priest, to pray for my father and give him last rites because he had married a Methodist and didn't send all of us to Catholic schools.

Even though the Catholic church did, God did not abandon us. His messenger was a caring and sympathetic British Methodist Minister, the Reverend Arthur W. Saunders, who gave my father a hero's funeral. The community knew that my father's death was attributed in part to his heroism in fighting a fire at the local administration building, which housed the post office, the District Commissioner's office, and our only telephones in town. Shortly after the fire, my father was hospitalized and died of pneumonia.

Because of my father's role in fighting the fire, the Reverend Saunders used his influence to help my 14-year-old brother Jimmy secure a job at the post office for $1.00 a week. Jimmy was a bright student and would have liked to continue his education, but knowing our dire circumstances he gladly accepted the challenge to be the man of the family. Simeona and I transferred to the Methodist school, and the whole family attended the Methodist Church.

Our survival depended on the charity of relatives and friends who were as poor as we. Welfare and public assistance were unheard of in those days. I remember Mother telling us, "I shed many painful tears when I looked at my children and knew there was no food to feed you. It was worse at night looking at your innocent sleeping faces, knowing that you went to bed hungry."

My family was a close one and began pooling its resources to help us survive. Our aunt, Ignacia Velasquez-Rivas, moved in and began baking bread for us to sell door-to-door as soon as we returned home from school. One day, my Uncle Luther Velasquez and his wife Pat arrived from Punta Gorda, British Honduras. Without my knowledge, he told mother, "Pat and I know you're having a rough time. We don't have any money to help you. But if we take one of your children that will be one mouth less to feed. Why don't you give us George? We'll share what we have with him." The following morning, after tearfully saying goodbye, and clutching a small brown bag which held all of my belongings, I sailed to a more difficult life.

Uncle Luther was a public works employee who cleaned the streets. I soon learned the truth of his motto: "You sweat before you eat." Each morning at 4:00 a.m., I worked beside him. After work, I hastily gobbled tea, johnnycake, and a piece of fried fish; then I ran as fast as my skinny legs would take me to beat the 9:00 a.m. late school bell.

Hard work became a way of life. After school, I worked with my maternal grandfather in his cabinet shop. If there wasn't enough work in the shop, I used the machete to chop overgrown weeds in our large yard or around the shop. Nighttime was reserved for homework under a kerosene lamp. My uncle was a strict disciplinarian who put work before play; therefore, my only play time was during recess at school. Occasionally, Mr. Saunders came to Punta Gorda and always did his best to help me overcome my increasing loneliness for my mother, friends, and my siblings.

In 1944, when I was 13 years old, I asked Uncle Luther to let me go back home. My wish came true at the end of the school year. I was elated to be home again even though it meant occasionally walking three miles one way to the farm and gathering plantains, coconuts, bananas, coco, or whatever was in season. When I didn't go to the farm, my siblings and I walked about a half-mile to the Stann Creek River, filled our buckets with water and carried them on our heads to fill the 55-gallon drums at the house. Life in Dangriga was better for me than it was five years earlier because Jimmy and Roberto had signed labor contracts with the United States Government. Faithfully, they sent money home every two weeks and mother no longer had to wonder where the next meal was coming from.

As I grew physically and socially, my spiritual growth increased also. The Reverend Donald Taylor, an educated Jamaican minister who spoke the King's English with a deep voice, listened to my dreams of becoming a minister. He even allowed me to assist him and conduct prayer meetings under his supervision.

"Son," he would say, "Ministry is a full-time responsibility and you never know when you are needed to assist those in need. But the joys of preaching, teaching, serving, and baptizing are some of the rewards of being a servant of God."

"Do you think I will be able to do that?"

"Of course, George, you are kind, caring and empathetic. People find it easy to talk with you. When you get the proper training, one day you will be a minister, and a good one too."

Pastor Taylor's encouragement fueled my desires to study diligently, and I became a serious religious studies student at school.

Even though I was at the mischievous age, it was hard to go too far because adults in our community were our "parents." Besides, our school teachers were also our Sunday School teachers. Consequently, we were in their presence six days a week, and they became an extension of our family who meted out punishment just as our parents did. Despite my teachers' strict discipline, I still remember their kindness, concern, influence, and interest in me.

I was fortunate that one of my "misdeeds" did not reach my mother. Although I was a teenager, it wouldn't have made any difference to her strap. During a dull part of the Reverend A. C. Alexander's sermon, I rolled a piece of paper into the likeness of a cigarette and put it into my sleeping friend's mouth. The minister noticed my antic and spread his lips into a restrained smile. After service, he sternly admonished me. "George, don't you ever do that again." I didn't.

Because school and church were very influential in my life, I wanted to become an accredited teacher, but there was no high school in my home town. Since my family couldn't afford to send me to the capital, Belize City, I stayed in school two years beyond Standard VI (8th grade) to study for the Pupil-Teachers Exam. But I didn't know how to study and failed both times.

Discouraged, I began working at the Agricultural Station as a laborer. While laboring in temperatures over 100 degrees, I talked with God: *"Lord it doesn't seem as if I'll ever get a chance to preach Your Word."* Even though my situation seemed hopeless, deep down I knew that *WITH GOD ALL THINGS ARE POSSIBLE.*

My biweekly wage for an eight-hour day, 5 1/2 days a week, was $6.60 cents. Generally, I gave mother $6.00. My pocket change paid for the Saturday night movie, ice cream, and church offering the following day. When the foreman threatened to lower our wages by changing to piecework, I organized the laborers and convinced them to strike. "Fellows, we have a serious problem. Our wages will be cut. We're going to have to stick together and refuse the piecework proposal." My suggestion met with resistance from Peter. "Man, you know a half loaf is better than none. If we protest, we might get fired."

"Peter, you always complain about our low wages. What are you going to do when you earn less?" I asked, annoyed with him. "Besides they can't fire all of us because they know we're good workers."

It worked. The piecework proposal was dropped and my followers went back to work. I was fired!

Two days later, I was working for the Sharp Citrus Company for $1.35 a day, which enabled me to buy a bicycle. Three months later, when the citrus was harvested, I was laid off, only to be immediately hired by the Public Works Department as a mechanic/laborer at twenty-six cents an hour. My supervisor, the Chief Mechanic "Uncle" Gus, soon complimented me for being a good, willing worker and made me his right-hand man in the garage.

Yet the yearning for the ministry kept nagging me. At one of our Methodist Men's meetings, Mr. T. V. Ramos, the men's leader and founder of Carib Settlement Day, said, "...Brother Castillo, don't give up. You'll occupy that mission house someday," pointing to the Minister's residence. His words encouraged me, but I realized that getting the needed education would require a move to the States. I, therefore, asked my brother Jimmy and his wife Iris who lived in Brooklyn, New York, to sponsor me. While waiting for my papers, I became ambivalent about leaving my family, friends, and my 11-month love child, Erick Anthony. But reality overtook doubt and emotions as I flew on July 31, 1952, from Belize, via New Orleans, to Brooklyn, New York.

The following day I reached my new home in Brooklyn. The cultural change was shocking!

I was mystified by everything around me: the tall buildings, heavy traffic, people rushing, subways, and electricity. When I saw someone touch a switch and the entire room instantly brightened, I thought of the kerosene lamps and candles I used at home. I had never used a telephone, radio, television, or kitchen appliance and wondered if I would ever be able to master them.

Luckily, employment was easy to find. Within a week I was working at the White Tower Restaurant and began my "Americanization." Even though I had never seen a hamburger before, I was soon cooking them by the dozens and handling the cash register. I quickly became the company joke after being caught by fellow employees putting my tips in the cash register. I couldn't believe that people would give their money away after paying for their food.

About six weeks after my arrival, I enrolled in Girls High School evening classes. Things went well until Christmas. Then I became depressed thinking about the Garifuna folklore, masquerade, Johnconnue and drums. Santa Claus didn't do it for me. Although food was plentiful, I lost my appetite thinking about the struggles people back home were going through. Guilt set in. Physically, I was in Brooklyn; mentally, in Dangriga, Belize.

Airman Castillo, You Are Untrainable!

As a legal alien, I was eligible for the draft. I also discovered that serving my new country would make me eligible for the G.I. Bill, and pay for my education to become a minister. I didn't want to be drafted; therefore, I enlisted in the Air Force, and on February 5, 1953, I became Airman Basic (A/B) George R. Castillo, AF 12424255. I was happy to be in the Air Force and proud to allot $51.00 of my $76.00 monthly pay to my mother.

My thrill was short-lived. During the two months of basic training, I took several aptitude tests. These tests were different from anything I experienced before. I felt I had done well and couldn't believe it when the sergeant looked at me and said, "You're untrainable."

I thought he was joking and I laughed. In a gruff voice he called me to attention. The stern look in his green eyes told me that he was dead serious. Venom was in his voice as he shouted, "What are you laughing at, stupid? Is it because you're dumb? Or is it because you can't learn? Wipe that stupid smile off your face."

Confused, I said, "No Sir!"

Being called "untrainable" was very discouraging and

depressing. I left Sampson Air Force Base despondent. I knew l wasn't dumb or stupid, or was I? I thought about my failing the first-year Pupil-Teachers Exams. Then I reminded myself that my grades were good at Girls High evening school. The memory of the folks back home saying, "George, you'll go far. You're a smart boy," flooded my mind. I wanted to believe them. But now those in authority have "proof" that I am "untrainable." Doubts, fear, and ambivalence set in. I was totally confused.

However, I did not let the label "untrainable" stop me. I continued to do my best and soon was promoted to Airman Third Class. I was the first in my group to have new stripes on his uniform. The word got around that I could sew. Airmen sought me out saying, "George, I'll give you a buck to sew my chevrons."

I made $20.00 that weekend and probably could have made more if I hadn't been threatened by a disgruntled customer who said he was going to turn me in to the IRS for making money without paying taxes. What a dilemma! I needed the money, but didn't want to get into trouble. Frightened, I quit sewing.

Two days later, three other classmates and I left for Mitchell Air Force Base, Hempstead, New York. I began making extra money again. Any time I was off-duty I took over another airman's KP duty. An airman said, "Buddy, I'll pay you $12.00 to do KP for me." My new American bargaining skill earned me $20.00 for his duty.

After I worked for a short while in supply, Mr. Joe Rudden, the civilian supply supervisor, said, "George, you're doing a good job. You can work weekends by yourself when the Reservists are training."

I began to realize that labels are frequently wrong. Maybe I wasn't "untrainable" after all. With this new confidence, I talked with Lieutenant Hefley. "Sir, I feel that I can be a good aircraft mechanic if given the chance. Will you consider me?"

"Airman Castillo, come back tomorrow after I've had a chance to review your records. Then I'll be able to discuss it with you more fully." "Yippie," is what I wanted to shout, but instead I said calmly, "Thank you, Sir."

On my return, Lt. Hefley told me the steps necessary to become an aircraft mechanic. He added, "It will be necessary to take the aptitude tests again because of your low scores at Basic Training." Needless to say I wasn't too eager to retake the tests.

Airman George R. Castillo
1953

But I did not let my fears stop me, and my old self-confidence and the "I can do it" attitude prevailed. A few days later, with prayerful thoughts, I stepped into the testing room. My self-esteem rose when I passed the aptitude tests with good scores.

This gave me the confidence to visit the Education Officer and request assistance in getting my high school diploma. He scheduled me to take the GED test. This time I wasn't as successful because my overall average was 35, but I needed a 45 average to earn a diploma from my home state, New York. The Education Officer encouraged me to enroll in some high school classes, then try again. "George, with a little higher score you could earn a high school diploma." I left his office on cloud nine thinking, *with a little work I could be qualified to attend COLLEGE, "Wow!" This is a long way from "Untrainable!"*

One afternoon I was told to report to the First Sergeant in the Orderly Room. "What for?" I asked. Usually when one saw the "First Shirt," he was in trouble. To make my apprehension worse, the First Sergeant wasn't in and I had to see the Adjutant. Nervously, I walked into the Adjutant's office and saluted, "Airman Third Class Castillo, George R., reporting as ordered, Sir."

He encouraged me to talk about myself, but I knew that wasn't the reason why I was there. Finally, he retrieved a folder from his desk, opened it and went over my aptitude test scores with me. "Airman Castillo, you aced the test. How did you do it?"

"Sir, I needed to prove to myself that I could learn."

"You did that. You can go to airplane mechanic school in December."

"Sir, can I go into administration"?

"No. The Air Force needs more mechanics than administrators."

"I'll do my best. Thank you." My broad smile conveyed my happiness. Maybe I can make it in America after all!

Citizenship and Prejudice

Being in the military had other advantages. It made it possible for me to become a citizen in a shorter time. As soon as I became eligible, I filed my application, and I became a United States citizen on October 26, 1953. But being a citizen didn't protect me from the uglier side of America.

On my way to Texas to attend Aircraft Mechanic school, I took a Trailways bus at New York's Port Authority building for $33.00. This not only saved me money but also gave me the opportunity to see my new country. I sat in seat #5, read for a while, looked at the unending glitter of the lights, and finally dozed. The farther I got from my starting point, the dictates of segregation made me move farther back in the bus.

The bus made several short stops, until finally we took a long break in Jackson, Mississippi. I innocently followed the other passengers to the terminal, not knowing there were separate sections for "colored" and "whites." I went to the white section. It was a cruel awakening. Immediately a white man shouted at me, "Nigger, you don't belong here. You belong over there," pointing to where I must go. I went with my stomach churning and my blood boiling.

While resuming my journey to Texas, a young white airman boarded and sat beside me. Wearing the same uniform, we immediately exchanged information about where we were coming from, where we were going, how long we were in the service, and where we took our basic training. As we were talking, the bus driver entered the bus and looked at his passengers. I immediately saw his anger as he walked to where I was sitting and said brusquely, "Boy, get to the back of the bus." Frightened, I quickly complied. The fellow airman tried to intercede on my behalf and told the driver that the way I was being treated was not right. The driver's reply to the white airman was just as blunt: "If you don't like it, you can get the hell off my bus!"

The airman's face flushed as he turned to the window.

During the last eight hours' ride to Wichita Falls, even though there were empty seats, I was forced to stand along with several other "colored folks." After riding five days, I was tired and my aching feet made me feel worse. As I looked around the rear of the bus, I saw the fatigue and helplessness on the other black faces. I closed my eyes and silently prayed, *"God, this is not right. I hope I can help change this one day."* My prayer for my new country, my America, was that the will of a just God would some day prevail.

In Dangriga, I had heard about United States' segregation from Belizean laborers who worked in the States and the Canal Zone. I thought I was prepared for racism, but nothing prepared me for the negative emotions aroused by having to obey unjust and unequal laws which treated some human beings as less than children of God.

Instead of becoming bitter, I claimed God's promise that all things, even the many humiliating racial experiences that I encountered during my 9 1/2 years in the Air Force, would work together for good, if I loved Him and stayed true to my calling. God kept His promise, and used these experiences to help me gain the courage and strength needed to overcome and become a leader. By talking with and reading about black people who succeeded despite the injustice, I learned the truth of my prayer: *"God, if they could stand for centuries and make it, I can too."* Then, whenever I felt put down by racial injustice, I thought of the many prior overcomers who became successful. With that assurance came the God-given strength to carry on and keep my Christian witness.

A Beginning and An Ending

After two promotions and a transfer to Loring Air Force Base, Limestone, Maine, a wonderful thing happened to me. While visiting family in Brooklyn, I met a lovely, vivacious widow, Muriel Jermain Seale. She didn't know it, but after dating about a month, I knew that she was going to be my wife.

She was everything I envisioned: a smart, responsible, slender, 5'5", warm, friendly, and good looking dark brown-skinned woman with straight, even white teeth that enhanced her pretty smile. Her warmth made the expression, "She never met a stranger" a truism. To this day, after 39 years of marriage, she remains my nurturing and caring special friend, my closest confidant.

When I proposed, she responded in her rich, lilting, Brooklyn-West Indian accent: "George, I care about you. But I want you to know that I will only marry you if you are willing to share my responsibilities of loving and caring for my son Joseph and my mother. Wherever I go, they go. We are a package deal. My mother is very special to me. She was always there for me. Now that she's older, I am going to do my best for her."

I responded: "In my culture, older people are revered. I'll be delighted to have the benefit of your mother's wisdom. Any man would be proud to have such a bright, loving six-year old son as Joe, and you're just special."

*George R. Castillo and Muriel J. Seale
are married on March, 23, 1957*

Muriel's mother, Mrs. Susan Jermain

George Castillo and his son, Joseph

Another photo of George and Joseph

I knew I had a deal and willingly accepted the package. So we tied the knot on Saturday, March 23, 1957, at Janes United Methodist Church in Brooklyn, with the Reverend Grant S. Shockley officiating. After a brief honeymoon, I was off to Sculthorpe Air Force Base, Fakenham, England, alone.

About a month after my arrival, I received the worst news of my life. A loud knock on my door the evening of April 29, 1957, was followed by an Air Force Chaplain entering my quarters. Knowing that Chaplains seldom brought good news I asked in a quivering voice, "What happened?" After a few moments, he told me, "George, your mother died on April 21st." I nearly fainted. I couldn't believe it. I knew Mama had not been feeling too well, but dead, NO! "She's only 55, it can't be," I shouted. The Chaplain prayed with me and assured me that he would remember me and my mother in tomorrow's Mass.

I spent the rest of the evening and night crying and thinking about my beautiful, kind-hearted, concerned, hard-working mother. In my grief her spirit seemed to fill the room. Instantly, many of her challenges flooded my mind: "Son, remember the three M's: Manners Maketh Man. Make us proud of you. Take God with you wherever you go." My anguish and loneliness were almost unbearable. I felt as if I were having a nightmare and wished someone would wake me up, but I was alone, far from my family. We couldn't comfort or talk with each other.

I hardly made it through the Pass and Review Parade the next day because my knees kept weakening. I kept thinking of my loving mother. With every thought my tears flowed.

God heard my prayers. I went to the Chapel Service on Sunday, as usual. I tried to control myself, but when we sang one of my mother's favorite hymns, "Pass me not, 0 Gentle Savior," I simply could not stop crying. Although the Chapel was full, I never felt more alone in my life. A Lieutenant and his wife saw my grief, changed seats, sat beside me, and held my hand. After the service they invited me to spend the afternoon with them. I was grateful for caring and concerned Christians. Little did I realize that someday I would be that helping hand for grieving men living far from home.

Life Goes On

The next day, with a heavy heart, I began evening high school. In July, Muriel, Joseph, and my mother-in-law, Susan Jermain "Ma," were finally able to join me. We moved into a 200-year-old rented cottage in Walsingham that had no hot water. The following year, Muriel and I met the Reverend Arthur Saunders and his wife Dorothy at a church service where he was the guest speaker. Pastor Saunders spoke about the mission field and what was happening in the Caribbean missions which the church helped to support. At one point he said, "A product of this mission is sitting here with us today, and he is on his way to becoming a Christian Minister. George, will you stand?"

At that time I was a local preacher with the Fakenham-Wells Methodist Circuit while taking courses for lay ministers. I helped the community and the churches by volunteering as a local preacher. This kept me involved every Sunday evening, conducting worship services in churches within the circuit.

My three-year tour of duty went quickly. Five days a week, I was in evening school. Saturdays, I spent part of the day with my family and the remainder preparing for Sunday services and school studies. Muriel and Ma busied themselves frequenting antique shops and collecting English bone china. Joe enjoyed all the boyish stuff, like bringing home stray animals. He especially relished the kidney pies prepared by his doting English "grandparents," the Williards, our next door neighbors.

By the time we were ready to return stateside, I had completed high school and earned 21 semester hours from the University of Maryland. I asked to be assigned to Castle Air Force Base in California. However, Uncle Sam said my skills were needed more at Dow Air Force Base, Maine. We arrived there in April 1960 with the entire family's support. Muriel said, "George, you did great in school. I'm behind you one hundred percent. We're firmly committed to helping you someday become 'The Reverend George Castillo'."

George R. Castillo and the Rev. Arthur W. Saunders
1958

EDUCATION CENTER
47TH AIR BASE SQUADRON
United States Air Force
APO 22, New York, N. Y.

4 March 1960

SUBJECT: Staff Sergeant George R. Castillo, AF 12424255

TO: WHOM IT MAY CONCERN

1. As Education Officer at 47th Bomb Wing, this station, I have known S/Sgt. George R. Castillo since he first enrolled in the off-duty education program here in June, 1957. During this period he has made impressive progress in furthering his education.

2. When he began his quest for further education he realized that his high school background was very weak, so for eighteen months he diligently attended evening high school classes. By February 1959 he had completed 8½ units and was awarded an academic diploma from Central High School, Third Air Force.

3. S/Sgt. Castillo then embarked on his college career with the University of Maryland and now has completed 21 semester hours towards a B.A. degree.

4. For his achievement in the off-duty education program he was awarded the USAFE Certificate of Distinguished Educational Achievement, given only to a few who have actively participated in the off-duty education program during their entire overseas tour of duty. He was selected by Third Air Force to attend a short resident course at the University of Cambridge from 5 to 12 January, 1959, and made good use of this opportunity to broaden his outlook on the world.

5. I have had ample opportunity to talk to George Castillo and am much impressed with his eagerness to further his education. He has indicated a genuine desire to use this education to prepare himself for service in the church, and I believe he has a strong interest to serve mankind.

6. His sincerity, capacity for hard work, modesty, and cheerfulness, and his keeness to learn have impressed me greatly and I do not hesitate to give him my unqualified recommendation for any position for which he applies, particularly for one where interest in other people is an essential quality for success.

GEORGE MARTINI
DAF Civilian
Education Officer

Chapter 2

Study To Show Thyself Approved

Although I enjoyed my time in the Air Force, I always knew that my calling was the ministry. I also knew that I needed a seminary education if I were to achieve my dreams. I prayed that God would show me where I was to attend. Through Divine order, my wife and I were invited to a sergeant's wedding in Veazie Congregational Church officiated by Mr. Samuel M. Lafferty, a white-haired senior at Bangor Theological Seminary. As might be expected, I immediately shared with him my plans to someday attend seminary when I finished my undergraduate degree in three years.

I listened in rapt attention as he said, "George, Bangor Theological Seminary is just the school for you. You could be accepted now under the 'Bangor Plan' that allows partially trained college students to reach the pre-theological level. Then you become eligible for the seminary program."

"Are you kidding? You mean right now I'm eligible to enter Bangor Seminary?" Sam beamed as he replied, "Of course, you can. I did, and so did many others seeking the ministry as a second career."

Needless to say I was at the administration office early Monday morning. My interview with the Dean, Dr. Marvin Deems, went well. My acceptance would depend on my school transcripts and church membership. "With hard work," he assured me, "You too could succeed."

My pastor, the Reverend E. Charles Dartnell of the First United Methodist Church, Brewer, Maine, noting the work Muriel and I were involved in the various ministries of the church, was happy to furnish the required recommendation. He told me, "George, I'll be happy to recommend you and tell them that you and Muriel are active members of the church — youth leaders, members of the fellowships, and Sunday School teachers. I'll also tell them about the good job you did substituting for me."

There was only one big hurdle standing in my way: getting released from the Air Force with over a year remaining on my six-year enlistment. My guardian angel was smiling on me again because, on September 6, 1962, I was honorably discharged with the stipulation that if I failed to graduate, I could be subject to recall.

I immediately took classes at the University of Maine, simultaneously with course work at Bangor Theological Seminary. Seminary wasn't easy and the dropout rate was high. With God's help, I made it. I wasn't at the top of my class, but I wasn't at the bottom either. My hands were full, holding down three part-time jobs as janitor, manager of the Dow Air Force Base bowling alley, and preacher at different churches when needed.

I loved preaching and doing the work of a minister. As the seminary improved my skills, God began opening doors for service. The Reverend David Bell of First United Methodist Church in Brewer, Maine, allowed me to assist him. Later I became Director of Christian Education at Universal Fellowship Church in Orono, Maine, under the leadership of the Reverend Herbert Houghton. Then, in my senior year, I pastored three joint United Church of Christ churches in Sangerville, Abbott, and Monson, Maine. One of my constant prayers was: "Father, I have always wanted to be your servant as a Minister. I'll do my best and if it be Your will, I'll make it. Thank you, Lord."

Our blessings abounded: good health, good friends, good marriage, and the baby we always wanted. Marcelle Angela was born on December 8, 1963. Ma took care of the baby so Muriel could finish her senior year at the University of Maine. The "perfect" mother-in-law, Ma was happy to take care of our home as her contribution to our ministry together.

A New Life in Ministry Began

In June 1966, the next step of my dream came true when I graduated from Bangor Theological Seminary and Muriel, along with the other supportive wives, received her Ph.T. degree (Putting Hubby Through). She deserved it for her unwavering support while at the same time graduating with distinction from the University of Maine in 1964, and inducted into Phi Beta Kappa and Phi Kappa Phi Honor Societies. Her annual $4,300

Marcelle Angela Castillo.
Baptized at Brewer First
Methodist Church in 1964

Brewer First Methodist
Church

Sangerville, Maine
United Church of Christ

Parsonage in
Sangerville, Maine

Monson, Maine
United Church of Christ

Abbott, Maine
United Chruch of Christ

Marcelle and
friend,
Karen Race

teacher's salary from Bangor High School allowed me to receive my Bachelor of Arts in Political Science from the University of Maine in 1967 and my Master's Degree from Bangor Theological Seminary.

With my education completed, my ordination into the Gospel Ministry took place at the First Congregational Church, United Church of Christ, in Brewer, Maine, on July 2, 1967. Pastor Raymond Wilbur planned the service and Pastor Dartnell delivered the sermon. I still remember the overwhelming sense of awe as ministers from both the Methodist Church and United Church of Christ participated in the traditional "laying on of hands." As I knelt at the altar, I whispered a prayer: *"Thank you God for allowing me to become a minister. Help me to be of service to my fellowman."*

I immediately applied for the United States Air Force Chaplaincy. I was not accepted, however, because I didn't have the required three years of experience. While looking for a full-time charge, I became the Interim Minister at the First Congregational Church, United Church of Christ, in Brewer, Maine, after Pastor Wilbur left.

The Shaping of a Young Minister

In the sixties, white flight from the inner cities to the suburbs presented numerous opportunities to black ministers as black pastors were needed for the newly integrated churches, which eventually became totally black. Unfortunately, fleeing whites expected black pastors to resurrect churches dying from lack of attendance and finances. But that didn't happen. Memberships didn't grow as quickly as hoped because too many blacks remembered when they were not welcomed in the former white churches. Therefore, many newly integrated churches became dependent on mission support. I pastored two such churches.

I accepted my first call from Christ Church, United Church of Christ, Detroit, Michigan. This ministry was more rewarding and more frustrating than I ever imagined. My role became that of comforter to the hurting and reassurer to those who had lost hope. I ministered to people's spiritual needs, performed life's important rites, shared joyous occasions, and empathized and counseled during life's woes. The United Church of Christ not

Brewer First Congregational Church
where I was ordained

only preached the Bible, but also urged its members to become involved in the lives of those less fortunate. So, as a leader, I involved my congregation in tutoring, supporting local organizations, and caring for a troubled community that many called hopeless. One of my church members who was also a community leader, Mrs. Mary McClendon, said, "Reverend Castillo, you're helping us through a difficult time. We appreciate the help you're giving our children by going to the schools, tutoring, and finding them jobs. You're a Godsend...a wonderful minister."

Detroit was struggling to come to grips with itself after the riots of 1967, and I too was struggling to balance my work involvement and my responsibility to my family. In my zeal to be all things to church members and community, I almost neglected my family. There was so much to do, at times it seemed overwhelming. I learned, grew, and "cut my teeth" in Detroit, but after two-and-a-half years, it was time to move on for my own personal growth, strength, and healing of my family life. Seemingly at the right time, Divine Providence set the stage for me to accept a call to East View United Church of Christ, Shaker Heights, Ohio. Several personal family tragedies in 1970 made it easier to move along. First, during the roughest year we faced as a family, my loving, faithful, and generous mother-in-law died after living with us for 13 years. During my ministry, I conducted many funerals, but hers was the most difficult emotionally, although, from a spiritual standpoint, her death was a celebration of the good life she led for 79 years.

In May, a month later, on Muriel's birthday, we suffered our second loss when our second daughter was stillborn. Making matters worse, difficulties during the pregnancy and delivery left Muriel's life hanging in the balance. Tired and depressed, I prayed with her and forced myself to deliver the sermon on Pentecost, the birthday of the Christian Church. In God's timing, the Pulpit Committee from the East View Church was in the congregation. After the service, they identified themselves. Mr. Harold West said, "Your reputation has travelled. We heard about your ministry, and we want you to be our Pastor as we need your expertise and leadership."

Mrs. Christine Bufford added, "After hearing you this morning, we are convinced we want you as our Pastor."

After Muriel recovered, we discussed the offer, made the decision to serve East View United Church of Christ, and tendered my resignation. Then the Reverend Ira Black, Coordinator of the Department of Church Development and Building for the United Church of Christ, sent me a letter which let me know that the long hours, calls in the middle of the night, endless meetings, etc., were all worthwhile. "I don't know of anyone who has had a more difficult church to serve than you, but Christ Church has moved ahead and developed a significant program under your leadership. You have become active in so many matters...that your witness in Detroit will be missed."

We began our service in Shaker Heights, Ohio, on October 1, 1970. I enjoyed this middle-class community. East View had great growth potential as it was the only church in the residential area bordering Cleveland and Shaker Heights. The church did grow rapidly, and I felt very comfortable and spiritually rewarded. So to better serve my congregation, I enrolled in a master's degree program for Pastoral Psychology and Counseling at Ashland Theological Seminary in Ashland, Ohio.

On November 10, 1972, six months before my graduation, I received a letter from the Reverend Leon Dickinson, Secretary for Chaplains of the United Church of Christ Council for Church and Ministry, which read in part: "There is only one Black Chaplain presently in the Federal Bureau of Prisons system. I am inviting Black Ministers to give serious and faithful consideration to the ministry of the incarcerated. Spiritual, emotional and physical resiliency are important for an effective ministry in the prison setting."

Mr. Dickinson's letter sparked my interest in prison ministry. I always enjoyed a challenge, and I was intrigued with the idea that I could serve where the need is greater. After some thought, I spoke to Muriel: "Honey, I've been thinking about the prison ministry. What's your feeling about it compared with parish ministry?" Muriel was instantly supportive. "It would be different," she said. "Your strong suit is relating to people and as in the past you could be very effective in turning someone's life around. East View has so much going for it, many ministers would love to serve here. But many may be reluctant to accept the challenge of a specialized ministry to the incarcerated. Think about it. I'll leave it up to you to decide whether you feel that your ministry

Council for Church and Ministry
UNITED CHURCH OF CHRIST

289 Park Avenue South, New York, N. Y. 10010, Tel. (212) 475-2121 and 254-7470

WILLIAM KOSHEWA, Chairman

HAROLD H. WILKE, Executive Director

November 10, 1972

LEON A. DICKINSON, JR.
Secretary for Chaplains
— Religion and Health

The Rev. George Castillo
15615 Chagrin Blvd.
Shaker Heights, Ohio 44120

Dear Mr. Castillo:

I have just received notice that the Committee on Pastoral Care in Institutions of the National Council of Churches, which Committee selects and nominates applicants to Chaplaincy positions with the Federal Bureau of Prisons, will be meeting January 29-31, 1973. The place of the meeting has not been selected.

There is one vacancy with a good possibility of another vacancy in the very near future. We of the United Church of Christ would like to offer two to six candidates for this Committee to review and recommend to the Federal Bureau of Prisons. There is only one Black Chaplain presently in the Federal Bureau of Prisons system.

I am writing to all Black Ministers of the United Church of Christ, either to invite them to give consideration to this ministry for themselves, or to ask them to recommend men or women who should respond to this ministry.

I am the first one to acknowledge that special training standards present a problem for many competent pastors. As one member of the Committee, I am pressing the acceptance of equivalencies of past and present performance, and general competence, in lieu of the more formal and academic degree programs of clinical training.

Would you give this opportunity for ministry to those who are incarcerated in our Federal prisons serious and faithful consideration. Ministers who are beginning a career in the Federal system should preferably be under forty years of age. Spiritual, emotional and physical resiliency are important for an effective ministry in the prison setting. If you acknowledge that this is not necessarily your expression of ministry, and you know other colleagues who would make excellent pastors to those in prison, would you encourage them to respond to this invitation and opportunity, and inform us of them.

The Rev. James H. Hargett, our Secretary for Black Ministries, concurs with this invitation and joins me in urging you to give this every consideration, and assist us in enlisting strong candidates for this ministry.

Faithfully yours,

Leon A. Dickinson, Jr.

LAD:elr

Church Vocations · Student Care · Personnel Records · Continuing Education
Military and Institutional Chaplaincies · Clinical Pastoral Education · Theological Education
Counseling Services for Ministers · Ministers' Overseas Exchange Program

will be more fulfilling serving the imprisoned. Whatever decision you make, I'll go along with. Why don't you go for the interview and find out more about what the Chaplaincy involves?"

The Interview

Reluctantly, I went to Atlanta for the interview, although I didn't really want to leave East View and certainly wasn't sure about prison ministry. The interview panel was made up of about 20 people representing various denominations of the National Council of Churches, Bureau of Prisons officials, including two Chaplains, and the Reverends Leon Dickinson and James Hargett who represented the United Church of Christ. One panel member asked me to describe myself.

"Gentlemen, physically, as you can see, I am a 42-year-old black man, 5'8" tall, weight about 160 pounds. What you don't see are my good character and my belief in God and the sanctity of the family. The essence of me is that I am a child of God. I'm made in God's image and because God creates only good I believe in the goodness of man. I also believe that we are here to help one another, even those who may have made wrong choices. I strongly believe in prayer and faith."

"Have you experienced discrimination?"

"Yes, like every Black person, I have. The color of a person's skin makes a difference in America. I can vividly remember many humiliating, painful, and hurtful memories. I can't forget 1960 when, even though I was in service, I couldn't rent an apartment for my family. In order to get shelter, my Christian landlady required me to ask a white man, Benjamin Ireland of Brewer, Maine, if I could live next door to him. For the first time in my life, this assault on my dignity made me feel inferior. To make it worse, my Commanding Officer, Colonel James Otis, angrily told me to 'wear-the-pants' in my family because my wife wrote letters to members of Congress about the discrimination we faced. That experience still riles me."

"Are you bitter?"

"No, I am not. Instead, I used the experience to learn to control my emotions. To be honest with you, if I had not been in the military, I would have punched my Commanding Officer in the face."

STATE OF MAINE
OFFICE OF THE GOVERNOR
AUGUSTA

JOHN H. REED
GOVERNOR

April 18, 1960

Mrs. George Castillo
c/o S/Sgt. Berkley Banks
33 Moosehead Boulevard
Bangor, Maine

Dear Mrs. Castillo:

I have read the copy of your very fine
letter to Senator Keating, and I certainly am
very much surprised and distressed to learn of
the difficulties that you and your husband are
having as to housing.

This is the first time that a case of
this type has been called to my attention, and
I feel certain that City Manager Coupal and the
Commander at the Base will do everything within
their power to locate housing for you. Throughout the State we do have negro families, and to
my knowledge they have never had difficulty in
finding housing.

I am sending a copy of this letter to City
Manager Coupal and to the Commander of Dow Air
Force Base so that they may know of my interest
in your behalf.

Sincerely yours,

John H. Reed
Governor

JHR:md
cc Joseph R. Coupal
   City Manager, Bangor
   Commander, Dow AFB

United States Senate

COMMITTEE ON THE JUDICIARY

June 4, 1960

Mrs. George Castillo
33 Moosehead Boulevard
Bangor, Maine

Dear Mrs. Castillo:

I am enclosing a copy of a letter I have received from
the Department of the Air Force in answer to my expression
of interest in your behalf.

I believe you will find the contents self-explanatory
and I very much regret that the information is not
favorable. However, I am sure you will understand
that while I can contact authorities in the military
services and ask that a serviceman's situation be thoroughly
looked into and given every possible consideration, the
final decision in these matters is still strictly within
their jurisdiction.

I sincerely hope that you will be able to obtain adequate
housing in the near future and if you still feel after
reading the attached letter that I can be of any further
assistance, I hope you will not hesitate to let me know.

With best wishes.

Very sincerely yours,

Kenneth B. Keating

K/AC
Enclosure

7 Gilmore Street, Brewer, Maine.
Our first house in Maine. We had to ask the white tenant
if we could live besides him before the landlady would
rent to us. Taken in 1960.

OPTIONAL FORM NO. 10
MAY 1962 EDITION
GSA FPMR (41 CFR) 101-11.6

UNITED STATES GOVERNMENT

Memorandum

Bureau of Prisons
Washington, D.C.

TO   Reverend George Ramon Castillo   DATE: February 16, 1973
        Shaker Heights, Ohio

FROM: J. D. Williams
        Executive Assistant

SUBJECT: Appointment as Chaplain, U. S. Bureau of Prisons

It is our firm intention to extend to you an appointment as Chaplain,
U. S. Bureau of Prisons, under the following conditions:

1) Your initial assignment will be as Protestant Chaplain at the
   United States Penitentiary, Atlanta, Georgia.
2) Your appointment will be at the base of the GS-11 grade
   ($13,996.00);
3) Your appointment will be effective on a date agreed upon
   between you and Warden James Henderson. Appointment date will
   depend upon the freeze that the federal government is now involved
   with;
4) You should contact the Business Office at Atlanta about your
   moving arrangements;
5) The responsibility of obtaining housing shall rest with you;
   but you may request the Warden to consider you for housing
   on the reservation;
6) You will agree to make yourself available to subsequent
   transfer to meet either the needs of the service or provide
   for your own career development as recommended by a Regional
   Director of Chaplain Services. In either case, such transfers
   will be in accordance with government regulations regarding cost
   of transfers and will be coordinated with the Committee on
   Pastoral Care in Institutions and your denominational representative.

Upon receipt of a personal letter from you indicating your acceptance
of this offer of employment, and the conditions cited above, we will
continue to effect your entrance into our service. The necessary
personnel forms are attached. After you have had your physical
examination at Milan, Michigan, please return the medical forms to the
Central Office. All other forms should be taken to Atlanta.

I have every confidence in your ability to provide an extremely effective ministry to the men and staff at the United States Penitentiary,
Atlanta, Georgia, and anticipate your acceptance of this appointment.
In accepting this appointment you will be joining a close-knit family
of dedicated Chaplains and outstanding personnel.

It is my belief, it would be wise to send carbon copies of your acceptance to both the Committee on Pastoral Care in Institutions and to
the denominational representative of your church as well as to any
others you feel should be made aware of your action.

Buy U.S. Savings Bonds Regularly on the Payroll Savings Plan

5010-108

"Can you minister to, and get along with, the Black Muslims?" I responded, "We disagree theologically, but Black Muslims are good people. Some of their philosophies are not new to me. As a youngster I was taught to protect my family, to stay out of anyone's way who does not like me, to be clean, and to act like a responsible man. It was driven home to me there is dignity in honest work and if you're going to be a friend, be a good one."

"You act and speak confidently about yourself. What makes you so confident?"

"I guess my confidence comes from spending my first twenty-one years in Belize, where we were taught that we are as good as anyone. Secondly, my struggle to overcome the label "untrainable," and my struggle to attain my education inspired confidence, especially knowing that I can adequately provide for my family."

As I exited the room I spoke with the other two candidates while I waited for the panel's decision.

Decision Time

After what seemed like an eternity, I was called back into the room. "George, we are recommending you to be a Chaplain with the Federal Bureau of Prisons. If you'll accept our call, as we hope you will, please make arrangements to report to duty as soon as you can. Chaplain Ezell will advise you pertaining to particulars and specifics. We wish you the best; we know that you can do it."

"Thank you," I responded.

I later learned that two of the three candidates were accepted. I wished that I were the one rejected. Now I had a dilemma.

Arriving home that night, tired and confused, I shared my interview experience with Muriel. But I held back the results to the end. Then I rapidly said, "I got the job." For a very long time, we were quiet.

"That's good, but what are you going to do?"

"I don't know. Right now I just want to go to bed. Let's talk about it in the morning."

The adage "There's no heavier burden than a great opportunity" was never truer. Tired as I was, I couldn't sleep for trying to decide whether to accept the challenge of prison ministry or staying comfortably put. Everything I had worked to achieve had materialized. My ministry was flourishing; my family was happy, healthy, loving, and supportive; and our good friends put flesh and bones to the meaning of friendship. God had truly blessed us.

Yet a stirring existed within me that I couldn't shake. God began reminding me of the people who helped me along the way. I realized that God had implanted in me a need to help others in a way that was not available at East View. Maybe the underdog, the underclass, the incarcerated would fulfill that need. Mixed emotions tore at me.

Over coffee, Muriel and I aired our feelings. "How do you feel about my accepting a new challenge of prison ministry? I know you like Shaker Heights, but how do you feel about moving? Do you think Marcelle will adjust well?"

"Well, George, let's look at the positives. We're blessed that you have the option of choosing how you want to serve. It's true I love our congregation and my teaching assignment, but with my experience and recommendations, I'm sure I'll get another job. As far as the family's adjusting to a move, we don't have to worry. Joe is on his own. Erick made an excellent transition from Belize and his grades are good. He can transfer his credits. As for Marcelle, she's so well-adjusted and happy, moving won't be a problem for her. As a former civil service employee, I like the security and the yearly raises you'll earn as a federal employee. But you'll have to decide what you want to do; we'll adjust."

"You make it sound so easy, and it seems as if you're ready to go, but I'm still not certain."

A few days later, I received a letter from the Reverend Jim Hargett, the black attendee from the United Church of Christ, who was supportive during my interview. He followed up with almost daily calls: "Have you made a decision yet?"

"No, I'm still thinking about whether I should accept the offer."

The Bureau of Prisons needed my answer and began calling. Chaplain Bill Ezell, from Atlanta Federal Penitentiary, also called and said, "I hope you take the job."

During a sleepless night of tossing and turning which ushered in the dawn of my forty-second birthday, I woke Muriel up around 2:00 a.m. to talk about the Chaplaincy again. She murmured before going back to sleep, "I haven't ever known you to be as crabby as you have been lately. Why don't you go ahead and take the job and get it over with?"

A peace, joy, and relief engulfed me after Muriel spoke. I know the Lord directs paths through inner urging and sometimes through other people. This time Muriel was His instrument. My tension was broken at 8:00 a.m. when I officially accepted the Federal Bureau of Prisons' offer to become a Chaplain. The guilt about leaving East View began to subside. Because my congregants and I cared about each other, I felt they would understand my call to the Chaplaincy.

Before calling Pastor Hargett, he called me. I didn't give him a chance to ask his usual question, I said, "Jim, I made the decision. I'll take the position and will begin on June 15th."

"Beautiful!" he exclaimed. East View will find another minister. We in the Council for Church and Ministry will help them. That's not your problem. Let us handle that. We need you in the prison because you are so very well-qualified."

As I made the many calls necessary to start the change, I prayed. God gave me an overwhelming feeling that He had used my past and years at East View to prepare us for a bigger ministry. Unknown to me, the second Master's Degree in pastoral psychology and counseling from Ashland Theological Seminary had more than qualified me for the Chaplaincy.

Yes, I realized once again that I was another Jonah. I knew that I had been called into the ministry; but, like Jonah, I wanted to choose the place and so I tried to run from the prison ministry. However, the Holy Spirit would not allow me to escape the words of Psalm 139:

Whither shall I go from thy spirit? or whither shall I flee from thy presence? If I ascend up into heaven thou art there: if I make my bed in hell, behold, thou art there. If I take the wings of the morning, and dwell in the uttermost parts of the sea; even there shall thy hand lead me, and thy right hand shall hold me. If I say, Surely the darkness shall cover me; even the night shall be light about me. Yea, the darkness hideth not from thee; but the night shineth as the day: the darkness and the light are both alike to thee. For thou hast possessed my reins.

Chapter 3

*Chaplain
George R. Castillo*

I knew, as I first walked into the Atlanta Federal Penitentiary on June 15, 1973, that I was not the only person to enter those gates who was nervous. My consolation was that I was there by Divine appointment as a Chaplain and not because of anything I had done on my own. As I stepped on the "hallowed ground," I could feel the words of Jesus that are recorded in Luke 4: 18-19 echoing in my mind:

The Spirit of the Lord is upon Me, Because He has anointed Me to preach the gospel to the poor; He has sent Me to heal the brokenhearted, To proclaim liberty to the captives And recovery of sight to the blind, To set at liberty those who are oppressed, To preach the acceptable year of the Lord.

Atlanta Federal Penitentiary

Spiritually, I was on solid ground. But looking at it practically, I didn't know what I was getting into. Had I known, I might have done more than momentarily pause to give God the thanks and the glory for sending me here.

The Atlanta prison was sometimes referred to as "Big A" and "A Warehouse." Entering a maximum security prison for the first time is always a shock. Facing me were two sets of locked gates. The first opened, allowing me to enter, then clanged shut and was securely locked. Only then did the second one open.

The clanging noise of the second gate caused me to pause, think, and shudder as a second, even more-deafening, noise startled me into reality. Loud voices of hundreds of men talking and yelling at the same time assaulted my ears. It was sobering to realize that about 1,300 men were housed at the prison. Even more sobering was the fact that I couldn't leave until a staff in the Control Center let me out.

I stood there feeling completely helpless until Chaplain Bill Ezell welcomed me. His warm handshake and assurance that Warden James Henderson was eager to meet me made me feel at home. "Welcome aboard," the Warden said. "You've got a lot to learn. Stick with Bill. He'll teach you."

"Sir, I intend to." Bill and I spent the day together as he introduced me to staff and showed me different parts of the institution: the Control Center, hospital, recreation areas, dining hall, and segregation cells (where they housed those who have committed infractions of the prison's laws). It was obvious as I walked through the facility that eyes were on me. Some openly sized me up, others looked with furtive glances, and even a few stopped their work to come over and shake my hand.

Into the Frying Pan

From the beginning, I felt comfortable working with Bill because his thirteen-years' experience provided answers to my questions. Uncertainty hit me when he went to the American Correctional Association's meeting in August, and I had to handle things by myself. Little did I know he would be promoted to Associate Warden of Programs at Seagoville Federal Correctional Institution in Texas and, less than two months after being hired, I would be *Senior Chaplain* — five weeks before my formal

OPTIONAL FORM NO. 10
MAY 1962 EDITION
GSA FPMR (41 CFR) 101-11.6

UNITED STATES GOVERNMENT

Memorandum CONTENTS NOTED

Staff Training Center
Atlanta, Georgia 30315

TO   : J. D. Henderson
          Warden, USP, Atlanta

DATE: September 21, 1973

OCT 1 1973

WARDEN'S OFFICE

FROM : JOHN W. ALLMAN
          Director

SUBJECT: George CASTILLO
          INTRODUCTION TO CORRECTIONAL TECHNIQUES –
                    SEPTEMBER 10 – SEPTEMBER 21, 1973

George was an exceptional student who was quite well liked by
his classmates and by his instructors. He was also able to
gain our professional respect early in the training period.

Test scores show that he has the solid base of understanding
of correctional work, contingent restraints, etc., that will
be necessary for him to operate within the penitentiary
setting.

In regard to further training, George expressed his desire to
establish active lines of communication with other prison
Chaplains and it may be well to consider him for attendance
at a Bureau Chaplains' Conference or for a visit to an
institution which has a widely diversified religious ministry.

Based on test scores which measure knowledge held and gained,
and others which measure career ambition, and also attitudes
toward security and treatment, and on our subjective observations,
we feel confident that George will be an above-average correctional
worker.

JWA/JMH:df

RECEIVED
PERSONNEL OFFICE

OCT 2 1973

U. S. PENITENTIARY
ATLANTA, GA. 30315

training *began!*

My co-worker was a new Roman Catholic Chaplain, Father Urban Cain, who began working a week after I began. We determined to work and learn together. There was no choice. We had to learn very quickly because our lives could well depend on it. Every new experience became an education.

Surprisingly, much of my initial "education and training" came from my inmate clerk, John, a tall, slender, nice-looking, articulate young man with an "All American" boy-next-door look. He was a convicted forger with eyes that sized people up quickly. He sensed my insecurity. "Don't worry about it, boss. You be the Chaplain and I'll run the office."

John was indeed a top-notch administrator. He knew the religious schedules and what had to be done to keep the office running smoothly. I learned the routine office responsibilities from him. I also learned that no matter how reliable an inmate seems, one always has to be on guard.

One morning, John put vouchers on my desk for my signature. Since no one in authority told me that it was my responsibility to approve the time sheets of the part-time employees, I was nervous about signing them. After all, I had not even been introduced to my immediate supervisor. Using this as an opportunity, I introduced myself to Associate Warden of Programs, Harold McKenzie, and explained the situation. My fears were eased when Harold said, "John's right. Check the number of visits against their contracts. If they're correct, sign the vouchers and carry them to the business office."

However, inmates' counsel wasn't always right. Many inmates use positions to "con" employees into meeting the inmates' own needs. Now and again I was "conned." It becomes a game of cat and mouse, and can sometimes bring deadly results to employees' careers. I soon realized that even my inmate clerk was not above suspicion when a purchase request apparently signed by me was sent to the business office without my knowledge. The forgery was masterful! As a result, beautiful all-occasion greeting cards, which I did not order, were delivered to my office. Bewildered, I wouldn't accept the cards and asked the business office to return them to the sender. Although I could never prove that John forged my signature and ordered the cards, I knew that he did have access to the Religious Department's purchase order numbers. Like so much of my "education" in prison work, I learned the hard way to pay more attention to John's work.

It didn't take me long to learn that in prison there are two roads: the staff's and the inmates'. Very rarely do they run parallel. If staff favors a certain idea, inmates will be against it, and vice-versa. It is always a we-and-they situation: "we" being the staff or inmate speaking, "they" the other side. Both sides watch the Chaplain closely to test whether he is one of "us." This left me in a very uncomfortable situation at times. My role was to be a reconciler in the "we-and-they" controversy without taking sides. As Chaplain, it was my responsibility to bring a caring, calming presence throughout the institution.

Helping to reconcile the desires of the inmates with the security needs of the prison system was always a challenge. One source of friction that remained constant was the annual inmate Christmas parties. The staff wanted to keep them small, but the inmates were always trying to find ways to make them bigger. Many times I prayed for the wisdom of Solomon as I walked the tightrope.

Chaplaincy, The Ultimate Melting Pot

The prison ministry is indeed a unique type of ministry. Men from all walks of life, with no religious background or with varying theologies, come together. I soon realized that my unique religious background of being Roman Catholic by birth, Methodist by rearing, and United Church of Christ by ordination, prepared me to respect and learn from every person. Regardless of their religious persuasion, it was my responsibility to supervise the endless religious programs that were conducted every evening and sometimes during working hours, as well as the occasional weekend seminars.

I decided early to maintain an open-door policy, and the men responded hungrily. I was constantly counseling as the inmates clearly needed someone to talk with who would listen. The Chaplain's office is the only place an inmate could unburden himself when he felt the need and feel safe in doing so.

Emotions ran the gamut. The outer "tough and mean" shells often evaporated in my office as some of the toughest men shed gallons of tears.

Frequently I became the recipient of angry outbursts and insults. It didn't take me long to realize that these outbursts were not personal attacks. To many inmates, I represented the entire society that many believed had treated them unjustly. They were simply angry with the system. I listened intently and compassionately because I knew that my office was a safe haven where they could vent their feelings about the policemen, the lawyers, the judges, and the system that was keeping them away from family and friends. After the counseling sessions came to an end and the tears dried, many inmates apologized for their outbursts. This opened doors to an effective ministry.

Dick Monihan was no exception as he pounded his fists on my desk. Like so many, it didn't take long for his anger to subside. With his anger spent, he said, "Chaplain, I didn't mean to direct my frustration at you. You have nothing to do with it. I'm just pissed off with the system."

I replied as I usually did, "We both know that you're seeing me as representing the system which may have treated you unfairly. I understand how you feel. Rest assured you can release your thoughts and feelings safely here and that my office is always open to you. Come and talk with me when you feel frustrated."

A Chaplain has to put aside personal feelings when dealing with those who are hurt, resentful, and confused, knowing that he's the bridge between staff, inmates, their families and, sometimes, communities. Defusing inmates' frustrations, anxieties, and tensions is an effective way to keep many from getting into trouble.

Tom was one of those inmates you wouldn't feel comfortable walking beside or behind you even in daylight hours. He frequently walked the recreation yard alone because almost everyone feared his anger. He was a rough-looking and gruff-talking, tattooed, big man whose only home for the past 15 years was Atlanta's maximum security prison. To say the least, he wasn't the sociable type. I caught him completely off guard when I greeted him: "Tom, how are you doing today?"

Surprised, he responded, "OK." Period.

Engaging him in light conversation wasn't easy, but I kept trying. As the length of our conversations grew, Tom's buddies were drawn like a magnet. They simply couldn't believe that any staff member would care enough about someone as mean as Tom to stop and talk with him that long.

That did it. Word got around that I was an understanding and sensitive Chaplain. Consequently, inmates were always waiting for me when I arrived at work. Like many ministers, I tried fervently to meet all their needs. Part of my problem was that I found it difficult to say "No" to inmates who really seemed burdened. My ever-increasing number of 12-hour days began leaving me physically and emotionally drained. Sleep no longer helped, and I stayed just plain tired. One evening, inmate Charlie Heron came to my office just as I was leaving. I was willing to listen to him, but he saw my fatigue and said, "Why don't you go home, Chaplain. I'll see you tomorrow. I have the time. I have ten years."

Ralph Graham, a kindly, soft-spoken, tall, handsome man, became Regional Chaplain during my early months. With adjacent offices, he became my sounding board and counselor. I shared with him my own frustration. "Ralph, there's so much to be done that I feel frustrated when I can't see everybody. I want to help these men get on the right path, but I must admit that when the gates close behind me at the end of the work day, I feel an emotional and psychological release."

Ralph, in his realistic manner, responded, "George, you're doing a great job, but you're trying to do too many things too quickly. You can't be effective that way. Your open-door policy is good if that's all you have to do. But it isn't. There's the paperwork. And what about the men in segregation who can't come to see you? They need to be seen as well as those in the hospital. Your visibility in the recreation areas is also necessary. You're spending too much time counseling in your office. Your aim and purpose are commendable, but these men had their problems before they met you, and they'll always have them. Don't let them drain you."

As Ralph talked, my mind went back to what the wise, seasoned Chaplain Bill Ezell had earlier advised me: "George, you can do your work in 40 hours or in 140 hours a week. You'll have to gear yourself accordingly." Eventually, I heeded the voice of experience and set more realistic goals and priorities.

There is always stress caused by the inner struggle of

ministry: caring and understanding while at the same time trying to protect oneself from some men who are not totally trustworthy. For instance, when my civilian parishioners came to
church, they worshipped. However, my prison parishioners didn't
always come to worship. I learned this when a distillery was
found in the Chapel ceiling during a routine shakedown of the
Religious Department. I was dumbfounded to say the least. Then
I wondered how the inmates were able to reach the ceiling without a ladder. Laughing, one of the correctional officers introduced
me to the reality of working in any correctional facility. "Chaplain, these men have years and years to think. While we're sleeping, they're thinking. If they don't succeed this year, they have
several years to accomplish their goal. Some of them know this
place better than we do. They find ways to do what they want."

Even Jesus Taught in Groups

Dedication brought Charles Riggs, a short, stocky Southern
Baptist minister who articulated with a Southern drawl, into the
institution as a contract worker who made several visits without
pay. He later became Southeast Regional Chaplain and the Bureau Administrator of Chaplaincy Services. In his early days, he
assisted every Tuesday with the orientation of new inmates in
our Admissions and Orientation (A&O) sessions. We told the inmates about the Chaplains' duties and the religious programs offered at the institution. These included church services, weekly
Bible studies led by various denominations' representatives, Alcoholics Anonymous meetings led by outside volunteers, transactional analysis, and Salvation Army weekly visits. We emphasized that we were available for counseling, leading group
therapy sessions, placing emergency telephone calls, and discussing any family emergencies.

Orientation was done in group sessions, which usually took
Charles and me all morning to conduct. These were followed by
individual counseling. One morning, while men were filing in for
an A&O session, I was caught off guard when a burly blond inmate hugged me like a relative he hadn't seen for years. I froze. I
didn't know or remember him. "Chaplain Castillo," he said, "I'm
glad to meet ya. I'm Calvin Brown. I heard you were coming
when I left in April."

I was so surprised that I responded in a way that was totally inappropriate for a Chaplain, "What are you doing back here? Do you like this place?"

Calvin loosened his grip, and we both relaxed.

"No, Chaplain, I couldn't get a job 'cause I've been in prison. So I lied on the stupid application and got a good job. The SOB's found out after three weeks and fired me on the spot. I looked for another job and couldn't find one, so I started stealing again and got caught. I'm back for parole violation. Then the State is waiting for me."

"That's a rough predicament to be caught in, Calvin. How do you plan to break the cycle when you're finally released?"

He didn't respond so I asked, "Why don't you come to group therapy and let's explore some possibilities to keep you out of prison."

Calvin on occasion attended group therapy, where he shared important events of his life. He once broke down and cried while discussing how he began his criminal career by running away from home at age 10 and landing in a juvenile center, then in jails and prison. When I left Atlanta about 18 months later, he was still there.

Through experience, I learned that many inmates share common problems. Thus my time could become much more productive by working with them in groups just as Jesus taught the multitude.

Infighting — Watch Your Back

I was taught to believe that God expected his children to work together in peace and harmony.

However, working in a melting pot of different religions quickly shattered that dream. Not everything that happened within the Chaplaincy ranks was holy.

Chaplain Ralph Graham, a certified Clinical Pastors Education (CPE) instructor, needed to keep his certification active so he invited Father Cain and me to take a CPE course under his supervision. I didn't need his course because my counseling degree more than met the Chaplaincy requirements, but I took it because I wanted to better serve my new constituents and understand the prison environment. Five of us enrolled, including

Father Cain, two contract ministers and one volunteer minister.

Ralph told us about the inner workings of Atlanta Federal Prison before we took a tour. He arranged for the custodial officers to show us parts of the institution I never knew existed. For example, safety tunnels for staff to travel underground from one part of the institution to another, and the storage area for the institution's guns, which are normally carried only by staff working in the towers. We also visited the towers and the Control Center, the communication pulse. Control really is *in control*. Officers on duty there know everything that is happening in the institution at all times.

Part of the classroom curriculum consisted of group therapy, which I found disturbing. Not that I minded sharing intimate parts of my life, but the mean spirit of some classmates made me feel as if I were a trampoline. These fellow ministers used the time to trample on my most cherished beliefs. In the process, my view of Ministers as kind, compassionate, and caring people who existed to heal broken spirits and uplift their fellow men spiritually was crushed.

My classmates' religious dogma differed from mine, and they used our theological and philosophical differences for personal attack. I became the object of their rending. They saw prisoners — and man in general — as evil. I became the subject of intense ridicule because of my conviction that even inmates are made in God's image and should be treated with respect.

I made it clear that I saw prisoners and people in general as having as much capacity for doing good as doing evil. I strongly believe that through the redemptive power of God, evil can be turned to good. I like the saying, "God isn't through with us yet. We're still under construction." I further explained that whenever I find myself getting smug, my inner voice reminds me: *There you go, George, but for the grace of God.*

This was too much for one fiftyish, white-haired, portly, round-faced minister who declared, "You're much too positive in your feelings....You're living in a Pollyanna world. That's not realistic. These inmates will never change. With your accepting attitude, they'll walk all over you."

In agreement, Frank Jones, the taller one with the receding hair line and piercing eyes, shook his head in approval and added, "They're devils out there, and there is sin in the world. Wake up! Get real! You're just too compassionate."

George Cadle, who had a bald spot on the top of his head and revealed a good sense of humor when he was away from the group, snapped, "You aren't a good Chaplain with your humble approach."

When they couldn't get to me, they turned on my partner. During one particularly searing session, Father Cain's theological beliefs were also scorned. "Why do you Catholics worship the Virgin Mary instead of our risen Savior?"

Calmly, Father Cain said, "Catholics don't worship the Blessed Mother. We love, venerate, and admire her."

I had enough of their criticism! The following morning, I shared my decision with Chaplain Cain, who also felt the group was too negative. My next stop was Ralph's office to complain formally about the destructive hostility in the group.

"Ralph, I'm tired of the negativity in the group. We all can benefit from positive, constructive criticism, but their hostility is destructive."

Ralph wisely did not allow me to just quit. "George," he said, "perhaps you're overly sensitive. But the group needs to know how you feel. Will you do me a favor and meet one more time and tell them why you are quitting?"

I agreed, and at the next session I looked directly at the three ministers, laid out my grievances, and said, "Gentlemen, I'm not getting anything from this group but insults. I had enough. Yesterday was my final session."

That ended my group participation, but I practiced the forgiveness that I preached and gave them the respect due to all of God's children. Our professional relationship continued in a cordial manner when we ministered to the prisoners.

Professional in-fighting is common. At some time, most of us struggle to keep our heads above water. But it's especially hard for black pioneers to paddle upstream and stay above water. I shared my group therapy experience with a friend, Doctor Norman Rates, Chaplain of Spelman College, who also felt that those ministers didn't like the idea that a black man had my position, especially since they preceded me. Chaplain Rates advised, "Now you're the number-one man. Normally, it's the other way around. Those guys want your job. You better watch yourself."

Indeed I had to watch my every action. One day I mailed two

boxes of personal property at government expense for John, my clerk, who was going home in two weeks. This had always been allowed in the past, but this time someone in the mailroom decided it was against policy and, without my knowledge, held the boxes in the mail room.

About a week later, Warden Henderson's secretary notified me: "Chaplain, the Warden wants to see you immediately."

I hurried to his office. He closed the door.

"Chaplain, it came to my attention that you refused to pick up your clerk's two boxes from the mail room after you were told about them."

"That's not so, Warden. I pick up my mail daily, talk and laugh with both guys, but neither one told me to pick up any boxes. I would have picked them up immediately."

My next stop was the mail room. Looking straight at them, I almost shouted, "Why didn't you tell me to pick up my clerk's boxes?"

Neither one of them said a word. Both officers continued what they were doing with blank expressions on their faces. They acted as if they didn't hear me. But I know they did because my tone was louder than normal.

About three weeks later, Chaplain Jack Hanberry visited the institution and inquired about my progress. He was told good things about me, except for the package incident. He told me, "George, I have always mailed packages for inmates at government expense, and as far as I know, that policy has not changed."

Policy changed when I became Protestant Chaplain. Practices that were acceptable and established were no longer applicable for me.

Chapter 4

Life in The Real World

The Bureau of Prisons has always encouraged the use of volunteers and visiting groups within the prison system. Most volunteers visit on a weekly basis; others come on a monthly or annual basis, as in the case of those who participated in the Fall Annual Revival. Both visitors and inmates looked forward to the Revival's five evenings of Gospel music, testimonies; and preaching of the Word.

Tradition reserved the Revival's opening night for a huge white Baptist Church. The joyful evening began with the Custodial Department processing visitors into the institution. For security reasons, each guest's hand was stamped before entering and proceeding to the theater/Chapel for the evening program. This was the first time that I had seen the over-500-seat Chapel almost full. Members of the 100-voice choir sang, church members gave testimonies, and the Pastor preached the Gospel. The supervising custodial staff, inmates, and I appreciated the spiritual worship experience.

The next evening, the Reverend Charles Stokes, from the all-black Rising Star Baptist Church, brought about 50 choir members. I thought this group performed beautifully, as did the choir the night before. The only difference was that this group was smaller and black. They sang the Word emotionally from the bottom of their hearts and shared their testimonies with joy and zeal. Their enthusiasm caused inmates to participate freely with frequent hand-clapping, "Hallelujahs" and "Amens"! The custodial staff was watchful and appeared apprehensive about the inmates' animated responses.

The next morning, Mr. McKenzie, the Associate Warden of Programs, called me to discuss the Revival services. The services went so well I said proudly: "Harold, our Revival services went great! The first night the Chapel was almost full. The visiting choir had over 100 members. Last night's service also was a wonderful spiritual event. Although that choir was half the size of the other, they made up in enthusiasm what they lacked in numbers."

He interrupted. "That's just what I want to talk about. The size of last night's group was too large. Keep the numbers down."

I stared in disbelief at the Warden. I couldn't believe what I was hearing and was dumbstruck because the Warden knew the facts but set two different standards. The black church's choir was approximately half the size of the white church's choir, yet he said to keep the black group's size down! I left his office desperately trying to understand his rationale. It didn't make sense until I looked through his words and saw the real problem. The real problem was not one of size, but style of worship and race.

I quickly learned that I couldn't put out brush fires and minister effectively. So I figured out how to play their games and work within the system. I made my peace with those staff members who were not supportive of me or the way I managed the Religious Department. I was to be the one to set the example for prisoners to follow.

A Prison Chaplain needs to learn quickly how to maneuver his way in and out of situations!

Rehabilitation

Rehabilitation programs are available to help inmates change, but most want to change on their own terms. Other inmates use the excuse that working toward change in a correctional facility is too difficult. The motivated ones take advantage of the rehabilitation programs and do improve their lives. When inmates have exhausted other resources of seeking help, they turn to the Chaplain. At this point, the Chaplain becomes an intervenor and a counselor.

I learned early that when counseling an inmate, it's important to get all the details, pro and con, and use all this information to help him think through his problems. However, sometimes the Chaplain can do very little except listen and give the inmate time to unburden himself and reach conclusions on his own. I always did the best I could for the inmate, but it is necessary to emphasize that I could only do so within the constraints of prison policy.

The fact is that prisoners are in prison *for punishment, and certainly not for rehabilitation.* They are not in the penitentiary for penance either. They are there to serve time as punishment for a specific crime or crimes they have committed. An inmate's prison life is meant to be punishment from day one until the day of release. A 37-year old depressed inmate who was serving a 7-year sentence for fraud described his feelings: "Chaplain, I feel like I have been asked to swim ten miles up river while hog-tied."

Rehabilitative programs are available, but it's up to the inmate to choose and pursue the program for his own rehabilitation. Any rehabilitation that is achieved is secondary to the primary mission of imprisonment. An adjusted black inmate put it this way: "Inmates have to change their bad values themselves while in prison if they want to change when they get out."

Attitudes do change in prison. I think of Jimmy, a former Grand Wizard of the Ku Klux Klan (KKK), who was imprisoned for killing an innocent black colonel on his way to military reserve duty simply because he was black.

"I didn't even know him. Chaplain, I just hated black people. We held secret meetings on how to eliminate and intimidate them. We felt they didn't belong in white America because they were corrupting the white race. Although they're white, we hate Jews and Catholics too. I was honored for killing a black, only to be deserted by my buddies when I was arrested. I was left all alone. In jail I had time to think, and I realized that I served a wrong cause, the devil. I'm really sorry."

When Jimmy committed crimes on behalf of the KKK, he was convinced that he was performing a Messianic function: "saving the United States of America from undesirables." He had taken his responsibility seriously. Later he repented and became a devoted, committed, and faithful member of the prison Christian community. His turnabout was amazing as I observed his relationship become brotherly to black inmates.

As our own relationship deepened, he confessed to me, "Chaplain, I have to make a confession to you. Before you arrived here last June, we were praying for a Christian Chaplain to come to this institution 'cause we felt that Chaplain Ezell wasn't preaching the Gospel but teaching psychology and transactional analysis. When we heard that you were coming, I was happy, but the thought of a black Christian Chaplain never even crossed my mind. There was no doubt that our new Chaplain would be a white man. To me, it was understood that only whites were true Christians. I guess, Chaplain, that God is still opening my eyes to the many things I failed to see."

Before Jimmy left my office that afternoon, we both knew that the Atlanta Penitentiary had become his "Road to Damascus." I realized that this counseling session needed to end with prayer. As my black hand joined with the hand of a former KKK leader, we thanked God for the change which only He and Jimmy's desire for change could accomplish.

Times of Testing

The penitentiary in Atlanta, like all prisons, needs the inside information that only inmate informants can provide. Naturally, these informers are hated by other inmates, but they are an invaluable asset to the custodial staff.

I didn't know that Steve was an informer when he came into my office. He was a tall, very muscular, regular-seeming guy who appeared to be a likable person. After a brief conversation, he said, "Chaplain, I'm in prison for counterfeiting. It's so easy I can show you how in two minutes."

"No, thank you," I replied emphatically, as I asked him gently and firmly to please leave, which he did.

Two months later, after his appearance before the Parole Board, Steve returned to my office and wept bitterly. Between the sobs of his uncontrollable crying he exclaimed, "I was promised parole because I cooperated as an informer. I needed the custodial staff's help for parole, and they let me down. They didn't do as they promised."

The contour of his face changed as the tears stopped. Anger and violence were written all over his face as it reddened. His eyes darted and narrowed, and his lips turned up in an angry frown as he began pounding on the desk with my paperweight while screaming, "I'm MAD as hell!"

For the first time since becoming a federal Chaplain, I was concerned for my welfare because I was behind closed doors with an angry and seemingly disturbed inmate. As he wiped his hands across his face to remove a tear from his cheek, I moved my telephone nearer to me so I could take the receiver off the hook if I needed help. That action would activate a silent alarm in the Control Center. Help would be sent immediately. Fortunately, it was not necessary. Rather quickly, an awesome transformation took place. His face softened as he gently replaced the paperweight on my desk and said, "Chaplain, I'm grateful that I can talk with you because I can't go to custody or other inmates."

"Steve, my doors are always open."

"Remember when I tried to show you how to make counterfeit money?" he asked.

"Of course, I do. I didn't want any part of it."

"Chaplain, custody sent me. They used me to 'set you up.' They wanted to test you. I feel bad for playing into their hands. I know you are a straight and upright man. I would like to be like you — to say 'No' to evil. What can I do?"

I was stunned, but I got up, put my hand on his shoulder and said, "Steve, this could be a new beginning for you. You have to be honest with yourself. It comes down to making choices. You know right from wrong. When faced with a decision, follow your conscience and choose the right course. Keep Jesus as your guide. He was human as well as Divine. As the son of God, He gave us guidelines to follow the will of God. We know God is good and God is love. We express our God-like qualities when we do the right thing. Ask yourself, 'What is the Godly thing to do?' Then do what you believe expresses the highest good for the love of God, yourself, and your fellowman."

I then handed him a tissue, a Bible, and the religious programs schedule, and prayed with him. Both Steve and I felt this was a new beginning for him. He continued to be an active member of the religious community. His changed behavior indicated that he was being rehabilitated.

Did his change of heart last? Only God can answer that. But as a Chaplain, I planted the seed of faith. By doing so, I shared the truth, which I totally believed, based on the revealed Word of God, to which I am Divinely called. No matter how far a person falls, the love of God, coupled with an earnest desire to change, can rehabilitate the hardest of hearts. This is the essence of my ministry.

Some inmates were so pleasant I couldn't imagine why they were in prison. Most would tell me why, but never the entire story. They shaded the truth to put their cases in the most favorable light. Usually, their stories were so well rehearsed that they actually believed the half truths they spoke. The stories seemed so plausible that even a trained professional listener could be duped. When I checked with case managers and heard the other half of their stories, however, it was usually as different as night and day.

For a while I began to familiarize myself with the inmates' records, but some were so long and thick that one record could require many hours to read. Besides, I couldn't read about the sordid lives so many inmates had experienced without prejudicing my thinking. I decided that I could better minister to them by accepting them as they were: INCARCERATED MEN WITH PROBLEMS WHO NEEDED DIRECTION AND SPIRITUAL KNOWLEDGE TO DEAL WITH THE FUTURE.

Instead of focusing on their records and their crimes of the past, I chose to focus on their spiritual growth. This gave me a new freedom to accept them as men with problems. It was gratifying to counsel people who never knew about the Bible, Sunday school, or church, and never had participated in religious activities. When they became acquainted with religious teachings, they acted like children who discovered Lego and all the things that a set can do.

Bert Langley knew no religion until he began attending Bible classes. He was constantly amazed at all the good "stuff" he found in the Bible. Every time he found something new he would excitedly ask, "Chaplain, you mean it tells us that in the Bible?" He became totally fascinated by Psalms 37:3, which commands us to Trust in the Lord and do good. He took it to heart, and several months later he said, "I wish I'd known about this Bible. Probably my life wouldn't have been such a mess."

Every once in a while I got to meet one of our former "celebrity" inmates. An aging Floyd Hamilton had been a driver for the Bonnie and Clyde gang during the 20's. He and I were asked to be the guest speakers at the Distinguished Public Service Awards worship service at Forrest Hills Baptist Church on October 20, 1974. His moving testimony told how he had found God in prison and used this knowledge to rehabilitate himself. He became the author of the popular book, *The Last of the Bonnie and Clyde Gang*, and spoke on the lecture circuit trying to divert youths from a life of crime. He mentioned how he regretted spending most of his life in prison.

After the service, Floyd gave me books for the Christian community in the "Big A." He autographed a book for Smokey, who was incarcerated with him in Alcatraz. I was surprised that Smokey had been incarcerated all those years while Floyd had become rehabilitated and made a life for himself.

There are three things extremely important to inmates: their visits, their families, and their mail. Inmates preserve these at any cost. Rehabilitation becomes easier when they know their families are safe and secure. The family plays a very large role in rehabilitation because loved ones symbolize the hope that a future lies beyond the somber walls of prison.

When I arrived at Atlanta Penitentiary, volunteers and inmates were planning a program to provide visiting family members low-cost lodging near the penitentiary. Five churches provided the funds to secure and renovate an old house that would lodge adult family members for $3.00 a day and children for $1.00.

By summer 1974, the project was ready to go and leaflets flooded the institution. A former inmate who participated in the original planning managed the house. I was very happy about it since it was the Christian thing to do. After all, Jesus had commanded us to help one another. This effort to help the families remain intact reminded me of His words: "As you have done it unto one of the least of these... you have done it unto me."

The administration's "hands-off" attitude neither encouraged nor discouraged the project. Shortly after the lodging was in operation, I better understood the administration's attitude. Before the year was over, the lodging was turned into a house of ill-repute. Some of the women who had been separated from their inmate husbands were introduced to men who paid a fee for their services. As this became known, the former-inmate manager broke parole and fled the area. About a month later, he cashed a check in Seattle, Washington. The inmates whose families benefited or would have benefited from the house were hurt and furious. Their outrage was summed up by John Thomas, a huge, raw-boned, fearless inmate: "Don't let him come back to this institution!" No one had any question about what John Thomas meant.

Turf Battles Split the Religious Community

The Religious Department offered rehabilitative religious programs seven evenings a week and some afternoons. These included group therapy, Bible study, counseling, prayer groups, and reading. In addition to the programs I conducted, Protestant churches such as the Salvation Army Cadets, Methodist, Baptist, Presbyterian, Assembly of God, Church of God, and Seventh Day Adventist were invited to lead the Sunday morning Worship Services.

One evening a group of Latter Day Saints approached me with a request: "Chaplain, we'd like our Bishop to lead a Sunday morning worship service too."

"Of course. All of you attend services regularly and meet weekly for Bible study with your volunteer so I'll be glad to have your denomination represented. I try to accommodate all denominations and this could be an opportunity for the rest of the prison population to learn about the Latter Day Saints."

I announced one Sunday that Latter Day Saints representatives had been invited to conduct services. That invitation split the prison Christian Community into two factions. When the service began on the appointed day, more people were present than usually attend Sunday services. I didn't know it at the time but, since there are few secrets in prison, the Mormon inmates knew that inmates of other faiths had planned a walkout during the service. Innocently, pleased with the size of the crowd, I opened the service with a Call to Worship and listened with joy as we sang the opening hymn,"Holy, Holy, Holy." After the invocation, I introduced our speaker. As the Mormon leader took his place behind the pulpit, several inmates walked out. But the LDS members had prepared for this by inviting all their friends to attend. They made sure there would be a good number listening to the message no matter how many walked out. Fortunately, the rest of the service continued without incident.

Many inmates in the Christian Community were furious that I had allowed a leader of a group some considered to be anti-Christian to lead "their" Worship Service. I listened, but later used this incident to talk about tolerance. "Each of us, as decent human beings, should respect other people's worship and religious belief just as we want ours to be respected. Regardless of our denominational differences, there is one God, Father of all."

Needless to say, I made an opportunity to talk with other Chaplains about the protest walkout. Several said that although the majority of inmates from different traditions come together in unity to worship, disputes among religious groups are common prison behavior. This was my first of many "Holy Wars" in the Bureau. In retrospect, this was a minor skirmish compared to what was ahead.

Steak and Wine for CONS

The Church of the New Song (CONS) was already in existence when I arrived. One of the first things that Chaplain Ezell advised me to do was to keep my distance from the group because CONS was a prison church, started by inmates with the goal of forcing monumental changes in the prison system under the guise of religious freedom. We furnished the other religious groups with bread and grape juice for communion. But CONS demanded 1" thick steaks and wine for its communion. If you attended CONS services, it could be interpreted that you condoned their goal.

The CONS was led by Donald James, a jailhouse lawyer. It didn't take long for the 44-year old, bright, short, potbellied, bald, raunchy "minister" to take Atlanta Penitentiary officials to court in an attempt to force them to recognize CONS as a legitimate religious body. Pending a decision in the case, the court granted CONS meeting time. In the meantime, the Bureau denied the request for steak and wine "elements" of communion.

CONS membership grew like wildfire in a dry wooded area. The hope of obtaining alcoholic beverages in a "dry" federal prison made the facility primed and ready for the Church of the New Song. Inmates came to my office in droves to change their church preference to the Church of the New Song after court action allowed them to meet.

The leaders of the CONS movement made promises to the inmates that if they joined CONS, they'd receive special benefits such as communion privileges and Certificates of Ordination which they could use upon their release. Although James could

"ordain" other inmates, he could not provide them with certificates. So he advised his followers to get credentials from a mail-
order firm. It didn't take long for inmates to begin to display
proudly their "ordained minister" mail-order credentials, which
arrived almost daily.

"Rev," one uneducated inmate said to me as he waved his 'diploma,' "You don't have to go to school to be a minister. See, I got
my papers."

"Do you think I wasted my time by going to school?" I asked.

With an obvious smirk on his face he snarled, "Yes. That's the
reason why you're working in prison. You can't make it on the
outside with your degrees. But now I have what it takes to *make
it*...." Like so many, this inmate wanted to be "special" without
doing the work to achieve his goals. I was disturbed to realize
that he had already developed schemes to use on the outside to
gain the confidence of unsuspecting people by representing himself as a legitimate minister.

Probably some decent inmates were sucked into the frenzy
too. Ray Brown, a stately, trustworthy, distinguished-looking former public official from Alabama, received a diploma of ordination. He assured me, "Chaplain, I just want it for a souvenir and
not for use."

Some used their "credentials" to marry homosexuals in prison. The "wedded" ones took their marriage vows seriously. The
situation became explosive. The administration had to control
the mail-order ordination diplomas pouring into the institution.
Instead of diplomas going directly to inmates, Mr. McKenzie announced, all mail-order ordinations were to be routed through
the Chaplain's office.

This gave me an opportunity to counsel with inmates and let
them know that their diplomas, which were legally their personal property, would be given to their case managers to file in their
records. They would be held there until the inmates were released. This procedure took away the inmates' "proof" that they
were "ordained ministers." As a result, they could not perform
marriages and the number of "marriages" dropped dramatically.

The counseling sessions also allowed me to help inmates see
the reality of their actions. I asked many, "Do you think the Parole Board is going to hold the diploma against you when they
see it in your records? Could they possibly think that you are

going back into the community to con people?"

My questions were effective in changing some inmates' minds. They asked me to destroy their diplomas instead of giving them to their case managers. However, since I would not destroy their personal property, I handed the diplomas to them to destroy in my presence. This was a simple solution to what could have become an even more complicated problem.

It turned out that holding back diplomas just created a lull in the "Cops and Robbers" game. The "ministers" who already had mail-order certificates soon began charging a fee to ordain others since no new certificates were coming into the institution.

Donald James, the CONS' leader, and I were on friendly terms. He came to my office frequently to talk about criminal justice, politics, religion, the Viet Nam war, social issues, and such personal matters as his family and the years he had spent in prison. He bragged that he ran for Governor of Kentucky and got votes while confined in a Kentucky jail. When the situation warranted, I helped James by making calls to find out how his sickly teenage son was doing. From a humanitarian point of view, I felt comfortable making these calls. Without them, James could only call — collect— every other month.

Inmate Setups and Federal Court

It didn't take long for "minister" James to show his true colors. Early one morning, James walked into my office and demanded that I make a phone call to his family immediately. Instead of being polite, he was belligerent and out of character.

I invited him to sit down and talk about it, but he refused. His shoulders went back as his chin and body leaned foreword. "My case manager, Mike Townsend, sent me to have you make a telephone call for me. If you aren't going to do it, then give me a note so I can give it to him."

I knew from experience that something unusual was going on. I also knew that the case manager wouldn't send someone to see me just to make a call because he had the authority to make the call himself. I faced James squarely and again said, "Sit down and let's talk. What's the problem?" Instead of answering me, James stormed out of my office in a huff. I decided to wait a couple of days before pursuing the matter further.

I didn't have to wait even that long to see James. The following day he returned with his usual demeanor and dropped a totally different issue in my lap. "Chaplain," he said, "I need permission for the Reverend Helen Leen to visit me. She's the minister from Northeast Atlanta I ordained."

"Tell her to send me a written request on her church's letterhead."

"Chaplain, that won't be necessary," he said emphatically. "She's legit. I ordained her myself."

"James," I said, slowly and deliberately, "every visiting minister goes through the same procedure without exception."

He pounded my desk and declared, "Okay, if that's the way it has to be done...." He murmured as he left my office.

He knew the system so he complied and passed on what I said to Ms. Leen. My decision was not acceptable to her. I was told by inmates and staff that she castigated me on her religious radio program, and I never received a letter from her requesting entrance into the facility.

About a month after that incident, we were in Federal court to respond to the law suit James filed against Warden Henderson for depriving him of his civil rights, and he asked for $250,000.00 in compensation. Even though I didn't know what I was supposed to have witnessed, I was subpoenaed as one of James' witnesses.

When I arrived in court the morning that I was scheduled to appear, Tom, a custodial member, asked me, "Is this your first time in court as a Chaplain?"

When I responded, "Yes," he chuckled. "Welcome aboard, Chaplain. You'll be lucky if you average less than four a year. That has been my average, and the average is going up every year because the courts believe everything the inmates say."

The egotistical James conducted his own trial with an American Civil Liberties Union lawyer as advisor. When I commented on this arrangement, Tom responded, "Where else but Atlanta Federal Penitentiary can an inmate practice law before a federal judge?" I sat outside the courtroom with Tom and other staff members. Our conversation was dominated by the seriousness of the trial. We all knew that if James won, we might as well quit and get another job because each one could be sued personally. Some of the correctional officers were complaining that inmates were taking over the prison with the aid of the federal courts. I listened to their concerns, but I doubted the feared result. What I didn't know was that James, in his role as advocate for inmates, had taken the prison system to court six times. Each cost him nothing, but it took a lot of time and money for the system to defend.

When it was my turn to testify, I was called into the courtroom and asked to be seated in the witness chair. As I looked at "Attorney" James, dressed in a natty three-piece suit with matching shirt and tie, I thought: *He looks like the epitome of success: an American citizen having his day in court. Where else but the United States, where freedom abounds, can an inmate question witnesses with the blessing of the court?*

It was obvious that the CONS minister was thoroughly enjoying himself, acting as a seasoned trial lawyer in a prestigious federal court and moving witnesses around like pawns in a chess game.

After I was sworn in, James began his questioning. "Chaplain, will you state your name for the records?"

"My name is George R. Castillo."

"Spell your last name."

"C—A—S—T—I—L—L—O."

"State your qualifications for the court. What schools did you graduate from?"

"I graduated from the University of Maine with a Bachelor of Arts Degree, from Bangor Theological Seminary with a Master's Degree in Theology, and from Ashland Seminary with a Master's Degree in Pastoral Psychology and Counseling."

"What denomination do you belong to?"

"The United Church of Christ."

"Where have you pastored before working for the Federal Bureau of Prisons?"

"I have pastored churches in Detroit, Michigan, and Shaker Heights, Ohio."

"Who is paying you right now?"

"Uncle Sam."

"A few weeks ago I walked into your office and asked you to make a telephone call to my family for me and you refused. Why did you refuse?"

"I refused because you demanded that I make the call

without explaining the reason you needed to talk to your family. I previously made several calls for you, but at no time were you so belligerent."

"Who authorized me to demand a telephone call from you?"

"Very good question. You'll have to ask and answer that question yourself." (The jurors laughed.) I should also add that you demanded a note from me to verify that I refused to cooperate with you."

"Chaplain, just answer the questions," he said with authority.

"Does the name Reverend Helen Leen ring a bell with you?"

"No, it doesn't," I said.

"Let me refresh your memory. A few weeks ago the Reverend Leen wanted authorization from your office to visit me and you refused. Do you remember her?"

"Yes, I do now. I didn't remember her name, but I remember the incident. You told me that you ordained her yourself."

"Why didn't you let her in as you let in other clergy?"

"You'll remember, I told you to ask her to write me. Well, she didn't. No one, not even clergy, walks into Atlanta Federal Penitentiary without taking the necessary steps for admission."

"Has Warden Henderson (pointing to him sitting in the defendant's seat) ordered you not to cooperate with me?"

"No, Warden Henderson has not said a word to me about you," I responded.

"What about his assistants or any other staff?"

"No one has talked to me about you," I emphasized.

"Did you meet with the staff and talk about this case?" he asked defiantly.

"Yes, I did," I answered.

"What did you find out?" James asked with superiority.

"I didn't find out anything. I left the group frustrated because I still didn't know why I was coming to court," I answered somewhat annoyed.

"How many times did you meet?" James asked triumphantly.

"I met with them twice," I responded.

"That's all I have, Your Honor," James said cockily as he looked at the judge.

"Your witness," the judge said to Mr. Henderson's Bureau of Prisons attorney.

"I have no questions for Chaplain Castillo, Your Honor," he

responded .

"Chaplain, you are dismissed, " said the judge.

"Thank you, Your Honor," I responded, relieved.

Heroes and Villains

I left the courtroom and went back to work, where I soon discovered that inmates have interesting ways of labeling their heroes and villains. Upon my arrival in the institution, several inmates asked me, "Chaplain, have you been on the witness stand?"

"Yes," I responded as I continued walking.

The inmates were having a field day. To many, James was a hero. At last, an inmate had the upper hand and had required the staff to answer him in federal court. But other inmates saw it differently. A former member of the CONS Church, Mike, said when referring to James, "That man is a show-off and con artist. That's the reason why I left his church. I know him very well. He told me he was going to set you up, but I knew that you wouldn't fall into his trap. You are too good, sympathetic, and honest."

"Thank you, Mike," I replied.

That afternoon I kept reflecting on the court scene. More curious than angry, I realized that this was a brand new world to me, and I concluded that this was part of being a Chaplain. It went with the turf.

Before the day was over, my supervisor, Associate Warden of Programs, Mr. Harold McKenzie, called me into his office.

"Chaplain, I heard you were a good witness."

"I only spoke the truth," I responded.

Muriel, a former court officer herself, remained in court all day. She assured me at the dinner table that night that she felt James didn't have a case. "George, it's a waste of time and taxpayers' money. Don't hold James' arrogance and cockiness against him. He was kind to you compared to how he questioned and talked to the other staff witnesses. It was obvious he didn't respect them, but he respected you."

Muriel went back to court on the second day of the trial. That afternoon the jury adjourned, and within an hour they returned a "Not Guilty" verdict.

It was rumored among the custodial staff that my testimony

was the turning point of the case. Officers Edward, John, and Andy were among those who congratulated me. I repeated to them, "I didn't say anything but the truth."

Andy said, "You're one of us," as he patted me on the back.

Although Donald James lost the case, as far as he and his followers were concerned, he won. After all, he practiced law which he had studied in prison, he sued the warden, and he disrupted the staff by having some of them spend time in court. His stock rose among the inmates. And he was elevated to hero status by some because he questioned staff disdainfully in court — something he wouldn't dare do in the institution. An inmate was overheard saying, "We got a celebrity among us. James took the bosses to court. Way to go, James!"

The national media's attention contributed to his aura. *Newsweek* mentioned him in an article entitled "The Jailhouse Lawyer" dated September 2, 1974. Before the article was on the newsstands, James joyfully came to my office and showed me the draft.

Chapter 5

Prisoners Are Human Too

During my eighteen months of service at Atlanta Federal Penitentiary, my knowledge of human nature greatly expanded. I saw families whose relationships were planted in love and sacrifice. Then there were prisoners who never had a visit or even a letter from family or friends. Forgotten by those outside the prison walls, these lonely inmates had relationships only with their fellow prisoners who became their substitute families.

Roosevelt, a tall, black, middle-aged inmate serving a 25-year sentence for armed bank robbery, was one of those forgotten people. "Chaplain," he complained, "I haven't received a letter from home in over five years and probably won't the whole while I'm here."

I instantly understood why he looked forward to his weekly counseling sessions and would wait even when I was late. Roosevelt seemed to be well on his way to rehabilitation, and I began to feel that it would be helpful for him to get at least a monthly letter from someone on the outside. "Roosevelt, I'll try to see what I can do to get you a pen pal."

Immediately, Mrs. Charlotte Durant, one of my former parishioners, an active Christian who never tired of doing good, came to mind. She gladly accepted the invitation to write Roosevelt, which she did regularly. About six months into the correspondence, Roosevelt asked her for money. Mrs. Durant sent his letter to me.

I wasn't happy about that. "Roosevelt, why did you request money from Mrs. Durant? You know that was not the reason why I arranged your pen-pal relationship. Besides, you know as well as I do that inmates do not need money in prison. Your every need is taken care of. The money you earn from work is more than sufficient for your commissary needs."

"But, Chaplain, I didn't mean no harm. My singing group wants to do some recording, and we needed the money to get it done. So I just thought she would like to help."

"Your behavior is unacceptable. Do not correspond with Mrs. Durant again," I admonished. Because he didn't see anything wrong with his action, he complied only grudgingly with my instructions. But I felt guilty for putting Charlotte in a bind and I apologized to her.

People can change, and Roosevelt did. About ten years later, while I was at Eglin Federal Prison Camp, Superintendent Michael Cooksey asked me to respond to a letter offering religious books to inmates. When I called to discuss the books, I was surprised to find myself talking to Roosevelt. He told me, "Chaplain, I'm now a minister with a prison ministry and want to help the imprisoned as I was helped." I accepted his offer.

The Love of Money Is the Root of All Evil

For obvious reasons, inmates are not allowed to handle money while incarcerated. Money is considered contraband. Their eleven cents an hour wages are deposited into their account along with any money relatives and friends send to the institution for them. When inmates buy cigarettes, snacks, and toiletries from the commissary, the purchase price is deducted from their accounts. Being creatures of habit, inmates like to deal with the familiar exchange — money. Therefore, they devise all sorts of means to get it.

Trusted inmates who work outside the walls are usually pressured to bring money into the institution. Bill Jones, one of our active worshipers had minimum custody and that enabled him to work outside under minimum supervision. He broke the trust within a short time. Bill was caught bringing money and drugs into the institution.

"What's the problem?" I asked when I visited him in segregation. Softly and slowly, he answered with his head down, without eye contact: "Chaplain, I was caught in the middle. The best way to get out of it was to have the authorities catch me. I was pressured by inmates to bring money and drugs in for them. If I refused, I could be maimed or killed as a lesson to those who didn't cooperate. If I was suspected of working with the authorities, they would also kill me. Either way I was a loser. I live here with these people 24 hours a day, and I couldn't stand the pressure. So I made my actions obvious to get caught and lose minimum custody."

After a week, Bill rejoined the general population, but as long as he remained in Atlanta he didn't go outside the walls.

Inmates also put a premium on money not because they need to buy food or other necessities, but because of gambling. Buddy Johnson, a jittery young newcomer to prison, tried to con his school-teacher aunt into sending him money for eyeglasses. I was somewhat surprised when she called from Jackson, Mississippi, and in a rather uptight voice said, "Chaplain, my nephew Buddy Johnson writes me often, and I just received a letter from him today in which he told me he needs $500 immediately to buy eyeglasses. That sounded exorbitant. I want to help him save his eyes, but don't want to be taken advantage of. Do you know, or can you find out, how much money he really needs to replace his glasses?"

"Miss Johnson, I am sorry to hear that. Your nephew does NOT need a penny for glasses or any medical needs. The Bureau of Prisons provides completely free health care for all inmates, even if they have health insurance. I will talk to your nephew."

Before I was able to call Buddy, he came to my office. He had just spoken with his aunt and knew that I was aware of his game. "Chaplain, I'm sorry I got you involved with my aunt. I really need $1,000 instead of $500 to settle my gambling debts. I've got to have the money. I'm in big trouble."

"Buddy, the best thing you can do now is talk to the Chief Correctional Supervisor. Tell him your story, and he will probably provide you protection."

Buddy was placed in segregation as a temporary measure to protect him. His gambling buddies knew he had talked to the authorities, and if anything happened to him they would be suspect. I don't believe Buddy ever stopped gambling, but he got it under control enough to keep out of further trouble.

Gambling is serious business in prison. Inmates' unwritten code of conduct states: "You gamble. You lose. You pay one way or another." It was common for inmates to check themselves into segregation for their safety because of gambling debts.

Inmates will gamble for anything. On one of my visits to the recreation building I saw men playing games around the shuffle-boards, pool and ping pong tables, weightlifting and other equipment. I commented to Wally Kline, the correctional officer who was supervising the area, "It's great to see the men making use of the recreation equipment. At least it keeps them healthy, occupied, and out of trouble."

The officer laughed and said, "Chaplain, even though no money is involved, they're gambling. I know they are because they huddle before each game. After the game, commissary items like cigarettes, cokes, and cookies are exchanged quickly and quietly. They know if I or any other officer catches them, they're going straight to the hole. But these slick cons are smooth, slimy, and fast."

"By looking at them, I never would have known," I said in disbelief. "They sure had me fooled. How's it done?"

"They manage to pay off big debts legally too. Sly over there (pointing to a tall, lanky, acned baby-faced inmate), just got permission from his case manager to send money from his account to Terry's brother who lives in Arkansas. We all suspect it's to pay off Sly's debt, but we can't prove it. If you were around here long enough, you'd notice that Sly and Terry are always shooting pool against each other, and Sly gets whipped each time."

The authorities could not do anything about the suspected gambling because, like the law on the outside, one is innocent until proven guilty.

Not All Requests Are Bogus

We tend to see people in the light of our experiences. Some inmates see a Chaplain as staff, while others think of him as a Man of God, set apart from the system and the institution. This allowed me sometimes to help inmates cut through red tape when the situation warranted. Such was the situation one Saturday morning when Tommy Harris rushed to my office. "Chaplain, I need your help bad. My fiancée flew all the way from D.C., and they wouldn't let her in."

"Why, Tommy?" I inquired.

"They said she wasn't on my visiting list."

"You know that anyone who comes to see you must be on your list regardless of relationship or distance he or she traveled."

"I know that, Chaplain. She's supposed to be on my list. Two weeks ago she got the forms, and she returned them right away because she wanted to be here this weekend."

"Tommy, wait here in the hall. What's your fiancée's name? I'll go and talk with her outside."

Strong empathy arose within me as I left my office to meet Gloria outside the main entrance. She was an attractive, tired-looking, upset, and very disappointed young lady. Her eyes were red from crying. I introduced myself and asked, "What's the problem?"

Gloria told me, "Sir, I came here all the way from D.C. to see my fiancé and now I can't get in. I don't understand why because Tommy sent me the forms two weeks ago, and I filled them out right away and took them to the post office myself the next day." Between sobs she continued. "I just knew everything was okay so I flew to Atlanta early this morning and took a cab to get here to see Tommy. Now I can't see him."

No promises were made because I didn't know what I could accomplish by interceding. "I know it's tough, but please try to get yourself together. I'm going to talk to someone."

Chief Correctional Supervisor Anthony Brown was the duty officer. He was in the Lieutenant's office talking with Lieutenant Mays when I explained the dilemma to him. I also assured him that I recognized the prison policy of only allowing visitors on the approved list to visit. "But something seems amiss," I continued. "Tommy Harris' fiancée claims that she sent her visitor's form in two weeks ago, and she seems sincere and certain. However, she hasn't been allowed to enter. I don't believe it will look good for us to have a lady fly from D.C., say she mailed her form, and then be denied a visit."

As the Captain carefully listened to me, Lieutenant Mays interrupted, "Chaplain, why don't you leave custody alone and stick with religion?" I ignored his remarks, paused a few seconds, and then continued speaking with Captain Brown.

"Because of this situation, I recommend she be allowed to visit now. We can document her story and bring the matter to the attention of the inmate's case manager on Monday." Captain Brown thanked me for my concern, but didn't say yes or no.

I left not knowing the outcome, and I returned to speak with anxious Tommy. "I just spoke with custody and pled your case but, as you know, custody makes the decisions. I really don't know what's going to happen. Just hang tight."

He clearly understood and reluctantly accepted my advice, yet I knew he was hurting. I also knew that the Captain had the authority to grant an exception and custody, having been burned too many times, had to be extremely cautious. I didn't think this was one of those times, but it was out of my hands. I was relieved, however, that before Tommy left my office an announcement came over the public address system: "Tommy Harris report to the visiting room."

Common sense ruled this time. His fiancée was allowed to visit him.

Casanova Is Alive and Well

As human beings, our security comes from being comfortable with associates and those who love us. Shaky relationships cause feelings of insecurity and uncertainty. When an inmate has been incarcerated for a long time, he becomes anxious to find out where he stands in his relationship with those he left behind. The inmate wants to protect himself from being without meaningful relationships on the outside.

My clerk, Charles Duncan, wanted to be sure that a woman would be waiting for him upon his release. He was rather thin and ordinary looking with a moody disposition, but he probably wouldn't have had too much difficulty finding a companion once released. However, he didn't take any chances. He became engaged to three lonesome, vulnerable ladies at the same time. That was bad enough, but he also used his position as Chaplain's clerk to legitimize himself. People assumed that "if he worked for the Chaplain, that made him a good prospect."

Unfortunately, many women are lonesome and without meaningful male relationships. It is not uncommon for such a woman in desperation to be willing to have a writing/visiting relationship with a prisoner with the hope that she'll have a man when he gets out. I began to get calls from ladies asking for information about Charles. It became apparent that about five or six ladies were waiting for his return home and that each planned an early wedding upon his release. Unfortunately, the inmate's right to privacy prevented me from providing personal information about him to my callers. Sadly, all I could tell each of them was, "Wait until he gets home before you start planning."

A concerned father called one afternoon, "Chaplain Castillo, my daughter hardly knows your assistant Charles, but she thinks she's in love with him. She wants to marry him when he's released. But before the relationship goes any further, I thought I'd better talk with you. First, let me ask you, do you have children?"

"Yes, Sir, I do. I too have a daughter," I said.

He continued, "Chaplain, then I feel as if we can talk father-to-father."

"Sir, before we go any further, let me correct your earlier statement. Charles is not my assistant. He's my clerk. I do not have an assistant."

"Has he always been your clerk?"

"Yes," I answered.

"Do you know that your clerk has been telling my daughter he's your assistant?"

"I didn't know that, but I'm not surprised. Thanks for telling me."

"If you were in my shoes, Chaplain, would you advise my daughter to wait for that convict?"

"Being a father myself, I would be concerned about my daughter's love affair also. I know how you feel. However, my advice would be for your daughter to wait until he is released from prison. It is only then that she can make a decision about marriage after she gets to know him."

"Chaplain, this is exactly what I've been telling Marcia — wait! I wish she were at home now to hear it directly from you. Thank you, Chaplain."

It was time to have a session with Charles. As I enumerated the calls to him, he started laughing. To him, it was a big joke and a game. However, he didn't consider that it was very serious for the women and their families.

"Which one do you intend marrying?" I asked.

"None of them," he said gleefully.

"What about all these ladies who are waiting to marry you?"

Without emotion, Charles began, "Sir, they're the ones who want to get engaged and married. I've already told them that I'm not ready yet. Since they're pushing it, I go along with them and tell them what they want to hear."

"Don't you know that you're hurting them? Charles, it isn't right to mislead those women. How about writing and telling them what you told me. Don't forget to add that you're *not my assistant.*"

Charles promised to "come clean." Evidently he did because the calls gradually ceased. However, through the inmates' grapevine, I learned he's back in another federal institution, this time as the "Sweetheart Swindler" who not only stole lonesome women's hearts, but their pocketbooks.

Till Death Do Us Part

Prisons are very hard on families, especially the wives. Knowing this, inmate Paul White tried to ease some of the burden for his wife. He had a good relationship with her and worked diligently in prison industries, where the pay rate was higher. By working many hours of overtime he was able to earn a monthly average of $100, which he joyfully sent to his wife. When Paul was about to go home, the relationship soured. His wife's attitude changed. Tearfully, Paul shared his experience with me and asked, "What do you think it is, Chaplain?"

Although I knew what that behavior usually meant, I didn't answer his question with my opinion. Instead, I asked him, "What do you think?"

"I believe she has a man at home, and she doesn't want me to return."

"Paul, I hope that is not the case. Before you jump to conclusions, talk with your wife now and continue the communication after you return home. Marriage counseling will help both of you adjust to your new roles."

Paul was so interested in saving his marriage that upon his release eight months later he encouraged his wife to go into counseling with their Pastor. My heart leaped with joy when I spoke to them about a year later and learned they were happily working on a "new beginning."

Sheroes

Wives and families are the second victims of crimes committed by the incarcerated. Many become the unsung "sheroes" who are a blessing. As the country song says: "They Stand By Their Man." It was not unusual for women to drive hundreds of miles to spend a weekend with their loved ones. Over the years, I have watched faithful wives, family members, and fiancées make tremendous sacrifices in order to be supportive of their loved ones behind bars. Many times the families pay a greater price for the crime than the incarcerated. The hands-on decisions and responsibilities are transferred from the inmate to the ones they leave behind. The inmates' sole responsibility is to abide by regulated routines of waking, eating, working, playing, and sleeping.

One "shero," Mrs. Helen Thomas, faithfully visited every month and every holiday during the eight years her husband William served for embezzlement. A middle-aged woman, she had been a privileged homemaker whose life revolved around her family and the community. Then everything changed when Bill was arrested, tried, convicted, and incarcerated. Their lives and their children's were turned upside down. The once-proud family went through agony and embarrassment. Their life savings suffered a blow; Mrs. Thomas had to secure a second mortgage to pay legal fees. She told me, "Chaplain, before Bill's arrest I never had to do anything but take care of my home. Now all the responsibility is mine. My driving was limited to getting around town to shop in the mall and the grocery store! No more! In order to see Bill, I have to drive 10 hours one way for our weekend visit. Thank God my children, who are suffering themselves, are so supportive. My son found me a job and keeps my car running."

Many times she left the institution in bad weather and too tired to make it home that night. She endured the extra expense of staying in a motel until the next morning to continue her journey. Even though Bill was always anxious when she left the institution alone, I only placed calls for him when the weather was bad to find out whether she arrived home safely. Despite the sacrifice, she never missed a monthly visit during his incarceration. I am happy to say that six years after Bill's release, we're still in contact. Bill is an appreciative man who has resumed his responsibilities and his family is doing beautifully.

There are many Helen Thomases waiting for their mates to come home. These loyal women are called upon to accomplish unfamiliar tasks. Through God's grace and their faith, they find the strength, courage, and ability, to meet the challenges. I salute and respect these faithful, committed mates.

To the inmates fortunate enough to have one of these "sheroes," I say cherish her. I remind the inmates of God's Words in Proverbs 31: "When one finds a worthy wife, her value is far beyond pearls. Her husband, entrusting his heart to her, has an unfailing prize. She brings him good, and not evil, all the days of her life. Strength and honor are her clothing...."

Welcome to the World of Parole Board

There are two sentences that an inmate receives. The first is the one given by the court. The second is the length of time the inmate actually serves, which is determined by the Parole Commission. Since I began my prison ministry, the name of the Parole Board changed to Parole Commission. They still perform the same function. However, since 1987 sentencing guidelines promulgated by a commission created by a "Sentence Reform Act" require that an inmate serve 85% of his time. Previously he was only required to serve two-thirds, at most.

The three board representatives have the power to determine when an inmate is released. As a result, the days leading up to board hearings were always filled with anxiety and tension. A hush filled the hallways of the entire facility whenever the parole officials entered.

Being new to the system, I didn't realize the role a Chaplain could play in the parole hearings. I was soon to learn that the inmates were fully aware of my ignorance of the process and were ready to use it to their advantage if given a chance. They might well have succeeded if it had not been for Tony, my inmate typist. With pride he claimed to have trained Chaplains before me. With a twinkle in his eye, he said that it was now my turn to receive my "on-the-job training" from him.

"Chaplain," he asked, "have you noticed the dramatic increase in inmate participation in the Religious Programs lately, especially the ones that you lead? Did you notice how many are asking you how to become true Christians?"

I have to admit that my ego had been telling me that my efforts, concern, and long hours caused the sudden increase and that the inmates were just responding to my concern for their needs. Something stopped me from saying what I was thinking. Instead, I put my vanity aside and asked, "What do you think is causing the increase?"

Tony started laughing. "The Parole Board is going to be here next week, Chaplain. The men are playing a game with you. Soon some of those new converts will ask you for a letter to the Parole Board about their religious rehabilitation and others will even ask you to accompany them to their parole hearings. You really care, Chaplain. Don't let them take you for a fool because you're new."

Tony was right. Because of his advice I was ready when several inmates asked for letters of reference and recommendations for their parole release. Although I didn't always give them what they asked for, I made sure I counseled with every one who made a request. The ones who had truly been faithful and showed signs of rehabilitation received my endorsement. Others were dealt with the way I dealt with Sam Whitehouse, one of our many convicted drug dealers.

"Chaplain, I'm going to the Parole Board next week. Can you please give me a letter to the Parole Board?"

I asked, "What kind of letter are you talking about?"

"A letter saying I have been coming to church and that I am ready for parole."

"Are you asking me to tell the Parole Board that because you came to church for the last two weeks you are ready to be paroled?"

"You don't have to tell them how long I've been coming."

"You want me to tell them the truth, don't you? Or do you want your Chaplain to lie?" I asked.

"No, I don't want you to lie. I just want you to say something nice about me."

"Such as?"

"You're an educated man. You know what to say."

"Sam, that's my problem. I don't know what to say about you because I have only known you for two weeks."

"Chaplain, I have been here for over five years."

"That may be so. Although I have been here for almost a year, I have known you for only two weeks. Where have you been?"

"I guess I haven't been coming around as I should cause I don't want to be known as one of the 'Kneelers and Squealers.' Religion in prison is for the weak."

"You mean you're embarrassed to come to the Chapel because of what other inmates will say?" I asked.

"Yes, but I believe. I used to go to church every Sunday with my grandmother. After I was about nine, I quit going and wouldn't listen to her."

Hoping to help him see his real problem, I replied, "Sounds like you continued in that pattern, even here. How do you feel about that?"

"Not too good," Sam responded.

"It's not too late to start again."

I knew that with Sam's attitude, he would have little chance of success before the Parole Board. I tried to get him to begin thinking about how he could prepare himself for release while in prison. "What have you been doing with your spare time?" I asked.

Sam looked at the floor and responded, "Nothing much."

"What do you mean by nothing much?"

"I work in industry and in the evening I do recreation."

"Have you given school some consideration? A few weeks ago several inmates, including my typist Tony, graduated from De-Kalb Junior College."

"I ain't interested in school right now. I'll go back to school when I go home."

Sam was like the majority of inmates, planning to wait until his release to make any meaningful changes. Knowing that this is usually too late, I recommended that Sam start his education NOW. "Yes, Sam, it is psychologically difficult to study during incarceration. But there are dozens of motivated inmates studying under the same conditions as yours."

Who Said Life Is Fair?

To enhance my growth, I sat through Parole Board hearings. As each inmate's past and present offenses were summarized, I felt frightened as I realized that I had been alone with some very vicious criminals during counseling sessions. Some of those men were criminals from their pre-teen years on and crime was the only life they knew. They had been in and out of prisons from an early age and would be in and out the rest of their lives because they had no desire to change.

Bobby Braxton was not one of these. I knew him very well as an active member of the prison Church Community, and I had counseled with him repeatedly. He was a distinguished, tall, and stately lawyer with mixed grey hair. In his mid 60's, he was serving his first conviction. Before coming to Atlanta, Braxton had attained a high public office in West Virginia and had enjoyed a good reputation in his community. But power and greed got the best of him. Along with his accomplice, John Jackson, he became involved in a kickback scheme and was caught. Because both men were involved in the same crime, Braxton was angry about being in Atlanta Federal Penitentiary instead of being with his accomplice in "Holiday Inn," as Eglin Federal Prison Camp is often referred to by the inmates.

To my disbelief, Braxton's future was decided before he entered the Parole Board's hearing. In their discussion, the board members acknowledged that Braxton had learned his lesson, was no threat to the community, and was unlikely to commit another crime. Yet because of his background there was concern that parole now would be viewed as preferential treatment and that this, in turn, might lead the inmate population to retaliate in some way.

The three board representatives agonized over their decision but, in the end, the reality of the moment prevailed. "Braxton," the board spokesman said, "you will not be paroled at this time. The severity of your crime and your betrayal of the public trust warrant your continued incarceration."

Like so many suffering a major disappointment, Braxton found my office a safe place to cry. With a choking voice he told me, "Chaplain, my parole was denied. John did the same thing I did and he got a parole date. I can't understand why this is happening to me. I'm a good man — a good father, husband, and church member. Everybody knows I served my community well. I helped people without hurting anyone. Ask anybody."

Braxton reiterated over and over: "Why? I can't understand it. Chaplain, if I'm asleep, please wake me up. I can't believe this is happening to me."

I listened patiently and let him cry it out, being able only to sympathize and empathize. At the close of the session, I put my hand on his shoulder and said, "Bobby, I'm sorry you didn't get your parole. Keep the faith; you've come too far to quit now. My door is always open. Come in for counseling whenever you feel the need."

It took a while, but Braxton gradually accepted the Parole Board's decision and continued to serve the church, using his skills and energy to help other inmates with their legal problems.

Chapter 6

Ashland, Kentucky: A Time of Growth and Change

Early one afternoon, Ralph Graham, the Southeast Regional Chaplain, called me to his office and asked whether I would consider a transfer to Ashland Federal Youth Center, Ashland, Kentucky, to fill a position that had remained vacant for several months. He added, "George, since it's a youth center, you could be very helpful to the young people there." After some discussion, I asked Ralph to give me 48 hours to think about it.

God works in mysterious ways. "Coincidentally," within that 48-hour period personnel from various institutions were touring the prison, and I saw someone's name tag with Ashland Federal Youth Center boldly printed on it. I quickly introduced myself to Fred Dickinson and asked him about the youth center. He said warmly, "You'll like Ashland, Kentucky. It's a small country town, full of nice people. The prison itself is running over with young people, and they need a Chaplain to help them find morals and values."

Helping young people had always appealed to me; I found it interesting that both men mentioned this need at Ashland. I thought *perhaps I could be helpful there because I find young people more flexible, open, and willing to change than older people. Besides, if we can change their focus at an early age, they and society would benefit tremendously.*

I became convinced that Ashland should be my new assignment, but I had one more step — talking with Muriel. We had been in Atlanta only eighteen months since the move from Shaker Heights, and Muriel knew that a move meant establishing another home and job hunting all over again. She knew, too, that the proposed transfer would require a period of separation because she would have to remain in Atlanta until Marcelle finished the school year. But she accepted all this as a way of life for civil servants. Fortunately, Marcelle was a good trooper too and would be able to adjust readily.

As usual, Muriel encouraged me to follow my desire. She supported my choice. Wives bear an unequal burden as they help husbands further their careers. I love my wife and respect her as I respect all the other wives who go the extra mile for their families.

After I told Ralph I would accept the Chaplaincy at Ashland, it became official and was announced in *The Key*, the official institution newspaper. Staff members who hadn't spoken before sought me out. Donald Green, a stand-offish correctional officer, was one of those. "Chaplain, I hate to see you go. You've been doing a good job here. Wish you luck."

Tom Hatfield, another of the quiet officers, said, "Chaplain, I have been observing you. You work hard and long hours, and you have made a difference with many of the inmates who were troublemakers. I hope you'll continue to be successful in Ashland. They're younger there and hopefully you'll have a hand in keeping them from coming here."

Inmates came out of the woodwork to tell me all about Ashland and what to expect. All assured me that I would like it there. Many, like inmate Marcus Washington, said, "Chaplain, you'll like Ashland. I was there in 1968. It's better than here."

January 12, 1975, was my last Sunday in Atlanta. More inmates than normal were present in the Chapel that morning. As I looked at my congregation, I realized that I would never see some of them again. Some would revolve in and out of institutions, a few would die in prison, and some would go into the larger society and be absorbed among the honest-living citizens. Some might one day be our neighbors. As I looked from the pulpit at God's multicultural mosaic expressions representing every race, color, belief, and unbelief, I whispered a prayer for them all.

While packing the car to head for Ashland, Marcelle said, "Daddy, I'll miss you." My heart was heavy to leave my beautiful, happy 6th grader. I forced a smile as I hugged her and kissed Muriel. "Take care of each other," I whispered to the beautiful females in my life. Our sons, Joe and Erick, were now men on their own. Joe was working for a Fortune 500 company in New York, and Erick had established his own home after marrying his childhood sweetheart, Martha, in 1974.

It was Dr. Martin Luther King, Jr.'s birthday, and I listened to tributes about him as I drove through the beautiful hills of Tennessee and Kentucky. What a difference between 1965 and 1975! In 1965, our country was not prepared to accept a black man as a messenger sent by God to help our nation attain freedom and justice for all. But this day, Dr. King was no longer considered a communist, an agitator, a troublemaker, a coon, or a foreign agent. He was now accepted as a caring Christian, an all-American patriot with personal convictions to right the wrongs in our society. I thanked God for Dr. King, His prophet to America, who helped to open the door for me and others.

I began reflecting on my life and how God had taken me from British Honduras and molded me into a successful prison Chaplain. I mentally tuned out the radio and found myself worshipping God. The weariness of travel was replaced with a feeling of indebtedness to the civil rights workers who had followed Dr. King's leadership. Those saints and martyrs willingly put their bodies on the line and laid down their lives for their fellow citizens' emancipation. Acts 7:52 was so appropriate. "Which of the prophets did your fathers not persecute....?"

Before I knew it, the 10 p.m. news had just begun and I was reporting to the Ashland Youth Center. After introducing myself to the control officer, he called the business manager, Joe Morales, who suggested that I check into a motel for the night. When I reported to work Thursday morning the first thing I learned was that I had broken Bureau policy by driving more than eight hours, or 300 miles, in one day.

Welcome Aboard, Chaplain

I was introduced to Roman Catholic Priest Chaplain Lee Trimbur, who was happy to see another Chaplain. With a warm smile and a firm handshake, he explained that he had been the only Chaplain at the facility for the past six months since the Protestant Chaplain had resigned to return to a church staff position. "Come on, let me show you the institution." With that, we began walking and talking as he introduced me to staff and inmates. "Father T," as the inmates addressed him, is a tall, greying, mild-mannered, friendly Priest with a good sense of humor.

I immediately noticed that Ashland Federal Youth Center was different from Atlanta. When we walked into the sleeping areas, several inmates were talking on the telephones. This pleased me because it meant I wouldn't have to be so intimately involved in placing inmates' emergency phone calls.

The Reverend William E. Garda, Pastor of Community Presbyterian Church, had been conducting the Sunday Protestant Worship Services and was present for my first service. I asked him to lead the service and introduce me to the congregation, which he did eloquently.

"Today is a new beginning for you and this man of God, Chaplain George Castillo, who is your new Shepherd. May God grant you a holy relationship...."

My first week-and-a-half was divided between the institution and house-hunting. I quickly learned the community, but I decided to remain in the institution's bachelor quarters until my family could join me. Warden Jay Flamm heard a false rumor that I was having a problem finding housing. Because of his concern, he called me into his office to confirm the rumor. I assured Mr. Flamm that what he had heard wasn't true. In fact, the realtors were very cooperative and showed me every house that I wanted to see, plus some others that they felt I would like. Mr. Flamm's big smile and relaxed expression indicated he was relieved. I shared my feelings with Father T, who laughed and said, "He's a good Catholic."

As our warm relationship developed, I soon renamed Father T, "Padre." We worked well together and always tried to arrange our schedules so that at least one of us would be present in the institution at all times.

Some of the few times we were both away from the institution were to attend local ministerial meetings. The first one we attended, Padre introduced me to several ministers and priests, who heartily welcomed me into their fellowship.

The morality of the protests over the Vietnam war was on everyone's mind and these ministers were no exception. The topic of this day's discussion was the Berrigan brothers, priests who had entered draft offices and destroyed registration records. One priest said in a confident manner, "I can't identify their actions as God's will. They are following the devil's will."

As the only black cleric among them, I felt it necessary to

share my views: "I am afraid to make such statements for not too long ago Dr. King's actions were viewed the same way. But were it not for him, our country wouldn't be liberated, and I wouldn't be here today. A hundred years from now those two priests and Dr. King may be sainted by the Roman Catholic Church." The sudden, uncomfortable silence was broken by the moderator's voice: "Please be seated. The meeting is ready to begin."

I was relieved to know that, in this group at least, opposing views did not mean the end of Christian fellowship. Ministers at the association spread the word that I had arrived and several preaching and speaking engagements at churches and civic organizations were forthcoming. The Christian community of Ashland not only opened its churches and homes to me, but also its hearts.

The Reverend Tom Vincell, Pastor of Normal Presbyterian Church, at 43rd and Winchester, asked me to preach in his absence. Because of my past racial experiences, I was somewhat apprehensive. I wondered if Tom knew that I was a black pastor. I later felt comfortable about accepting the invitation as Padre spoke highly of him. Nevertheless, I decided to visit the church the Sunday before I was to lead the Worship Service. My apprehension grew as I looked around and saw only God's lighter expressions throughout the congregation. *Am I going to be accepted or will I face an indifferent congregation?* I wondered. I prayed for God's guidance and direction and silently repeated the 23rd Psalm as I took my seat.

As the Reverend Tom Vincell issued the call for the congregation to prepare for Communion Service, I wondered *if I, a black man, would be welcomed to take communion?* I knew that I was included, though, when he said, "Every member of the body of Christ is invited to the Lord's table. Come one and all."

I felt comfortable with the services because my Belizean worship experience was very similar to their Anglo-Saxon Protestant religious practice. The social time in the Fellowship Hall was filled with Christian love. It was the beginning of a very positive experience that continued through the years. It wasn't long before I was speaking at local churches almost every Sunday.

After a few short months that seemed like an eternity, Muriel and Marcelle finally arrived, and we settled into a small comfortable house in Summit, about a mile from the institution. Muriel, as usual, was instantly accepted and began substitute teaching at the local schools. We joined several bowling leagues and Marcelle made a new set of friends. Ashland quickly became home.

Community involvement is always an integral part of any Chaplains' duties. At Ashland, the religious programs flourished with the support received from the Christian community. It delighted me each week to be an ecumenical minister and welcome different denominations to the prison.

Various groups visited the institution weekly, monthly, or occasionally. Among the regulars were Meade Station Church of God; Normal Presbyterian Church; the Friends (better known as Quakers) of West Virginia; Tri-State Christian Businessmen; Kentucky Christian College, Alcoholics Anonymous, Jehovah's Witnesses, Christ Temple AOH of Huntington, West Virginia, under the leadership of the Reverend Sister Katherine Jackson, who had a standing invitation every Mother's Day; and the Reverend Elsie Thomas, with his faithful and dedicated family.

The nearest church of my denomination was the First Congregational Church, United Church of Christ, in Huntington, West Virginia, 25 miles away. The distance prevented me from taking an active role in church activities. However, for the three years I was at Ashland, Pastors William L. Allen, Ray Woodruff, and I represented our denomination in the World Wide Ecumenical Communion Service. I always looked forward to participating on that Sunday as hundreds of Christians of different persuasions worshipped and broke bread together in the Name of our Lord, on one of the busiest streets of Huntington.

Because Chaplains' duties are so varied, I received a two-page job description of my duties upon my arrival at Ashland. However, I soon realized that my immediate supervisor, Dana Straight, Associate Warden of Programs, was unaware of my many responsibilities and how I spent my time. I've always found amusing the number of people who think ministers only work the couple of hours a week they are in the pulpit preaching. Therefore, for Straight's information, I kept a detailed log of each day's activities from April 1 to June 17, 1976, that included my involvement with staff, inmates, and the community. I didn't realize the impact this log had made until two years later, when Bob Horn replaced Dana Straight. After reading it, Horn sent me a complimentary memo:

George, I have read your activities log which covered the three month period of time during 1976. I must admit it was most enlightening concerning the time spent in direct contact with inmates. But even more important is the obvious sincerity and dedication you demonstrate toward the inmates. I certainly appreciated reading the time study and learning more about you as a highly dedicated employee. Thanks.

Prison Change Turns Deadly

In April 1976, the entire mission of the institution changed as the Ashland Federal Youth Center became Ashland Federal Correctional Institution. Younger inmates were sent to other institutions and were replaced by older inmates. Inmates between the ages of 23 through 25 remained.

Two months after the conversion, the first murder occurred. That was the first time I had to notify a mother that her son had died. It wasn't an easy task for me, and I wished I could do it in person rather than over the telephone. To help myself, I wrote out how I would deliver the tragic news.

"Mrs. Coffee, this is Chaplain George Castillo from Ashland Federal Correctional Institution. Are you Arnold Albert Coffee's mother?" I could hear the apprehension in her voice as she answered, "Yes, I am. Is there anything wrong?"

"Mrs. Coffee, I am sorry to let you know that Arnold was involved in an unfortunate incident at the institution.

"Is he all right?"

"No, Mrs. Coffee, I'm really sorry, but Arnold died late last night...." The sudden silence on the phone was replaced by a loud thud, followed by an even more deathly silence. My carefully planned announcement went out the window. In its place I kept asking, "Are you there?"

After what seemed like an eternity, another female voice shouted into the phone: "What's going on? Who are you?"

Before I could answer, she said, "My co-worker passed out. What did you tell her?"

"I am Chaplain Castillo. Unfortunately, I notified Mrs. Coffee of her son's death."

Abruptly, she said, "Call back in an hour," and hung up the

phone. I did as she instructed and precisely one hour later I called again. This time Mr. Coffee answered and I repeated the message I had given Mrs. Coffee earlier. Mr. Coffee's reaction stunned me: "I'm going to have a congressional investigation. You people are responsible for my son's death...."

I felt sorrowful as I listened to him vent his angry feelings. I knew he was hurting and I didn't take his angry remarks personally. Instead, I tried to leave him with the feeling that there was someone within the institution who actually cared about him and his family's feelings.

Like most first-time experiences in prison, this one came complete with several lessons. The ordeal drove home the fact that inmates will almost always believe any other inmate rather than a member of the staff.

Normally, I don't have any confidential conversations in the presence of an inmate. However, I didn't consider Arnold's death to be confidential when I spoke with his family since everyone knew about the murder and who committed the act. Moreover, his death came during an unusual time, when inmates were in and out of my office helping me move furniture from one building to another. This meant that the door was open during my conversation with Arnold's mother. By the time the moving project was over, inmates had spread the rumor that I had told the deceased's parent her son's death was due to an *accident*.

The inmates who respected me asked me to verify the rumor. Others, like John Kelley, were visibly angry. "How could you call a planned and calculated murder an accident?" After the third inquiry, I retrieved my note from the trash and shared it with Kelley and many others. They read the word I used, *incident* and not *accident*, and peace was restored.

All this reminded me again of the truth behind the axiom: *"Prison walls have ears."* From then on, I made sure that regardless of the circumstances, my door stayed closed at all times whenever I was talking to anyone!

Ashland's conversion from a Federal Youth Center to a Federal Correctional Institution elevated the institution to the criminal "Big Leagues." Prior to the change, fist fights settled arguments. Now stabbings and attempted murder became the means to end squabbles. While this was disturbing to me, I wasn't frightened for my own safety because I treated inmates decently, as human beings, and they respected me for it.

Since several inmates were young enough to be my children, I frequently had "father/son" type chats. Their response was heartening. "Pup," as my clerk liked to be called, summed up the statements of many when he said, "Rev, I appreciate your speaking to me like a father. I never had a grown-up man speak to me like you do."

Pup taught me a lesson I'll never forget. One day I raised my voice in disapproval to express my dissatisfaction with him after he typed a memo incorrectly twice. Without any change in expression, he responded, "Rev, I have fifteen years, man."

I realized that he was really saying that being shut away from society for fifteen years carries with it an even tougher set of problems than a couple of mistakes in a memo. As a result, perfection in typing was not a priority. "I've got plenty of time to do it over. How do you expect me to function normally?"

Sometimes I did forget and expected inmates to function normally in spite of their abnormal community. While constantly helping inmates to seek improvement in their work, I had to remind myself to be more patient with them regardless of the length of their sentences. Both those with long and short sentences suffered feelings of separation and guilt.

The truly mature inmates adjusted to their environment and learned to cope by finding strength within themselves. They dealt with one event at a time. The emotionally weak inmates were usually frustrated and angry. Their dysfunctional behavior led them in and out of segregation in B-cell house.

Living in solitary confinement is a lonely experience and my weekly visits to B-cell house were welcomed. I made friends with those who were segregated there by listening to their concerns. Upon their release, many made my office their first stop to get to know me better or to have me answer questions about the Bibles which I had given them. This presented an opportunity to invite them to Worship Services and Bible study as well as to group therapy sessions where they could learn from men who were coping well. Positive attitudes do rub off.

The Answers Are Within

Prisons are full of angry men. As a result, the conversations in my office were frequently heated. Some felt that the system had railroaded them. They were bitter and looked at me as a member and supporter of the status quo. James Clark angrily asked me, when I didn't agree with his negative stand, "What kind of minister are you, supporting the system?" He wanted to vent his anger and he expected me to see things his way and be against the warden and the other staff.

I learned to listen with empathy and not take sides. I have always been told that I am a good listener, but dealing with people whose script was so different from mine and from the norms of society was a special challenge. I had to listen very carefully to understand what they are feeling. To do so, I vicariously entered their world to be able to lead them to a better one. Doing this required that I create a safe environment when counseling so that the counselee could air his feelings freely and know that he was accepted and understood. I knew that "real" communication couldn't take place unless trust existed between the listener and the person unburdening his problem.

Inmates usually went to their counselors for advice on legal matters, half-way-house placement, furloughs, and personal and family matters. Sometimes they went to get information on different institutions and their programs. My function differed from that of the counselors. Besides answering inmates questions, I also included spiritual and religious guidance, without proselytizing, while allowing them to choose their own faith.

Fortunately, I was able to get through to many inmates by allowing them to feel comfortable while I acknowledged their feelings without voicing agreement or disagreement. While at ease, they usually either found the solutions to their problems or attained the inner peace and strength necessary to live with them under unnatural prison conditions.

Many times, however, I became frustrated with young men who wasted their time without taking advantage of the rehabilitation opportunities offered by the Education Department. Some would not work toward a high school diploma or even read a book. For these, looking at pictures in girlie magazines was as close as they got to reading. Some even refused to do their job assignments. I simply couldn't understand that type of mentality, remembering how hard it was for my classmates and me to attend school in Belize and how we would have done anything to get an education. It greatly displeased me to see inmates whose lack of initiative made them waste good opportunities. It was even more troubling to watch salvageable young men get stuck without doing anything to prevent themselves from getting caught in the revolving door of recidivism.

It's times like these that the "preacher needs a preacher." One day I asked Nick Stemill, a case manager, "What makes them so apathetic?"

"Chaplain," he said, "we're working with losers. These men are angry at everyone, including themselves. They will not accept what society dictates as the norm. Hence they are antisocial and refuse to accept responsibility. It's a common feeling that the world owes them a living, and they are collecting the debt in prison. They're not incarcerated because of what they did, or because they wanted to come here. Instead, it's always somebody else's fault."

Willie Corder personified Stemill's description. Willie claimed to have lived in ten foster homes before his first incarceration. When I started the choir in 1975, Willie was one of my original members. He left the prison but was returned because of parole violation. Again he joined the choir. I introduced him to the others as one of the charter members. Instead of being embarrassed, he was joyful to be back "home" and have the status of a charter member.

In Willie's situation, I felt he probably was in prison because of a family that neglected him and caused him to be shifted from foster home to foster home. Yet, I wondered, *When does one take responsibility for the bad breaks that life deals?*

During my three-and-a-half years at Ashland, Willie was paroled three times and returned three times. Once he was returned for making telephone calls and charging them to the FBI's telephone number. Prison life was almost a common family pattern for Willie. He asked me, "Chaplain, will you say hello to my uncle, Chad Corder, when you go to Atlanta Penitentiary for your conference?" Over the years I've met many men from the same family who were incarcerated at the same time.

Unfortunately, Willie's revolving door was not unusual; parole violations and prison were the norm for many inmates at Ashland. Many even became so institutionalized that they were afraid to return to society.

Prison was home for Strict, a model inmate with a fifteen-year sentence for armed bank robbery. After he served five years, the Parole Board gave him a parole date at the end of his sixth year. We all thought he was ready and several staff members, including myself, wrote letters of recommendation on his behalf. However, as soon as Strict got his parole date, he messed up. Knowing that it's a violation to bring food out of the mess hall, Strict brought out a plate of food in full view of the custodial staff. His infractions continued until he served his full sentence and could no longer legally be held.

Some inmates got worse instead of better. It became obvious that many Ashland Federal Correctional Institution inmates were potential candidates for Atlanta Penitentiary and similar higher-security institutions. Their penitentiary games, though small, were being perfected and getting bigger.

Too many people inside and outside our penal institutions appear to be spiritually bankrupt, which contributes to our decline in morals and values. My belief is that religion is the answer to most of our problems. Religion teaches us to go and "sin no more" and look for the answers within. Therefore, in counseling from a religious point of view I helped the inmates establish a relationship with God and others, gain inner strength and acceptance of self, and alleviate guilt by learning to forgive themselves and others.

Why Try?

When I arrived in Ashland, inmates and their families worshiped together in the Chapel to enhance family ties. These visits took on an added dimension when many of the families used the Chapel to pass drugs. An inmate who received drugs in the Chapel had his drugs stolen by another inmate as he was heading to his unit after the service. Drug passing and related incidents became so prevalent that the administration ended the family worship privilege. This brought a dramatic decrease in Chapel attendance. Inmates who stopped coming were branded "drug pushers," "female-lookers," or "phonies."

Drugs were not the only problem. Many inmates' morals and values were skewed or lacking, and they would do anything to get money, legally or illegally. All one had to do was walk through the prison to learn the truth that the love of money is the root of all evil. Most inmates are in prison because of money. Mike, a 24-year-old high school dropout who had never worked at an honest job, exemplified the prevailing thinking. One morning he complimented me on the attractiveness of my suit. "Rev, you sharp this morning. How much these folks paying you to work here?"

"One hundred dollars a week," I responded facetiously. He looked at me quizzically, for he knew that I made more than that.

"When I was on the street, I averaged $10,000.00 a week as a drug pusher."

"How much are you earning now?" I asked.

He laughed, gave me the high five, and said, "Okay, Rev, you got me." Mike was my priority for the next hour. I had hoped to establish a relationship so that in the future I could introduce him to upright thinking, which hopefully would lead to his earning an honest living. Instead, Mike tried his best to convince me that his life-long habit was the right way to act.

"Rev, when you get home and you're hungry, you go to the refrigerator, right?"

"Yes," I responded.

"If you broke, whatcha do?" he asked.

"I would borrow money or go look for a job if I were unemployed."

He replied, "Not me. I would go and hold up a bank, where the money is."

After three months of weekly counseling, I accomplished what I set out to do by introducing him to moral alternatives. But to be honest, I rather doubt that Mike ever became a nine-to-fiver.

Although I couldn't change everyone, I didn't give up. To keep from being discouraged by the many negative responses, I accepted the fact that no matter how hard one tries, people make their own choices and are responsible for their own thinking and actions.

In an effort to help promote positive change, inmates were allowed to spend Sundays with local ministers. The privilege was given only to adjusted inmates who completed a substantial portion of their sentences and exhibited acceptable behavior, work patterns, and character.

Inmate Earl Pratt, a good electrician and church member, wanted to participate in this program. He approached me: "Reverend James Lowe invited me to attend services with him on Sunday and visit his home afterwards. I would love to go. Can I?"

I didn't think he was ready, so I said, "Pratt, it would be a nice opportunity for you, but you can't go because you do not have community custody, and there isn't a thing I can do for you."

However, a few days later, Pratt's team, made up of his counselor and unit and case managers, gave him community custody because the institution needed him to do electrical work outside the confinement area. I questioned this in my mind but didn't say anything. I had always thought that community custody was earned and not based just on the institution's work needs.

Since Pratt had community custody, he got a furlough to his home in Indiana. What a furlough he had!!! Pratt held up a drug store and was clocked driving his getaway car at 125 miles an hour. The last time I heard of him he had graduated to one of our toughest prisons, Leavenworth Penitentiary.

Suicidal Inmates Are Common

Suicide and attempted suicide are common in prison. If an inmate displays suicidal tendencies he is immediately taken to the hospital and given treatment. However, sometimes the signs are not apparent.

Inmate Frank Miller, a very quiet, introspective young man, was a loner who didn't take advantage of any recreation or rehabilitation opportunities. During our counseling sessions I encouraged Frank to get involved and pleaded with him to participate in constructive activities. With a sullen expression and few words, he said, "I don't feel like it."

Psychologist Earl Washington and I worked with Frank for months, when a breakthrough came. I finally convinced him to participate in the religious programs, and he joined the choir. As our counseling sessions continued, he appeared to be gradually adjusting and interacting with other inmates. One day Frank told me he wanted to leave Ashland. This desire was not unusual; many inmates believe, without any factual evidence, that they would be better off in another prison, not realizing that they carry their thoughts and problems with them.

I was shocked to learn one morning that Frank had committed suicide. I was troubled as I thought, *Did I blow it? Did Frank give me any signs that I failed to pick up? Could I have done any more?*

The psychologist and I exchanged notes, talked, and tried to determine if and when Frank indicated he would take his own life, but we couldn't find any indications. Frank's death saddened both inmates and staff. We held a memorial service for him in the Chapel. I thought about him for weeks and offered many prayers for his soul.

Let God Do the Work

Inmates frequently think they have unlimited abilities and can do anything they desire without going through the agony of preparatory training. Some inmates expect God to instantly give them the ability to do ministry work. Robert Gibson was such an inmate.

Parole day came and I watched Gibson walk out of the institution to freedom with the goal of becoming a Christian minister. Several years later, I was taken aback by his call from London, England. "Chaplain Castillo," said Gibson, "I just want to talk to you and tell you what I didn't say before. You're the most together person I have met and I would like to share my future plans with you." He continued, "Upon my release, I joined a church at home in the Bahamas and shared my goal with the pastor. She put me in charge of the Youth Fellowship but didn't give me a chance to preach, and that's what I wanted to do. So after six months, I quit."

Knowing Gibson, I understood that he wanted to be an assistant pastor immediately and became upset when it didn't happen. He expected to find greener pastures in England but, to his surprise, the pastures in London were even dryer than those in the Bahamas.

I responded to him with the same recommendation I had given at the prison. "Gibson, I can understand your frustration, but it's self-inflicted. You want to be a minister without making the sacrifice of going through formal training. Since you have an undergraduate degree, you're halfway there. With effort you can do it. Join a church and become active in its ministry. After you have proven yourself, I'm sure the church will aid in your seminary training."

Gibson really didn't want to hear that advice. He still wanted a shortcut to the ministry, and I didn't know of any.

He's still a layman putting his energy into finding an easy way out instead of using his God-given intelligence constructively to attain his goal.

Some Inmates Become Winners

Successful inmates realized that in order to win they needed both a plan and the "guts" to put their desires into action. One of the joys of prison ministry was helping and encouraging winners. Several discussed their problems with me and tried to help themselves become better citizens.

Russell Davey became tired of getting into trouble and decided to change his life. Being motivated, he enrolled in education and often used one of the Chapel rooms to study. Besides encouraging him, many times I tutored him. During the three years I knew him in Ashland, Russell completed high school and two years of college. To earn his undergraduate degree, he requested a transfer to Texarkana Federal Correctional Institution, where he could complete his last two years of school. The officials cooperated and he got the transfer. I heard that Russell got his undergraduate degree and left prison and his former life of crime behind. He is now a working, taxpaying citizen. Winners like him made my efforts worthwhile.

Doc was another winner. Before incarceration, he was a professional organist/pianist, and he continued to use his talents while at Ashland for our Worship Services. Being very bright and personable, he made friends easily and became a "Big Brother" to a number of inmates, some of whom were older but less mature than he. When he wasn't able to get results with resistant inmates, he referred them to me. Because Doc talked to me about them beforehand, I was prepared to take an effective course of action. Doc was my valued helper.

People in the Ashland community recognized and appreciated Doc's talent too. For several months, under my escort and supervision, Doc voluntarily played for the Christian Methodist Episcopal Church (CME), on Greenup Avenue. As we were returning to prison one Sunday afternoon, Doc said, "Rev, I appreciate your taking me out to help the church. I always look forward to the trip, but returning is hard and depressing."

I understood how difficult it was for him to leave the warm, accepting, and appreciative Christian community and return to the hard, cold prison environment. But with encouragement, he went back each Sunday until he was paroled. He learned to savor the good and carry it over during the difficult times. He's still out.

While some inmates avoided work, others looked for it. Paul was a very ambitious and pleasant black Vietnam veteran about 26-years old. He had no work assignment and when he heard that I needed a clerk he applied for the position. Many others applied, but I eliminated them because they couldn't type a Sunday Worship Service bulletin. After struggling with the "hunt-and-peck system," many admitted in frustration that they couldn't type. But Paul completed the bulletin much more quickly than I expected, and with no errors. I hired him.

I discovered that Paul had learned to type in high school and continued typing all through his military experience. "I was born in D.C.," Paul told me. "I had two years of college before joining the U.S. Army and going to Nam, where I learned to perfect my typing skills fast to avoid going to the front lines. During the day, I typed the names of the daily casualties, and I performed extra guard duty at night."

"What are you here for?"

"Drugs."

"Are you addicted?"

"No, I sold for survival. I came back from Nam ready to go to work and settle down and start a family. But I couldn't get a job. It seems that people hated Vietnam vets, and when you're black it's another strike against you. So I did what was available. Rev, believe me, I knew better, but it was a matter of survival."

Paul was a very good clerk, and since he liked to be busy, he constantly asked for more work. When there was no office work, he studied the Salvation Army's religious correspondence course. To help him fill his spare time, I brought in my trumpet and gave him lessons. He was such a fine young man that I really missed him when he transferred to Tallahassee (Florida) Correctional Institution. Once when my family was passing through Florida on a vacation, I visited him in prison and was delighted to find out that he was continuing his course work.

Since his release, Paul has held a steady job for the last six years.

Many inmates promised to write or call me upon leaving but few did. I learned not to take their promises seriously. I was surprised, therefore, to get a call which began, "Chaplain Castillo, I bet you don't remember me."

The caller was right. I didn't remember Lee until he identified himself as a former choir member and reminded me that he left over a year earlier. He added, "Thank you for the help you gave me while I was at Federal Correctional Institution. I am working and doing well now."

"Lee, I'm really glad to hear from you. Thanks so much for calling. You made my day. May God continue to bless you. Keep on doing the right thing." His call was so gratifying that I paused to utter a word of silent prayer as I placed the phone back on the hook.

Volunteers Want To Do It Their Way

Volunteers are an integral part of a Chaplains' ministry. At Ashland every opportunity was given inmates to become rehabilitated and find creative outlets for their emotional and spiritual development. This went along with my philosophy that we must align our thinking with the presence of God and listen to the still, small voice. Therefore, I encouraged support groups and behavioral-modification classes as well as religious programs. To achieve my goals, I had three groups conduct weekly meetings in the Chapel: Jehovah's Witnesses, members of Alcoholics Anonymous, and the Tri-State Christian Businessmen. Eventually, the businessmen were assigned to different units for the purpose of reaching every inmate.

Under Warden J. Flamm's administration, religious

programs flourished. He believed that if our young men were to change religion needed to be involved. Warden Flamm's acceptance of our religious activities enabled the Religious Department to broaden the programs to include Ashland Ministerial Association members.

Those visiting ministers worked with the inmates one day a week. However, this program was short-lived as most ministers already had overloaded schedules. The one remaining volunteer, the Reverend Clarence Coleman, continued to visit, but he began putting his emphasis on spreading his own denomination's doctrine rather than teaching the good news of Jesus Christ, which was the aim of the program. He was asked to leave.

One evening I called the three volunteer groups to pray together for Divine Guidance before ministering to the inmates. The Jehovah's Witnesses, who call God "Jehovah," refused to pray with us because when we prayed we called our Divine Father "God." Another time, the Reverend Willie Hamilton brought his Church of Christ members and a 15-voice choir. As Doc played the congregation hymn, "Jesus Shall Reign," we expected our guests to join in this well-known Christian hymn. But they stood, folded their arms, and gazed at the ceiling without singing a note. When Mr. Hamilton began his part of the service, he explained, "I'm from a tradition that doesn't use musical instruments in worship because the early church didn't use it. We sing a cappella. That's why we didn't sing along with you."

Prison ministry is different from ministry on the outside. On the outside, worshipers can change churches if they don't like a particular denomination; inmates don't have that option. An institutional Chaplain must be an ecumenical minister, capable of working in a multi-denominational setting. This requires a great deal of flexibility to accept, respect, and bring varying beliefs together in harmony.

Scheming Inmates Kill a Good Program

Since volunteers supported the Religious Department, our Chapel choir was allowed to sing in the volunteers' churches under staff supervision. The inmates really looked forward to these town trips. They would have liked to go out weekly, but they were restricted to one Sunday a month. During the trips, some of the choir members gave Christian testimonies of what Christ had done and was doing in their lives. I frequently delivered a message appealing to the congregation to give the incarcerated a chance when they return home.

Our community trips went well until two schemers escaped. When they got to the church, they asked Padre for permission to use the rest room; of course, he consented. In a split second, both had escaped through the rest-room window. It took the authorities less than 24 hours to catch them. Later they were tried in court and given additional sentences!

Their escapes made the Religious Department the butt of jokes and admonitions from some of the staff: "Chaplain Castillo, are you letting them go too?" asked Jim Childs, correctional supervisor.

"You Chaplains are being conned. When are you going to learn you can't help these cons?" chided Ralph Thomas, case manager.

"We're here to hold them, not to let them go," added Ralph Brand, correctional officer, with a big, hearty laugh.

"Have you Chaplains learned your lesson yet?" asked typist Helen Allen.

Louise Brown, personnel secretary, piped in with, "They're worse than animals. A dog wouldn't run away from a friend."

Padre and I took the teasing good-naturedly. We did notice though that our hecklers didn't mention that the Religious Department was the only department taking inmates out of the institution to participate in developmental and rehabilitative programs. We also observed that the inmates didn't like the escapees any more than staff did because it meant their little taste of freedom was threatened.

The most awkward moment came when Warden Flamm, a devout Roman Catholic, handed Padre a letter of reprimand. Since the Warden saw the Priest as his pastor this was an uncomfortable moment for both of them.

Chaplaincy Extends into the Community

Occasionally I was called by people in the community to perform pastoral functions. About 7:39 a.m. on my day off on April 8, 1976, Mrs. Jean Trawick called my home to tell us, "We need your help. Yesterday an apparently homeless lady, Mrs. Hattie Day, was wandering in the vicinity of the bus station. We don't know anything about her. The Police Department, the welfare agency, and I all suspect that she came to visit a relative inmate at the institution. Reverend Castillo, could you check if there's a black man by the name of Day at the prison?"

"I don't know any, but I will find out and let you know."

The prison record office couldn't find anyone with that last name. Because Mrs. Day had no place to stay, a kindly senior citizen, Mrs. Ballinger, allowed her to stay free in her home for a few days. Hattie was uncommunicative and didn't reveal anything about herself, not even where she lived or where she was going. A search of her belongings showed a Belle Glade, Florida, address.

I called that address and learned from Mrs. Day's aunt, Annie Mae Jones, that her niece was emotionally disturbed. "She left Belle Glade last August, and we haven't heard from her since and don't want to either. She's caused us nothing but trouble," Mrs. Jones said emphatically.

Days, then weeks, passed and Hattie remained at Mrs. Ballinger's home. No one, not even city officials wanted to take responsibility for her. After about two months, the Police Department notified me that Mrs. Day had attempted suicide by trying to jump off the Ohio-Ashland Bridge. A diligent policeman saved her and returned her to the now distraught senior citizen's home. I tried talking with the stranger in our midst, but I couldn't break through her silence. I again contacted Mayor Welch and other city officials, urging them to get her out of Mrs. Ballinger's home and get her professional help. All the officials sympathized with Mrs. Ballinger, but they told us they couldn't forcibly put Mrs. Day out since she was an "invited guest."

Police officer Manny Halle shook his head and said, "It's a bad situation, but we can't do anything because Mrs. Day hasn't broken any law."

The problem landed in my lap. I had two people to check on: Hattie Day, who carried on lively conversations with herself and showed other signs of emotional unbalance, and Mrs. Ballinger, who was terrified by her lingering "guest."

I continued conversations with Mrs. Jones and finally convinced her to take responsibility for her niece. She agreed to come to Ashland and take Mrs. Day back to Belle Glade. The day before Mrs. Jones and another family member were to leave Belle Glade for Ashland, Mrs. Day packed her belongings and left town as mysteriously as she had entered.

Chapter 7
Into The Lion's Den

Consider it pure joy, my brothers, whenever you face trials of many kinds, because you know that the testing of your faith develops perseverance. Perseverance must finish its work so that you may be mature and complete, not lacking anything.   (James 1:2-4 NIV)

I t has been said that all good things must come to an end, and they did when Padre and I heard of Warden Flamm's retirement. It was a sad day for us as we would miss his considerate manner and great support for the Religious Department. Regional Director G. R. McCune named Earl Aiken, his long-time friend, as replacement.

Warden Aiken came in with a big stick. Prior to Mr. Aiken's coming, the local federal employees union worked in close harmony with Mr. Flamm's administration. But that changed quickly with Mr. Aiken's unyielding dictatorial stance. He and the union became adversaries. Small things became big issues. Staff members complained that smooth-running operations were now coming under microscopic scrutiny. Employees who previously had had no problems were in trouble. Things that were all right a few weeks before suddenly became "federal cases." Those who could resigned. Others transferred. Some stayed and fought the system. I wanted to remain neutral, but soon it became my turn to be singled out.

My problem came over a judgment call. Homosexuality is a very real part of prison life. Although it is not officially condoned, "everyone" knows that it is physically impossible to stop. Consensual sexual contact among inmates was ignored by some security staff, as long as it was kept private. Many homosexuals came to my office for counseling, some looking for ways to escape their lifestyle, others hoping to gain my blessing, and still others hoping for me to assure them that they, too, are God's children. I knew that before I could help any inmate to change he would have to understand that I would not compromise my Biblical value system. Yet, it would also have to be made clear to him that I would not reject anyone because of his lifestyle.

John Cruz and Tom Deal were practicing homosexuals who regularly participated in the religious programs. John sang in the choir and was also an informer for Lieutenant Earl Mueller. Occasionally, I coordinated meetings between John and Lieutenant Mueller by putting John on a "call-out," which excused him from being counted along with the other inmates. This made it appear that he was talking with me and not with the Lieutenant. It's unwise for an inmate to speak to correctional officers in private; it could be detrimental to his health and life.

It appeared that John, Tom, and I had established a trusting counseling relationship. Both told me that they wanted to change their lifestyle, and I accepted their desire to go straight and encouraged them to do so. During a session, Tom told me he was leaving for Springfield Medical Center in Missouri. "Chaplain, I'm going to miss our church here. Would you mind sending me Chapel bulletins so that I'll know what is happening?"

As I had done with other inmates in the past, I agreed: "Sure, Tom, I'll be glad to send you bulletins every two weeks."

About two months later, John asked if I would send his letter to Tom. I agreed, knowing that security requires all incoming and outgoing correspondence, except legal mail, to be read by staff. I had in mind that by reading John's letter I would be made aware of any changes in his behavior. However, much to my dismay, reading his letter made it obvious that John's homosexual lifestyle had not changed. The letter contained explicit sexual references which were repulsive to me. This placed me in an ethical dilemma between my role as a Chaplain and my role as a member of the prison staff.

Because the Bureau justifiably fears coordinated uprisings, direct inmate-to-inmate communication is against policy. However, John's letter was *indirect* communication from inmate, *through staff*, to another inmate. There was nothing in the regulations that covered this, and I had to make a decision about whether or not to send the letter. In my mind, I pondered how

Jesus handled His encounter with the prostitute caught in adultery. I was in a quandary: *Do I follow my Biblical dictates and not be judgmental; or do I follow my emotions and refuse to mail it?*

My heart was heavy as I weighed my options. I knew that if I were to continue counseling John, I had to keep my credibility with him. Although I didn't condone John's and Tom's homosexuality, I mailed the letter along with the bulletins. I had several reasons: like other professional counselors, I realized that lifetime habits do not change after a short time in counseling. Besides, repulsive as the letter was to me, it was strictly personal and did not violate the security of the institution. If the letter had presented even the slightest hint of a threat, I would have quickly handed it over to the chief correctional supervisor.

The decision I made still haunts me. After I mailed the letter with the church bulletins to Tom, I called John to my office. We had a heated counseling session because of the contents of his letter. Apparently that had some effect. Later he wrote a second letter to Tom, and this one was friendly but without sexual references. I mailed that to Tom too. I quickly learned that both letters were intercepted in Springfield Medical Center. Copies were made and sent to G. R. McCune, Southeast Regional Director; Warden Earl Aiken; and my immediate supervisor, Associate Warden of Programs Robert Horn.

I was in "BIG TROUBLE." My action was considered as serious as if I had given guns or drugs to inmates.

The Hot Seat

Wednesdays and Thursdays were my regular days off. As I entered the institution on Friday afternoon, April 14, 1978, I was given a message to see Mr. Horn in his office immediately. I didn't think this strange because I often received such messages after being off for two days.

Mr. Horn took John's letter out of his desk, showed it to me and asked, "Do you know anything about this?"

"Yes, I mailed it."

"Don't you know that direct inmate-to-inmate communication is against policy?"

"I must admit the letter is against my principles. Repulsive as it is, though, the letter isn't a threat to the institution and it doesn't come under the policy of direct communication because staff read and mailed it. To me that comes under the category of indirect communication."

"OK, write me a memo explaining why you did it."

"I will." Then I added, "I mailed two letters to inmate Deal. The one you have and another John later sent without sexual references."

I shared the matter with Padre when I returned to my office.

"Oh, George it'll blow over. You know, lately molehills are becoming mountains."

I focused my attention on my ever-increasing demands and at the end of the day wrote a memo explaining the situation and delivered it to Horn. Content that this would satisfy administration's needs, I put the matter behind me and actually forgot about it. They had not. Two weeks later I learned that an investigation was in progress that would leave no stone unturned.

April 25, 1978, was not a pleasant day! Acting Warden Horn called me to his office for questioning and announced that Karl Fant, the personnel officer, was the recorder. I felt like a criminal as Karl read my rights to me and required me to sign the document from which he read. During this "interrogation," I learned that I was in bigger trouble than I thought.

Horn started, "Tell me everything dealing with the mailing of John's letter." Having nothing to hide, I said, "I know that John and Tom are homosexuals. During our lengthy counseling relationship both indicated a desire to change their lifestyle. I encouraged them to follow Biblical teachings. Tom asked if I would send him Chapel bulletins as he was leaving for Springfield Medical Center. I agreed. Later John asked if I would send his letter to Tom. I consented because I knew that I would read it and would know whether John was really trying to change his lifestyle. To my dismay, John hadn't changed. I wrestled with the question of whether I should send the letter or not."

Horn then asked, "Don't you know that inmate-to-inmate communication is against policy?"

I responded, "Yes sir, I do. But the letter was not going directly from one inmate to another. Before sending John's letter, I read it. I knew, too, that staff in the mail room also open and read incoming and outgoing communications."

Horn began a series of rapidly fired questions: "Why did you do it?"

I replied, "I feel I have a responsibility to work with anyone who is dissatisfied with his life and wants to change for the better. I thought that's what John wanted to do."

"This is a serious matter. Did you know you were breaking policy?"

"No, I did not know I was breaking policy or that this is a serious offense. There is nothing in policy or any briefing that covers what is considered indirect mail."

"George, it was direct mailing," Horn snapped, with force.

I left his office distraught. Initially I thought that I did the right thing, but in retrospect I realized that I could have treated the matter differently. It would have been better not to send the letter but to use it as a counseling tool with John. Even so, deep down in my heart I knew I didn't break policy, nor would I have intentionally done so. However, I now fully realized that the administration and I didn't see it the same way.

I put the investigation behind me, and I went about my responsibilities of meeting the needs of the 700-plus inmates. But the matter didn't drop. On May 15th Karl told me, "See me in my office." I asked Padre to go with me for moral support. My heart sank as we walked into Karl's office, and he said, "IT IS BAD!"

I was expecting a letter of reprimand at the worst, but I was dead wrong! Instead, I was handed a copy of a letter sent to the Southeast Regional Director recommending my DISMISSAL. I had thirty days to respond. Padre and I walked to the Chapel silently. I couldn't believe what was happening to me.

Padre put his hand on my shoulder and said, "In my thirteen years, I haven't seen anything like this. Your punishment is overkill. It's like swatting a fly with a hammer. George, we'll fight it together." He was angry and reminded me that although two prisoners escaped while under his supervision, his punishment was a letter of reprimand.

I arrived home emotionally drained and weary. "You don't look good. Is something wrong?" Muriel asked with concern. Knowing that she had a major exam in her master's degree program that evening, I decided not to cause her any anxiety before the test. Instead, I looked at my loving wife and simply said, "I have a headache."

UNITED STATES DEPARTMENT OF JUSTICE
BUREAU OF PRISONS
FEDERAL CORRECTIONAL INSTITUTION
ASHLAND, KENTUCKY 41101

May 11, 1978

To whom it may concern:

This letter is written on behalf of Reverend George Castillo, Protestant Chaplain, Federal Correctional Institution, Ashland, Kentucky.

I am the Catholic Chaplain at the Federal Correctional Institution in Ashland, Kentucky and have been in this position since June 21, 1964. I am also the Chaplain at Our Lady of Bellefonte Hospital in Ashland, Kentucky. In the past years I have become very active in the American Correctional Association and am at present the President of the American Catholic Correctional Chaplains' Association. This is said with the intention of giving more weight to what I have to say about Reverend Castillo.

In August 1974, our Protestant Chaplain at this institution resigned. During the interim, I was the only Chaplain until January 1975 when Reverend Castillo came to Ashland. A Protestant Minister came to the institution for Protestant Services on Sunday and visited the institution for several hours each week. Naturally, I was very happy when a Protestant Chaplain was assigned. Reverend Castillo has been in this position since January 1975.

In the past three years working with Reverend Castillo and socializing with him and his family, I have come to know the Castillos quite well. Reverend Castillo has been with the U.S. Bureau of Prisons for the past five years, working at Atlanta's Penitentiary before coming to Ashland.

From a fellow chaplain's point of view, working with Reverend Castillo has been a pleasure. He is a compatible, friendly, understanding person. I see him working well with inmates of all faiths and denominations. The Protestant Choir is a tribute to him; the Bible Study and other groups he has are also the successful work of his hands. It was heartening to see that since he is such a successful Chaplain, he was recently promoted to a higher GS step (Gs-12).

Besides his work at this prison, Chaplain Castillo has become active in the Ashland community. At present he is the vice-president and Chairman of Programs for the Ashland Area Ministerial Association. From time to time, he is asked to preach in various faith's pulpits in the area. This, too, is a sign of his versatility and adaptability.

Bishop Grutka, our Catholic Episcopal Advisor to prison chaplains has recently said that "A Prison Chaplain is truly the Minister of Divine Charity. He is the one who has to prolong God's presence in a most inhospitable place and has to possess within his own heart the profound sentiments of the Lord Himself. Charity can cope with stubborn opposition and unite complex diversity. The expectations, of the residents in a Correctional Institution from the Chaplain, are in direct proportion to the power inherent in Charity and they can become frightfully exacting."

I think Reverend Castillo has found a hospitable place in the hearts of the inmates and staff here with whom he works. They both respect him and have high regard for him. To this prison service, Reverend Castillo has brought nine years of military service and many years of experience as a Pastor of a Church outside the confines of a prison. Any Chaplain will know that this is an excellent background for the type of work involved in the chaplaincy.

The Prison Chaplain is a shepherd of his prison inmates; even though he is a "man of God" he still is in every respect a "man" and as such is subject to make mistakes and to err. The pressures under which a chaplain works may tend to increase his vulnerability to fall short of perfection. Strains, stresses, and frustrations of the prison life may tend to bring out in the Chaplain the real, utter humanness of his being a "man"; yet one given to God.

I hope that these sentiments about Reverend Castillo, my fellow Chaplain with whom I have worked the past few years--a man whom I admire deeply--will convey some message of what probably the one person in this institution who knows him best thinks of him. These are my thoughts.

Lee F. Trimbur

Lee Francis Trimbur, priest
Catholic Chaplain

After Muriel returned from school, I told her what had happened and gave her the letter. Her tears turned to inner strength as she said, "George, I can't believe this. We'll fight this together. Everyone knows that you wouldn't do anything that would be harmful to anyone or the institution."

Sleep didn't come easily that night. We tossed and turned, experincing anxiety, disbelief, anger, and every other disturbing emotion known to humankind. Mercifully, the dawn of a new day finally came, and with it a new resolve to see justice done.

Fighting for Survival

Early that morning, I called Joe Pitchford. For 13 years he had enjoyed the reputation of being a good worker until he became a union representative. Then his problems with the administration cost him three suspensions and his job. He was in the middle of a long, painful, five-year struggle that eventually saw him reinstated and awarded $65,000 in back pay, an outcome reported in the May 1983 issue of *The Government Standard.*

Joe advised me to call Gregory Monge, an attorney who was representing other personnel whose jobs were threatened. Upon hearing my story, Mr. Monge shook his head in disbelief that such drastic action would be taken, especially on a first offense and since the words "direct" and "indirect" communication were not spelled out in policy. He was frank, though, when he told me, "You will have to be prepared to go to court."

He made no attempt to minimize how tough the fight would be. Yet he encouraged me to continue because what was involved was a judgment call which did not cause harm to any inmate or the institution. Once the decision to go ahead was made, he said, "I will send a letter to Mr. McCune, the Southeast Regional Director, advising him of our appeal, along with a copy to Mr. Aiken." He then gave me the assignment of collecting character-reference letters from leading citizens.

Thus the fight began. The citizens of Ashland knew me to be an honorable, ethical, respectable man with high moral principles, a man who was an outstanding leader and a community volunteer. Without hesitation, many agreed to write a character reference.

Several staff members sought me out and asked, "Is it true,

CARL D. PERKINS
7TH DIST., KENTUCKY

COMMITTEE:
EDUCATION AND LABOR

Congress of the United States
House of Representatives
Washington, D.C. 20515

July 5, 1978

Father Lee F. Trimbur
Reverend George Castillo
Federal Correctional Institution
Ashland, Kentucky 41101

Dear Father Trimbur and Reverend Castillo:

Thank you for your nice note sent to my Ashland office about my efforts to improve conditions at the Federal Correctional Institution.

I have been in touch with the Department of Justice here in Washington again about the situation and also have other inquiries underway. I hope it can be functioning as it should, in an efficient way, as soon as possible.

With best wishes,

Your friend,

CARL D. PERKINS, M.C.

CDP/ih

Chaplain, that you received a 'Bad Letter'?" I acknowledged the fact. Officer Tom Hayden put into words the attitudes of many: "If that happened to you, it could happen to any staff. We have a Hitler on our hands."

Because news spreads rapidly in prison, the inmates appeared depressed and openly discussed the matter. One of the Chapel program regulars, Aaron Hall, a stocky inmate with crystal-clear blue eyes and a crew-cut, stuck his head in my door and said, "Chaplain, we really feel bad 'cause you're the only person who cared for us. Now you're being ill-treated and fired. That's the damned system for you."

Joe Shipley, a young man serving time for auto theft added, "Rev, we are sorry what happened to you. You are like a father to us, and now you're being messed over." I thanked Joe and Aaron for their concern and added, as much for myself as for them, "Keep the faith. God is in control."

Although prayer was constantly on my lips and in my heart, my zeal was diminished. I was concerned about my reputation, my future, and all the implications of losing my job. When I got down emotionally, Isaiah 35:4 picked me up: Be strong, fear not; behold your God will come. He will come and save you.

Stress began to take its toll with the constant emotional see-saw I was experiencing. Immediately after Worship Service at the prison, Muriel and I left for my preaching engagement at Meade Station Church of God. The word was already out so I briefly shared my problem with the congregation. "If I'm not my usual enthusiastic self, you know why. I ask for your prayers, patience, and understanding." The congregation was sympathetic. Following the service, the Mattinglys and several other families asked, "Is there anything we can do?"

"Yes," I replied, "please write Congressman Perkins and give me a character reference. He is already aware of my situation and that of the six other employees who are under adverse personnel action. He recently met with us and our wives."

I hadn't slept or eaten properly for a week. I now felt weak and was losing weight. Doctor Manuel Garcia gave me two prescriptions and wanted to put me on sick leave. I was caught between a rock and a hard place. I needed the rest and to be away from the stress, yet I knew that my mind and body could not be at rest at home so I went to work, heavily burdened.

Mr. G. R. McCune
Regional Director
U. S. Department of Justice
Bureau of Prisons
Southeast Region
3500 Greenbriar Parkway, S.W.
Building 300
Atlanta, Georgia 30331

RE: Proposed Action of May 5, 1978
on George R. Castillo

Dear Mr. McCune:

Pursuant to letter under date May 5, 1978 and received by me May 8, 1978 from E. V. Aiken, I hereby exercise my right to reply to the proposed action to be taken against me. The proposed action concerns three charges all of which deal with my having allowed two letters to be mailed by me along with a chapel bulletin from inmate Wade to inmate Evans. I must disagree vehemently with the proposed action to be taken against me on the basis of the charges outlined in Warden Aiken's letter. Even if the charges were sustained, my removal from my position would be in no way fully warranted and in the interests of the efficiency of the service.

Throughout my almost five years in the Bureau of Prisons, my record has been completely spotless and my evaluations have been without derrogatory comment. Additionally, I am certain you are aware of the chaplaincy services that Father Trimbur and myself perform. As recently as February 28, 1978 a memoranda from Mr. Tyson to yourself and Warden Aiken illustrates clearly that I have performed in an excellent manner.

As I stated in my memoranda which was directed to Mr. Fout under date May 1, 1978, I certainly did not believe that the letters that I enclosed were violating the spirit and intent of the regulations governing the inmate communication. I certainly believed that since I had read and screened the letters, since I was counseling both of these individuals with regard to their activities and since I saw nothing in the letters that would violate the policies of the prison, I used my professional judgment in allowing the letters to be mailed.

Obviously, had I wished them to be mailed without any one knowing, I could easily have placed them in an outside mailbox with no return address. I am not foolish enough to think that the screening of mail would not have picked up these letters. If I made an error in this regard, my error was simply one of bad judgment and not a deliberate attempt to break any policy or regulation, which incidentally I feel strongly I have not done. Based upon what has been brought to my attention, I obviously will not permit any letter to be mailed in the future.

Since I have been in the area of the Federal Correctional Institution, I have maintained a spotless record, I have worked exceedingly hard to build community relations and have instituted various ministerial programs at the institution. As shown by my previous job performance ratings, I have carried out all of the duties and responsibilities of my position with no complaint of any kind or nature.

I might also add that had I realized when Mr. Honsted asked me to talk with him that he was going to recommend my suspension and reassignment, I certainly would have requested some additional grounds or a statement from him as to why this would follow. Clearly a review of charges 1, 2 and 3 in light of my previous record indicates that the action proposed by Warden Aiken is totally unreasonable and is absolutely without basis in fact or law.

I am hoping that you will agree with me and see fit not to take the proposed action.

Yours truly,

GRC

George R. Castillo

cc: Mr. E. V. Aiken
     Warden
     United States Department of Justice
     Bureau of Prisons
     Federal Correctional Institution
     Ashland, Kentucky 41101

     Hon. Gregory L. Monge
     Attorney for George R. Castillo
     1416 Winchester Avenue
     P. O. Box 1111
     Ashland, Kentucky 41101

Decisions Require Answers and Support

My fight with the administration had become a central issue. Everywhere I went, inmates' and staff's eyes were on me. I always waved and said "Hello" as I passed, even when I didn't feel like it. I knew God would see me through, but my mind was torn. *Should I return to the parish ministry or remain with the Bureau of Prisons? If I can be fired for this incident, maybe I don't belong here. I love my work, and have been effective in bringing God-like changes to many, but perhaps I should exercise my options.*

Reality took over, and I began realizing that before I could make intelligent decisions, I needed to understand my options. The next morning, I asked Personnel Manager Karl Fant, "What are my rights if I were to resign?"

Karl answered, "You would be paid for annual leave, but not for sick leave. George, I'm caught in the middle and am obligated to advise you as well as Mr. Aiken. It seems that you're thinking about resigning. I wouldn't if I were you. You have a perfect record with the Bureau. If you want to go to the regional office to talk with the Director, the institution will pay for it."

I thanked Karl, but I knew that a visit to the regional director's office would be in vain since the likelihood of a regional director's supporting a Chaplain against a warden is slim to none.

When I reached my office, I called retired Chaplains Ralph Graham and Dick Summer. After I told them my story, both were surprised that such a drastic action was recommended for such a minor incident. Both promised to help. I also called the Reverend Leon Dickinson, who represented my denomination during my interview almost five years earlier. Leon became angry after I told him my predicament. "George, I can't see what you did wrong. I'm here with some officials interviewing future Chaplains. When it's over, I'll talk to the officials."

It was becoming obvious to everyone during the next two weekly staff meetings that Warden Aiken was not about to soften his unyielding control of the institution. Addressing the staff, Aiken crowed, "Rumor has it that I'm going to retire. That rumor is false! I don't plan to retire until June 1979. Listen closely and pass the word. I lost money when I was transferred here from Eglin Federal Prison Camp in Florida, and I'm not going anywhere!"

Psychologist Earl Washington had been the duty officer the Memorial Day weekend. During the staff meeting that followed, he reported: "Inmates had a great weekend because many had visitors, ate lots of food, and participated in competitive sports. On the other hand, staff morale is low because of the several adverse actions pending against staff."

With that, Warden Aiken removed his cigar from his mouth, blew the smoke upward, and said callously, "I'm glad it's their morale that is low and not mine."

My heart sank as a sickening hush blanketed the room. I had worked under Wardens J. D. Henderson, Marvin Hogan and J. Flamm and had never heard these professionals speak about staff in such a manner. I was suddenly overwhelmed with the realization that even if I "won" Aiken wouldn't be leaving in a few weeks as everyone thought. I didn't know if I could endure another year with him in control.

Discouragement filled the air. Tired, exhausted, distraught, and depressed I went home, took my newly prescribed medicine, and prayed for a good night's sleep.

Same Song, Different Verse

The physical strain was bad enough, but the emotional turmoil was worse. Along with concern and fear about my career, I was filled with self-doubt, resentment, and an overwhelming sense of the unfairness of it all. This was so unlike me because I had been positive and on an even keel most of my life. At times I was like doubting Thomas; other times I was like a Spirit-filled warrior claiming the promise of Psalm 56:11, "In God I trust without a fear."

Just three months earlier, in January, Regional Chaplain Charles Tyson had audited the Religious Department. We had received our usual high marks and I got promoted. Now, I could do nothing right in the administration's eyes.

Traditionally, each May the Salvation Army conducted the service on Correctional Services Sunday. As I did each year, I gave Horn a memo requesting permission to allow the custom to continue. He refused to sign it until I answered all his questions — questions that had never been asked in the five years I had served as Chaplain.

"Do you know all the people who are coming?" he bellowed.

"No. The Chaplain only needs to know the leader. He identifies his congregation," I responded.

"Has any one of them been in jail?" he queried.

"I don't know. I'll have to call the Salvation Army Captain to verify that. If he doesn't know, I may have to call the FBI in Washington, D.C.," I added sarcastically.

His battery of questions continued nonstop.

"Is anyone related to an inmate?" "What will they be doing in the service, apart from singing?" "Do you know the individual ages, sex, and occupation of all these people?" "What....?"

My frustration was obvious as I answered, "Sorry, but I just can't answer these questions without time to look into them." The facts didn't matter. We both knew that the Salvation Army was never under any cloud of suspicion that required this interrogatory, nor did we have any problems with any group coming to the institution. Without giving me time to find out the answers to his questions, the program was cancelled.

Horn's actions spoke loud and clear. I was out of the administration's grace. Everything I tried to do to run the Religious Department efficiently was hampered. The administration had begun arbitrarily curtailing many of our programs, and every decision I made was questioned.

Angels Come in Interesting Forms

On May 26, 1978, Dick Summer, a retired Bureau Chief of Chaplains, who still lived in Washington, D.C., returned my call. "George, I have good and bad news for you. Which one do you want first?"

"Let me have the bad first," I requested.

"Based upon the complaints received in the Director's office from Ashland you are in the worst institution in the Bureau."

"I agree," I responded.

"The good news is this. Because you are a Chaplain, under current regulations you are allowed to go directly to the Director of the Bureau of Prisons. Thus, if you write a letter to the Director, Mr. Carlson, stating the situation and your specific request, it will take your case out of the Southeast Region. Be sure, at the same time, to send a copy to Roy Gerard, his assistant. If your case stays in your region, you are a dead duck."

"Thank you Dick, I'll write the letter promptly."

Just as angels comforted Jesus during his times of trial, I had many to comfort me. Although mine were human, they were sent by God to strengthen me just the same. For the first time, I found myself receiving instead of giving comfort. During this time, Muriel, of course, was my closest ally. Friends were very supportive also. I had to admit it was an emotional lift to be soothed when I was hurting.

Usually I consoled, but now my friends were consoling me. Whenever I discussed my situation, help was offered. My friend and Pastor Ray Woodruff promised to write a letter to his Congressman. The Quaker leader, who regularly led services at the institution, said, "Chaplain, it's part of our responsibility and function to humanize the system. We're here to help you." They both wrote many letters to governing officials.

Association Minister Dr. Reverend William G. Brandt declared, "We can't let Aiken get away with something like that, George. We have representatives and offices in D.C. I'll act on that immediately."

Many inmates were outraged, frustrated, and depressed over my proposed firing. Without my solicitation, knowledge, or consent, many wrote President Carter because he was a "born-again Christian." Paul Gooden summed up the sentiment expressed by others, "We want you here to be our Pastor!"

I responded, "There are times when we don't get what we want. But what I want you to do is put my difficulty behind you. It will pass. Because of my education, several doors are open for me. I want you to focus on getting an education. Then when one door is closed, others can be opened."

The Muslim community became involved, too. Imam (Minister) Samuel Richardson told me, "Our Imam Mikal Huda Ba'th is in D.C., and he has access to the Chief of Chaplains, Father Houlahan. I'm sure that he can help."

A few days later, Imam Ba'th was on the phone, "Chaplain, I have heard about your predicament, and I am working on it right now. I talked to Houlahan and promised to write him up in our newspaper, *The Bilahain News*." This case is bigger then you think. I talked to Jack Anderson, and he's also interested."

UNITED STATES DEPARTMENT OF JUSTICE
BUREAU OF PRISONS
FEDERAL CORRECTIONAL INSTITUTION
ASHLAND, KENTUCKY 41101

May 19, 1978

Mr. Norman Carlson
Director Bureau of Prisons
U.S. Bureau of Prisons
Washington, D. C. 20534

Dear Mr. Carlson:

I wish to inform you of my situation at Federal Correctional
Institution, Ashland, Kentucky. On June 15, 1973, I entered on duty
in the Chaplaincy service. My record has been impeccable, and I was
promoted to GS 12 in February 1978.

Without realizing that I violated policy, I forwarded correspondence between inmates that I am counseling. When I was made aware of
this error of judgment by my supervisor, Mr. Honsted, I apologized and
stated that I have not done that before, and I shall not do so in the
future. Therefore, I was shocked to receive Warden Aiken's letter
proposing my removal from the position of chaplain.

I might add that the staff at FCI Ashland is demoralized to learn
that a person, whose relationship with staff and inmates is excellent,
first infringement in five years can result in his termination of
service.

This extreme action is unwarranted in view of the outstanding
reports from the regional directors of chaplaincy services; my ministerial services to the institution and the community; also my performance standard and evaluation reports.

Mr. Carlson, I am asking you to intercede on my behalf. After
14 years of government service (9 in the Air Force; 5 in the Bureau
of Prisons), without even an oral reprimand, I feel that I do not
deserve to be dismissed from a position which I have so faithfully and
ably served.

The three enclosures are for your information.

Copy furnished:
Mr. Roy Gerard

Very truly yours,

George R Castillo

George R. Castillo

3 enclosures
1. letter from Warden Aiken dated 5/5/78
2. Letter from Dept. Head dated 5/11/78
3. Letter to Mr. McCune dated 5/13/78

I felt uncomfortable when he mentioned Jack Anderson, the nationally and internationally syndicated columnist. Anderson might discuss the case on his "Good Morning America" program, and I didn't want the publicity.

"With your permission, can I give Jack your telephone number?"

"No," I responded, "I would like you to help me out quietly and diplomatically."

God does move in mysterious ways. I was scheduled to attend the UCC Ohio Conference Black Empowerment Implementation Committee meeting. Of all places, it was being held in East View United Church, where I formerly pastored. People there knew, loved, and respected both me and my family. The committee empowered the chair, Mrs. Carolyn Miller, to call the Director of the Bureau of Prisons and Houlahan's office to intercede on my behalf. On my way home, I praised God for smiling on me and providing me with another avenue of support.

After the meeting, I met my classmate Glenn Royer and his wife Millie for lunch. Naturally I unburdened my heart. Both were angered. "George," Glenn said, "that's not right. With such a short time left, I may have to call Houlahan instead of writing. I promise you, they'll hear from me."

Back at work I noticed a change in staff's behavior. Many staff members who had openly talked, laughed, and shared with me earlier felt uncomfortable talking or eating in the mess hall with me now. However, in many instances staff members used nonverbal communication, such as head shakes and winks, as their verbal communication decreased. Padre was the only staunch supporter who did not waver. He showed me a copy of his letter to Mr. McCune, the Regional Director. Then he shared his feelings: "I have been praying for you from the day we discovered their intentions to fire you. Since our Father is the same yesterday, today, and forever, it will be interesting to notice the unfolding and the final solution of your case. Justice is the foundation of God's throne. The more I prayed, the more the Spirit has been directing me to the words in I Chronicles 16:22 and Psalm 105:15. "Touch not my anointed ones, do my prophets no harm."

Mr. G. R. McCune
Regional Director
U. S. Department of Justice
Bureau of Prisons
Southeast Region
3500 Greenbriar Parkway, S.W.
Building 300
Atlanta, Georgia 30331   RE: Proposed Action of May 5, 1978
                                      on George R. Castillo

Dear Mr. McCune:

    Pursuant to letter under date May 5, 1978 and received by me
May 8, 1978 from E. V. Aiken, I hereby exercise my right to reply
to the proposed action to be taken against me. The proposed action
concerns three charges all of which deal with my having allowed
two letters to be mailed by me along with a chapel bulletin from
inmate Wade to inmate Evans. I must disagree vehemently with the
proposed action to be taken against me on the basis of the charges
outlined in Warden Aiken's letter. Even if the charges were sustained, my removal from my position would be in no way fully warranted and in the interests of the efficiency of the service.

    Throughout my almost five years in the Bureau of Prisons, my
record has been completely spotless and my evaluations have been
without derrogatory comment. Additionally, I am certain you are
aware of the chaplaincy services that Father Trimbur and myself perform.
As recently as February 28, 1978 a memoranda from Mr. Tyson to yourself and Warden Aiken illustrates clearly that I have performed in
an excellent manner.

    As I stated in my memoranda which was directed to Mr. Fout
under date May 1, 1978, I certainly did not believe the letters that
I enclosed were violating the spirit and intent of the regulations
governing the inmate communication. I certainly believed that since
I had read and screened the letters, since I was counseling both of
these individuals with regard to their activities and since I saw
nothing in the letters that would violate the policies of the prison,
I used my professional judgment in allowing the letters to be mailed.

Obviously, had I wished them to be mailed without any one knowing, I could easily have placed them in an outside mailbox with no return address. I am not foolish enough to think that the screening of mail would not have picked up these letters. If I made an error in this regard, my error was simply one of bad judgment and not a deliberate attempt to break any policy or regulation, which incidentally I feel strongly I have not done. Based upon what has been brought to my attention, I obviously will not permit any letter to be mailed in the future.

Since I have been in the area of the Federal Correctional Institution, I have maintained a spotless record, I have worked exceedingly hard to build community relations and have instituted various ministerial programs at the institution. As shown by my previous job performance ratings, I have carried out all of the duties and responsibilities of my position with no complaint of any kind or nature.

I might also add that had I realized when Mr. Honsted asked me to talk with him that he was going to recommend my suspension and reassignment, I certainly would have requested some additional grounds or a statement from him as to why this would follow. Clearly a review of charges 1, 2 and 3 in light of my previous record indicates that the action proposed by Warden Aiken is totally unreasonable and is absolutely without basis in fact or law.

I am hoping that you will agree with me and see fit not to take the proposed action.

Yours truly,

GRC

George R. Castillo

cc: Mr. E. V. Aiken
      Warden
      United States Department of Justice
      Bureau of Prisons
      Federal Correctional Institution
      Ashland, Kentucky 41101

      Hon. Gregory L. Monge
      Attorney for George R. Castillo
      1416 Winchester Avenue
      P. O. Box 1111
      Ashland, Kentucky 41101

God Provides Strength in the Storm

By now the situation had become so strained at the prison that the administration communicated with me through Charles Tyson, the Regional Chaplain. Tyson asked if I would consider resigning, insinuating that I might have some skeletons in my closet. As he spoke, the thought went through my mind: *Perhaps the administration thinks that since I was so understanding of homosexuals I might be one.* I assured Tyson that I had no skeletons in my closet. Further, my God and I knew that I was not a homosexual, nor had I ever participated in any homosexual activity. As we ended our conversation, I told him emphatically, "I have nothing to hide. I will not resign!"

Surprisingly, Tyson's call strengthened my resolve to fight my case all the way up to the Supreme Court if necessary. I told myself: *Such innuendos and gossip can destroy a man's reputation and his family. I am not going to take it!*

A day or so later, Horn called me to his office and began a strained conversation, "George, I heard you were born in Belize."

"Yes, I was," I replied, without elaborating.

He dropped that subject, then asked, "Have you talked with Tyson lately?"

Knowing that he was referring to our most recent conversation regarding resignation, I responded, "Charlie and I are always talking. He's my Regional Chaplain."

"When he calls you again, please let me know, will you?"

"I will."

He then awkwardly added, "We received calls to the institution on your behalf. George, you seem not to understand the gravity of your act."

Feeling the strength of the Lord in my soul, I looked him straight in the eye and said, "Bob, I'll use Father Trimbur's words: 'Your administration's punishment is like swatting a fly with a hammer.' I'm being treated unjustly. It's not fair that I served my government commendably for 14 years without a blemish on my record and now I face dismissal for a questionable judgment call. I still can't believe it. I've shared this with others, and they can't understand it either. Do you really think I deserve what I am going through?"

Horn did not answer but changed the subject by expressing a concern about the time I spent speaking in area churches each Sunday. However, as he spoke, we both knew that community participation was included in my position description. He had the power to stop almost everything else I was doing at the prison, but this was part of my ministry and that he could not control. As I left his office, God lifted a burden from my shoulders. Even if I were to be fired from the Bureau, God had not fired me from the ministry.

Judgment Day

As the fateful day approached, I was able to share with Padre how God had removed the fear from my heart and replaced it with courage and faith. With a smile, Padre replied, "I noticed that when you walked in today." With a sigh of relief, I admitted, "I'll still be glad when the resolution comes."

I had been promised an answer by the 15th, but on the 14th there was still no word. I called Chaplain Tyson to get a status update. "George, though the 15th is almost here, I still don't know the status of your case. There are so many people involved in it, I don't know where it stands."

"Thank you, Charlie. If you hear anything, keep me informed please, will you?" He promised to do so.

Since I didn't get any feedback from Tyson, I decided to call Father Richard Houlahan at the Bureau. He didn't provide any information either but asked, "George, is keeping your job all that you want?"

"Yes," I responded.

"I'll get back to you," Houlahan answered.

"Before the fifteenth?" I asked eagerly.

"As soon as I can," he said with finality.

Houlahan's question made me wonder if the Bureau expected me to file a discrimination complaint? Although I hadn't raised the issue of race or associated my "sentence" with the color of my skin, everyone knew that unequal treatment and harsher punishment were usually meted out to blacks. The fact is that I was still a trailblazer in the federal prison system. It wasn't easy being one of the first black Chaplains in the history of the U. S. Bureau of Prisons!

Mr. George R. Castillo
Chaplain
Federal Correctional Institution
Ashland, Kentucky 41101

Dear Mr. Castillo:

On May 5, 1978, you were issued a notice which proposed that you be removed from your position. A copy of the notice is attached. The proposal was based on the charges of: (1) Circumvention of Correspondence Regulations; (2) Aiding and Abetting Inmate Circumvention of Correspondence Regulations; and, (3) Violation of "Standards of Employee Conduct and Responsibility" - Policy Statement 3735.1B. In making my decision, I have given full consideration to the charges and the specifications in support thereof, to your written reply of May 13, 1978, and to all the revelant evidence contained in the adverse action file which has been made available to you.

After careful consideraion, I find the charges sustained and fully supported by the evidence in the file. However, it is my decision that you be suspended for ten (10) calendar days. Your suspension is fully warranted and in the interest of the efficiency of the service in that I believe that having to serve this suspension will have the desired corrective effect on you. Consequently, you will be suspended for the period June 16, 1978 through June 25, 1978, inclusive. You are to report for duty at your regularly scheduled hour on June 26, 1978.

If you consider this action improper, you may request a review of this suspension on its merits under the negotiated grievance procedure (Master Agreement, Article 29) by commencing at Step 4 of Section e. If you choose to make such a request for review, it must be made in writing within fifteen (15) calendar days from the date you receive this notice. You may also request a review of the procedures utilized to effect this suspension by appealing this action, in writing, to the Federal Employee Appeals Authority, U. S. Civil Service Commission, 1340 Spring Street, N.W., Atlanta, Georgia 30309. An appeal to the Civil Service Commission may be filed at any time, but no later than fifteen (15) calendar days from the date your suspension is effected.

Should you desire any advice or assistance on this matter, contact Mr. Carl L. Fout, Personnel Officer, phone number - (606) 928-6414.

Sincerely,

G. R. McCune
Regional Director

I have received the original and one copy of this letter on this date:

Name:_____ Date:_____

During those last 24 hours, I agonized, prayed, talked, gave my problem to the Lord, revisited it, took it back, and then finally and completely turned it over to God. "Father," I prayed, "it's in Your hands. You sent me into the prison system. I'll accept your will. Thy will be done."

After one of the longest nights in my life, Judgment Day, June 15, 1978, finally arrived. As I was leaving the house that morning, the phone rang. It was Karl Fant from personnel.

"George, I have a letter from the Regional Director for you."

"Will you please open it and read it to me," I asked.

"It's for a ten-days' suspension," said Karl.

"Effective when?"

"Right now."

"I'll be right there to get the letter."

As soon as I received the letter, I wanted to share it with Muriel, who was now a typing teacher in the Education Department. But I changed my mind and decided to wait until she got home. "After all, I'm suspended. I'm getting out of here!"

As I drove back home, I began thinking, *HOW IRONIC. MY SUSPENSION BEGINS ON MY FIFTH ANNIVERSARY WITH THE BUREAU OF PRISONS. THANK GOD IT IS OVER. A TEN-DAY SUSPENSION WITHOUT PAY IS SOMETHING I CAN ACCEPT.*

A Word of Warning to All Employees

What I had fallen for was something common in prisons: "the inmate set-up." Many inmates see concern and caring as weaknesses and will frequently target caring people to achieve their own goals. Although I accepted responsibility, I was really the victim of an inmate set-up by John and Tom. They used our counseling relationship to gain my trust and then conned me into mailing a letter they knew they could not mail directly. Both knew that if any problem arose, I would be the one to get into trouble instead of them. They did not care. They simply wanted the power to do things their own way no matter how much it might hurt me.

Nobody is immune to being conned. Contrary to popular belief, it is usually not the weak employees who are victims. Instead, it is usually good, strong employees who couldn't conceive

UNITED STATES DEPARTMENT OF JUSTICE
BUREAU OF PRISONS
WASHINGTON 20534

June 8, 1978

George R. Castillo
Protestant Chaplain
Federal Correctional Institution
Ashland, KY 41101

Dear Chaplain Castillo:

This letter is in reply to your correspondence of May 19, 1978 regarding the proposal of Adverse Action which was presented to you by Warden Aiken on May 8, 1978.

As you are aware by now, Mr. McCune has reduced the penalty from removal to a suspension. Although I have not closely examined this disciplinary action on its merits, I trust you will accept Mr. McCune's decision as a fair one.

Sincerely,

NORMAN A. CARLSON
Director

of their ever being charged with doing something that would get
them fired.

Prison work requires many judgment calls. I learned almost
too late that there is a way to keep from getting conned. After my
experience, whenever faced with anything that might have even
the slightest appearance of breaking a rule or going beyond the
limits of professional ethics, I talked it over with my fellow Chaplains or supervisors before making a final decision.

Chapter 8

Recovery And Redemption

Endure hardship as discipline; God is treating you as sons...No discipline seems pleasant at the time, but painful. Later on, however, it produces a harvest of righteousness and peace for those who have been trained by it. (Hebrews 12:7a, ll NIV)

The incident that almost got me fired was finally over, and I had to put the past behind. I would miss two weeks of pay, but l realized that if I were to continue my calling I needed to pull myself together and rely on God's promise in Isaiah 43:18, "Do not cling to events of the past or dwell on what happened long ago. Watch for the new thing I am going to do. It is happening already — you can see it now! I will make a road through the wilderness and give you streams of water there."

Trusting in God's Word, I decided to go forward, pray for Divine Guidance, and continue serving the incarcerated and offer them hope through the love of Christ. As I prayed, I could hear the still, small voice of Jesus found in Matthew 5:16, "Let your light so shine before men, that they see your good works, and glorify your Father which is in heaven." I decided to obey this command and do my very best, just as I had always done. I knew that God would use my experience to help me grow stronger and make me more empathetic toward those who suffer. I also knew my "test of fire" would make me a better Chaplain.

We all needed a relief from the heavy tension that permeated the Ashland prison. Fortunately, it came the second day into my suspension at a happy occasion, the marriage of Mr. and Mrs. Bill Brittain's daughter, Kimberly Dawn, to Alan Robinson at Rose

Hill Baptist Church. Differences were put aside as the Bureau of
Prisons' family rejoiced with the Brittains.

As I entered the church, I spotted Warden Aiken and his
wife. It was important that I show no animosity, so I went over
and greeted them in my usual warm manner. "How are you?" I
asked, as I reached out to shake their hands.

"Very well, thank you, Chaplain. How are you?" Mr. Aiken responded.

With the confidence of God's love, I replied, "Just like this
sunny day, Sir. Beautiful." After a few minutes of idle chitchat I
moved on to greet the other guests.

You Cannot Leave, Request Denied!

Although Muriel had remained in the background during our
ordeal, she suffered just the same. Our life and important family
decisions had been put on hold. One of them was a business trip
Muriel needed to make to St. Martin. Now that my tribulation
was over, I wanted to go with her, so I requested 15 days of vacation leave.

Horn emphatically denied my request, "You'll already be gone
ten days, but if you're gone for 25 days, it will adversely affect
the morale of the staff and inmates. They'll think that you are
fired."

Even though I felt angry, Muriel and I couldn't help but
laugh at the sudden turn of events. "Isn't it funny," I quipped. "If
Aiken's recommendation had been accepted I would be gone per-
manently. Now they're saying my brief absence would lower morale. How ironic! A few weeks ago. Aiken said he wasn't concerned about the staff's low morale."

As usual, Muriel's calming voice brought me back to reality:
"George, our faith will see us through. God will give you the
strength to face whatever they throw at you. In the end, I know
that right will prevail and victory will be ours. We just have to
hang tight. As my mother used to say, 'Everything is going to be
all right; just trust in the Lord.'"

I was unhappy about having my leave denied, but I also
agreed that the morale of the staff and inmates was at its lowest
ebb. Staff had become reluctant to make even minor decisions on
their own. Tom West, a seasoned correctional officer with 15

years of experience, reflected the prevailing mood of the staff when he said, "It'll be my butt if I make a mistake in judgment. I'm not going to take the chance. Let the supervisors do it."

Welcome Back

On Sunday, June 25, 1978, I returned to work and a hero's welcome. To my joy, the Chapel was filled to capacity for the morning service. The service began with a prayer of Thanksgiving to God before my sermon, "God Is in Control," based on verses from Psalm 139. I preached not only to the congregation but also to myself as I concluded: "Search me, O God, and know my heart: try me, and know my thoughts: and see if there be any wicked way in me, and lead me in the way of everlasting."

To the men in the institution, my ordeal had become a testimony to God's unending help in time of trouble. I left that service with my faith strengthened and with the realization that God was preparing me for whatever lay ahead.

Soon after my "40-days' travail" was over and the waters began to calm, the storm raged again.

George, Pack Your Bags!

In early July, I received an abrupt phone call from Father Houlahan: "George, you're scheduled for a transfer to Federal Correctional Institution, Danbury, Connecticut. This transfer is NOT negotiable." I was tired of fighting, so without resistance I asked, "When do you want me to leave?"

"You'll have to work that out with the administration."

I was stunned, but yet I realized that God was involved with this too. My mind went to Isaiah 40:31, "But those who wait on the Lord shall renew their strength. They shall mount up with wings like eagles. They shall run and not be weary. They shall walk and not faint." To me, God again used His word to give me the courage to face the changes that were about to happen in our lives and to know that "Everything was going to be all right."

Praise the Lord, I shouted to myself. Danbury is only 65 miles from New York City, where Muriel grew up and my siblings live. I began fantasizing about attending Broadway plays and having pleasant Sunday afternoon family visits. This transfer could be a blessing.

Muriel became just as excited as I was. Being a Brooklynite, she welcomed the opportunity to move closer to familiar territory. As usual, she immediately wrote the Chamber of Commerce requesting real estate information. We were determined to make lemonade out of lemons.

Our positive thoughts and dreams were crushed two days later by a second call from Father Houlahan: "George, your transfer has been changed from Connecticut to Eglin Federal Prison Camp, Eglin Air Force Base, Florida."

To him I said, "Okay." Inwardly I said, "Thank God!" I knew that with so many people retiring, vacationing, and moving to Florida there must be some real positives. Besides, the brief Florida vacation we took in December 1974 had been a delightful experience. This move could be even more exciting than Danbury, and a savings, too, because I knew Florida did not collect state income tax.

Again, Muriel wrote the Chamber of Commerce to get information about the schools and housing available in the Fort Walton Beach area.

On Tuesday, July 11, 1978, Warden Aiken's secretary, Mrs. Haney, interrupted a counseling session: "Chaplain, please see Mr. Aiken immediately about your transfer." Upon my arrival, I found Aiken and Bob Horn, his assistant, waiting for me. After the usual greeting, and with a smirk for a smile, Warden Aiken said, "Chaplain, you'll like Eglin Federal Prison Camp. Harrison Yancey and Dave Hart are there and they'll help you. They're good men."

"I'll do my best," I responded.

"How much time do you want to straighten out your affairs?" he inquired.

"We have a house to sell; I'll need at least six weeks." Without hesitation or explanation he reduced my request to three weeks. I figured that he wanted my replacement, another black Chaplain, Ed Saxon, to begin work as soon as possible. He needed to do something to calm the large black inmate population and convince the religious inmates that race had nothing to do with my disciplinary transfer.

As I signed my papers to join the union, Joe Pitchford gave me a dose of reality. Morosely, he said, "George, you're still in big

UNITED STATES GOVERNMENT

memorandum

DATE: July 11, 1978

REPLY TO ATTN OF: E. V. AIKEN, WARDEN

Chaplains

SUBJECT: PROTESTANT CHAPLAIN

TO: THOSE LISTED BELOW

We were advised last week that Chaplain George Castillo will be transferring to Eglin AFB, Florida. The effective date of his transfer will be August 13. His replacement will be Edward H. Saxon who is presently a Captain in the U. S. Army. Rev. Saxon is affiliated with the African Methodist Episcopal Zion Church. His reporting date is July 24, 1978. Let's all welcome him to Ashland.

EVA/rh

cc: AW(O)
AW(P)
Spt. FPI
CCS
Cf. Psychologist
Business Manager
Chaplains
Chief, Case Mgt.
Spvr. Education
Food Service Spvr.
Cf. Facilities Mgr.
Hospital Administrator
Personnel Officer
Safety Officer
Record Office Adm.
Unit Manager, C
" D
" G
" K
" L
" M

Buy U.S. Savings Bonds Regularly on the Payroll Savings Plan

OPTIONAL FORM NO. 10
(REV. 7-76)
GSA FPMR (41 CFR) 101-11.6
9010-112

trouble. Your problems aren't over yet. You remember where Aiken came from, don't you?"

"Eglin."

Then he continued, "You'll be in the PENALTY BOX for a long time. Aiken still has contacts there. Everything about you is already known in Eglin and they're waiting for you. You have to be extra careful. Aiken does not like to be beaten. Expect them to do their best to get rid of you. Just don't forget that your *real boss* is God. He is sending you to a better place, which you'll like. God even works through an SOB like Aiken."

Joe's words caused me to think of the old African proverb: "Every skin teeth ain't a laugh." I suddenly realized what Aiken's smirk and words meant: "Harrison Yancey and Dave Hart are there and they'll *help* you."

The many changes that had happened at the prison and the attempted firing had been tough on my family. We all needed a break before leaving Ashland, so we took a short vacation. Marcelle was now 13 and because she had never ridden in a train, we decided to take AMTRAK to Washington, D.C. Marcelle loved the train; her enthusiasm helped us unwind as we discovered the treasures of our nation's capital.

I took a few minutes to visit Chaplain Houlahan's office to thank him for his support. I expected to receive some practical down-to-earth survival skills drawn from his many years of service to the Bureau. Instead his only words were, "George, you were very lucky."

Deep inside I knew that luck had little to do with it. God had been in control all along. My "luck" was due to God's love and mercy and was my reward for obedience to His will. I left Chaplain Houlahan's office with a renewed vow to always follow God's leading, even in times of darkness.

During my last few weeks at the institution, the administration acted almost as if I did not exist. This really didn't matter because packing and attending going-away parties kept every hour occupied. Padre gave the first party, followed by our friends at Normal Presbyterian Church. The biggest surprise came at a party given by Ben Bradley, a black community leader and businessman. At that party I was presented with a copy of a petition from several prominent community leaders recommending that I be made an Honorary Kentucky Colonel because of services I had

COMMONWEALTH OF KENTUCKY

JULIAN M. CARROLL

GOVERNOR

To all to Whom These Presents Shall Come, Greeting:

Know Ye, That HONORABLE GEORGE R. CASTILLO, ASHLAND, KENTUCKY

Is Commissioned A

KENTUCKY COLONEL

I hereby confer this honor with all the rights, privileges and responsibilities thereunto appertaining.

In testimony whereof, I have caused these letters to be made patent, and the seal of the Commonwealth to be hereunto affixed. Done at Frankfort, the 8TH day of AUGUST in the year of our Lord one thousand nine hundred and 78 and in the one hundred and 87TH year of the Commonwealth,

By the Governor:

Secretary of State

rendered the city of Ashland. The certificate, signed by Governor
Julian M. Carroll, was sent to me   at   Eglin   Prison   Camp.
Needless to say, it decorated my office in a place of honor.

Many of the staff were afraid of Aiken's wrath and kept a safe
distance. However, Paul Helo, a white case manager, held a going-away party at his home for us and staff members who dared
to attend. We found ourselves discussing a headline in that day's
Ashland Daily Independent: "Report Awaited from Director of
Prisons, GAO Poised To Investigate U.S. Prison Here."

Moving Day Miracles

Moving day came and our house was like Grand Central Station, with packing boxes and people everywhere. Movers were
constantly tracking in and out, realtors were showing the house,
and neighbors were coming to help and to say their "good-byes."
Muriel gave plants to neighbors as going-away gifts, and our son
Joe, who came to help, packed the remaining plants and our devoted dog, Faith, into our Volkswagen.

By 5:00 p.m. it was all over. The movers had left, the house
was cleaned, the lawn mowed, and the keys turned over to the realtor. After putting the last items in the car, we had dinner
across the street at the Mattinglys' home. As we were eating des-
sert, a realtor drove up with Kentucky State Trooper Cussell and
offered us a sales contract that Cussell had just signed.

Yes, God is still in the miracle-working business. As is often
said in our black churches, "God might not come when you want
Him, but He's always on time."

Florida Becomes Home

Our drive to Northwest Florida was a pleasant one, even
though Marcelle was sad about leaving her friends. We encouraged her to write them as soon as she got to Florida, and we
talked about the beaches we would soon see and the other new
adventures awaiting us. We arrived on August 15, 1978, and for
the next thirty days Aloha Village Motel on Okaloosa Island,
Fort Walton Beach, was our home. We were immediately dazzled
by the beauty of the Emerald Coast's startlingly white "sugar"
beaches. As our family walked on the fine sandy beach in the

evenings, we reflected on God's creation and His ability to turn adversity into joy. We thanked God for His goodness. I asked His continuous guidance as I faced the unknown at Eglin Federal Prison Camp.

On Wednesday, August 16, 1978, I reported to the minimum security, all-male Federal Prison Camp located inside Eglin Air Force Base. The first thing I noticed was that the facility had no bars or guard towers like all the other facilities I had seen. In their places were well-manicured grounds with landscaping so beautiful many college campuses would envy their perfection. I was welcomed by the personnel officer Mrs. Rose Spinner's warm smile. She informed me that, "Superintendent Peters is not at the camp. But I'll introduce you to his assistant, Dave Hart."

Dave took me on a tour, introduced me to staff, and explained that Eglin's inmates were trusted to work both inside and outside the institution. Under agreement with the Air Force, inmates provided the base with an auxiliary work force. I was amazed to see inmates sitting at desks with telephones, working in tool cribs without staff supervision, and even walking into and out of the Control Center. *What a change,* I thought to myself. *Inmates are even performing tasks that staff did at Ashland and Atlanta.*

Most of the inmates were first-time offenders from the southeastern United States, and were between the ages of 20 and 65. They were primarily white-collar criminals without records of violent or sexual crimes and without medical or psychiatric problems. They were trusted to work in every part of the base: the grounds, the offices (including the Judge Advocate's), the commissary, the housing areas, and the hospital.

After the tour, Dave and I shared information about Eglin and other institutions where we had worked previously. He quickly steered the conversation to the Ashland/Aiken incident. When he asked me what had been the problem at Ashland, I told him, "Dave, I consider the matter closed and do not wish to discuss it. I look forward to a fulfilling ministry here."

While I was still getting acquainted with my new assignment, Muriel and Marcelle were having a great time exploring the Fort Walton Beach area. We didn't have to worry about Marcelle because she made her usual quick adjustment. Our baby was growing up; she got her first babysitting job soon after we arrived at

Eglin. Under her mother's supervision she ably cared for a military family's two children. During the day, realtors kept my family busy looking at houses. After work and on my days off, we looked on our own. We saw lots of homes but nothing that excited us until one afternoon we drove around the Shalimar area and spotted a "For Sale" sign on a two-story house that grabbed our attention. It was love at first sight. I immediately contacted the agent: "We want to see that house." The minute we walked into the house we knew that we had found our home — 175 Country Club Road.

We moved in a few weeks later and realized that this house was literally a dream come true. As we unpacked, we came across a "Find-A-Home" magazine which had been sent to us in Kentucky. In it we had circled this very house as the one we would love to own. I used the words of Thomas the Doubter: "My God and my Lord!" Not that I doubted that my transfer was Divinely inspired, but the manifestation of this Divine plan was awesome. To this day, we are amazed that we had actually chosen our home while in Ashland, and that God had directed us to the place where we were to spend 12 happy years.

Miracles Happen, Even in Prison Camps

A few days after my arrival, Superintendent Peters transferred from the camp. In his place came J. Michael Quinlan, a former assistant to the Director of Prisons, Mr. Norman Carlson. Quinlan was later to become the Director of Prisons.

I liked Superintendent Quinlan immediately. He was a concerned Christian who was people-oriented. He was firm but he demonstrated openness, warmth, gentleness and, most importantly, fairness. Superintendent Quinlan also made it clear that he did not hold the Ashland/Aiken incident against me, which restored my confidence in myself and in the system. Quinlan certainly reinforced my conviction that the system depends on the person sitting behind the desk. Thank God for the "Quinlans" who counteracted the "Aikens."

The new Superintendent confidently assumed his responsibilities as he made known his philosophy of corrections: "A person is in prison *as* punishment and not *for* punishment. When a person has lost his freedom; is separated from family, friends, and community; and is unable to support his family, that person has been punished enough."

Quinlan's advice to staff was, "Help the inmates. Their lives should be better when they leave this institution because of their contact with you."

Time proved Quinlan to be a real humanitarian in the Hebrew-Christian-Islamic tradition. He was concerned not only about the prisoners, but also his staff's welfare. Staff could talk with him any time. Department heads affectionately called him "Mike."

Mike's concern for people extended beyond the institution. In September 1979, Hurricane Frederick devastated Mobile, Alabama, 135 miles west of Eglin Federal Prison Camp. Each Saturday he sent inmates under staff supervision to help restore the city. I was happy to volunteer in the clean-up effort too. In addition, he allowed inmates, under Prison Fellowship's supervision, to refurbish homes for the elderly indigent in Atlanta. Their initial venture was so successful that he authorized inmates to do the same in our local area.

Mike Quinlan was also a Captain in the Air Force Reserves and he encouraged me to join. I immediately investigated the possibility of entering as a Protestant Chaplain. Unfortunately, no vacancies existed. However, the Air Force needed aircraft mechanics, and since I was trained in that specialty I was accepted immediately. I was elated when a Chaplaincy position became available within a few months. I discussed the appointment with the reserve unit commander, Colonel Billie Parker, who said, "I'll be just too happy to have you serve as a Chaplain in my unit." With those words of encouragement I quickly applied for the position. I was disappointed to learn, however, that I was too old to be commissioned. It wasn't long, though, before reservists and Air Force Reserve Technicians were bringing their problems to me and asking for counseling. Even without a commission I was, in essence, a Chaplain in the Air Force Reserves.

After weighing the pros and cons of remaining as an enlisted man, I decided to stay in the reserves until retirement at age 60.

Different Philosophies

As Mike brought his liberal philosophies from the Bureau, I

brought my conservative experiences from Atlanta and Ashland. For example, I had difficulty leaving the Chapel open when I wasn't there. Although my inmate clerk assured me that the Chapel was always left unlocked from 7:00 a.m. to 10:00 p.m. whether the Chaplain was present or not, I wanted to hear it was okay from my immediate supervisor, Dave Hart. But Dave wouldn't give me a direct answer. It wasn't until I was told, "Chaplain, don't worry about it" by Harrison Yancey, the chief correctional supervisor (CCS) in charge of security, that I decided to leave the Chapel unlocked. Even then, I was still concerned. Aiken's promise that Yancey would "help me" was still fresh in my memory.

In Matthew 5:44, Jesus said, "But I say unto you, Love your enemies, bless them that curse you, do good to them that hate you, and pray for them which despitefully use you, and persecute you." My heart went out to Mr. Aiken when Mrs. Linda Paulk, the Superintendent's secretary, announced that Aiken had suffered a severe stroke only six months after his early retirement. I immediately began praying for him and his family.

As I prayed, my mind went back to a lesson my grandfather had taught me in his cabinet shop. My friend Jim had done something wrong to me. I complained to his mother, who not only verbally chastised Jim but gave him a whipping. Jim screamed as the strap stung his bottom; I yelled with joy.

"That's not right," my grandfather said. "No one should laugh when someone is in pain."

Years later, Rabbi (Chaplain) Marvin Labinger repeated this philosophy using a Talmudic illustration: "...The angels in heaven broke out in songs of jubilation when the Egyptians were drowning in the Red Sea. God silenced them and said, 'My creatures are perishing, and you sing praises?'"

Not Enough Hours in the Day

Since I was the only Chaplain, my hands were always full. Handling problems didn't stop when I left the prison. Frequently, my home telephone rang all hours of the night. Some callers were staff reporting emergencies or seeking counseling themselves; others were volunteers or the unchurched asking for pastoral help. Parents from the community wanted information regarding their children's participation in the Christmas program. Senior citizens wanted to know how they could get inmates to refurbish their homes. Inmates' wives needed someone to listen to their family problems. And so it went. Staff members found that I had a sympathetic ear and frequently stopped by my office. So staff was part of my ministry too. It seemed that requests for assistance or special consideration were never ending.

The life struggles of the 400 inmates at Eglin were quite similar to those in other institutions. To nurture their religious growth, I continued some religious programs and developed others so that all religious-faith groups could be served.

But somehow my supervisor, Dave Hart, didn't feel I had enough to keep me busy. So he required me to sponsor the inmates' Toastmasters Club. This education/recreation program had over 200 speakers and would-be speakers, making this the largest club like it in the world. Not only did I attend all their meetings, but I shopped for their photo supplies and supervised the picture-taking the club did as a fund-raising activity. They took photos of inmates who wanted pictures to send home and used the profits to buy refreshments for all the camp-sponsored organizations. This also meant that I had to assume the responsibility for buying the refreshments for Black Awareness, Jaycees, Latinos, Jewish Fellowship, and Alcoholics Anonymous.

The Toastmasters annual banquet was an important part of the club's existence. It was at these banquets that the members polished their new-found skills. Under my sponsorship, they completed preparations for their banquet and were ready to mail invitations to Toastmasters Clubs throughout the area. I was proud of those responsible for creating such beautiful invitations. Not wanting to be "caught" again, however, I showed Dave Hart the invitations before mailing them. I knew he was against the Toastmasters' hosting the banquet, but I expected him to appreciate a job well done. Instead, even though he couldn't find anything wrong with the invitations, he still managed to delay the mailing.

"Where did the inmates obtain the stationery?"

"They did the art work on paper provided by the institution," I responded.

He then said, "Since I won't be in on Monday, let's talk to Mike about the stationery on Tuesday."

"But, Dave, that means the mailing will be delayed for another four days," I reminded him.

He retorted, "So be it."

On Tuesday morning, when we met in Mike's office, Dave's criticism turned from the stationery to the invitations. He looked at me and asked, "Who authorized the duplication of the invitations?"

"Toastmasters is an educational program. Since I was off and time was of the essence, Roberta Stewart, Supervisor of Education, authorized the duplication of the invitations. It's supposed to come under her department anyway," I emphasized.

Hart stated, "George, you should have initiated the authorization and not Roberta."

Mike interrupted the conversation at this point and authorized the mailing of the invitations. I mailed them immediately.

The banquet was a wonderful, fun-filled experience with eloquent, articulate inmates and local Toastmasters sharing the podium. The room rocked with applause and laughter at the many extemporaneous presentations, short stories, and humorous speeches given to an appreciative audience.

The responsibility of the Toastmasters and the related duties remained mine until April 1980, when Hart assigned it to teacher/activity coordinator Shirley Minter-Smith, who had recently transferred to Eglin.

Padre's 25th Anniversary

Padre had been such a close friend that Muriel and I wanted desperately to help him celebrate his 25th Ordination Service at Holy Family Roman Catholic Church in Ashland. However, at that time I had to find my own replacement for any time I wanted off, and I couldn't find anyone for that weekend. Muriel and I decided that she would go alone and take my place by reading the Scripture lesson.

Within minutes of her arrival in Ashland, our old friends began bombarding her with questions about our transfer. She happily told them that God had turned our darkness into light and our affliction into joy. "We couldn't have been assigned to a better place. George loves the different religious programs and is excited about a Sunday School being started for inmates' children.

The weather in Northwest Florida is absolutely beautiful year round. Although the winters are cool, we don't have to worry about shoveling snow. Okaloosa County schools are very good, which helped make Marcelle's adjustment smooth. We're both doing well in school, as I'm working on my Master's degree in public administration part-time while holding down a full-time civil service job. Erick and Martha will make us grandparents in the spring. Joe is doing well."

Upon her return home, we felt so blessed, and we prayed for those who were at war within and fighting wars without, such as poverty, disease, crime, confinement, illness, and those other things that make life difficult. We felt so thankful and grateful for our health, inner peace, children, friends, jobs, and all else that made our lives worthwhile. We affirmed that God is in control and God is good. We loved Eglin and needed no convincing that our transfer to Eglin Prison Camp was a Divine transfer. However, everyone didn't see it that way. At the Southeast regional Chaplains' Conference in Atlanta, several Chaplains asked me, "George, how were you able to get Eglin, the Bureau's plum?"

I said to Jim Moore, a tall, heavily bearded Chaplain, and to the others listening, "God sent me there."

My reply was hardly out of my mouth when Chaplain Paul Simms' booming voice a few feet away said, "Maybe you have to screw up before you get a good assignment."

Changing of the Guard, and Healing

From the day of his arrival, I had known that Mike Quinlan was destined for greater assignments. Even so, all staff at Eglin felt a sense of loss when we bid Mike Quinlan God's blessings on his next assignment, to Otisville Correctional Institution in New York.

I was flattered when he asked me to consider transferring too. I would have enjoyed working with him, but economic considerations made me say, "No, thanks." The transfer would have meant almost doubling my mortgage to between 15 and 18 percent in addition to my having to pay New York State income tax. Besides, I was content continuing as a one-man department and felt very pleased to have the opportunity to try new programs.

Chaplains of the southeast region

However, there was one nagging concern that continued to haunt me; the institution did not have any official designated to supervise the religious programs when I was off for extended periods of time. Outside volunteers told me that when Chaplain Stump was here, they pitched in during his absence. But I realized that they had no authority to make official decisions in emergency situations. Before something happened that could turn into another major incident, I wanted an answer from the administration. Each of the many times I had asked Hart and Yancey, "Who supervises programs when I'm off for an extended time?" I received the same responses. Hart said, "George, find your own staff replacement." Yancey frankly admitted, "I don't know." Needless to say, this added burden of finding a staff member who would volunteer to be my replacement placed me in an uncomfortable situation.

Finally, on May 20, 1980, I met with the new Superintendent, Larry Kerr. "Larry, I need your help. For the past twenty months I've been unable to take leave unless I can find my own replacement. Everything else here works under an established chain of command except me. I'm tired of the additional responsibility it places on me to find another staff member willing to volunteer in my absence. It's unfair to have me handle an institutional problem. I've tried, but no one is willing to address the question of who's responsible for the religious programs during my absence."

The Superintendent was obviously caught by surprise and immediately called his assistant, Dave Hart, to get an explanation. "Dave, who supervises programs when the Chaplain is away?"

After a long pause, Hart looked down and said softly, "I don't know."

Hart's answer prompted me to ask, "Larry, why did it take twenty months to get my question answered? I've been working under a double standard since my disciplinary transfer here. Only last month I was relieved of the Toastmasters responsibility. That too was part of my punishment. Haven't I had enough?"'

Without waiting for Dave to answer, Larry said, "Dave, take care of it. It's the *institution's* problem."

I left Superintendent Kerr's office relieved. A few days later, Hart gave me a memo he had sent to all department heads:

As you are aware, Chaplain Castillo is the only member of his department, and when he is away on Annual/Military Leave or Training he has had to seek assistance from other departments to supervise activities where outside guests are involved. To minimize this problem and avoid interruption of religious programs during the Chaplain's absence, the duty officer will supervise the Saturday and Sunday morning worship services and custody will supervise the Friday evening Jewish services.

With the replacement issue resolved, I was able to minister to the inmates and staff more effectively. Work became a pleasure. I found myself growing spiritually and able to concentrate on the religious programs. I felt rewarded because the programs flourished. Within a few months, religious programs were available to inmates seven evenings a week. Under the leadership of Attorney Richard Powell, I was even able to add a very popular group called Christian Businessmen.

Win a Few, Lose a Few

Positive changes became apparent. The number of inmates who voluntarily attended the 4:30 p.m. prayer group dedicated to prayer and praise increased. Prayer was a new religious experience to many inmates, and like most new converts they couldn't get enough of God's Word and teaching. In this prayer group, the inmates found good things happening in their lives. As a result, the Chapel walls began vibrating 365 days a year with prayer, testimony, singing, and spiritual support of each other.

Inmates Tom Harris, John Clanston, Bill Hall, and Paul Shaw each used almost the same words: "Our entire group is deriving spiritual support and benefit from this prayer group....It's the strongest Christian fellowship we have....When I get released, I'm gonna attend prayer meetings at church....I feel such caring and compassion in our group."

With these positive affirmations, word got around, and after a short time we had a core group of about 25 inmates. One afternoon there were a record-setting 72 worshipers. Other inmates noticed the positive coping skills in the participants. As a result, the Jewish, Roman Catholic, and Muslim inmates soon formed their own prayer groups.

As in all prisons during the 80's, the inmate p
increased daily. To accommodate the increase, the room
dormitories that had previously been used for reading ano
playing were converted to sleeping areas. Part of the visiti
room was opened for inmates to play cards after the 4:00 p.m.
and 10:00 p.m. head counts were completed. Inmates were also
authorized to watch TV in any dorm after the 10:00 p.m. head
count. Not surprisingly, "skin flicks" had the largest audiences.

Those inmates who weren't card players or didn't want to
watch skin flicks, were short-changed after 10:00 p.m. Several
Christian inmates asked me, "Chaplain, can we have permission
to use the Chapel for prayer and meditation after the 10:00
o'clock count?" Acknowledging that it was a very good idea, I
agreed to ask permission from Chief Correctional Supervisor
Martinez to leave the Chapel unlocked for prayers and meditation. Martinez's resounding response was, "NO!"

"Are you saying you prefer to have inmates watch skin flicks
rather than go to the Chapel for some quiet time?" I asked.

"Yes, I am," he responded adamantly.

I couldn't stand the idea of skin flicks winning over Christian
values. The Chapel was open unattended during most of the day
already, and I couldn't believe the administration would rather
have healthy, sexually starved males watching skin flicks instead of reading, praying, and meditating on God's Word. So I
took my argument to our supervisor Williams. Again the movies
won. Score: Skin Flicks-2, Religion-0.

Religion frequently lost. A few months earlier, Mrs. Donovan
had brought her family to visit her husband Bill. A gung-ho correctional officer, known for being a stickler for the rules, saw her
Bible and refused to let Mrs. Donovan bring it into the visiting
room. He followed Supplement Policy 5267.3A to the letter: "The
only leisure time items allowed in the visiting room are playing
cards, coloring books, crayons, children's educational books and
one rubber or plastic toy per small child, which must be utilized
in the outside patio area."

Mrs. Donovan was outraged. She said, "I will not take my
Bible back to the car. This is America, where no one don't need to
be ashamed of the Holy Bible." Since Mrs. Donovan didn't comply, the unbending officer did not allow the family visit that day.

When I brought the issue to the attention of Assistant Superintendent Cox, he expressed annoyance because he had directed Chief Correctional Supervisor Martinez months earlier to allow Bibles in the visiting room. Cox said, "Chaplain, I'll take care of it, again." For a while there was no problem, but when the shift changed the old standard prevailed. Again, Bibles were prohibited from the visiting room.

Welcome to the Religious Department

Being a minimum security prison, inmates arrive at Eglin differently than in higher-security-level institutions. Although some are brought in by the U.S. Marshals, most are allowed by the courts to get their affairs in order and turn themselves in to the facility on the specified date. Regardless of how they arrive, they are processed by Receiving and Discharge, assigned to different teams, and scheduled for Admission and Orientation (A & O) lectures covering every phase of institution life.

Chapel orientation was scheduled for each Tuesday afternoon. I knew that this period might be my only chance to convince some of the inmates that the Chapel was a place of refuge, healing, and restoration.

By nature I am an easy-going and rather laid-back person, and this made it easy for me to put new inmates at ease. While making it clear what I could and could not do for them, I told them how to make a successful adjustment to prison life. I also used the time to schedule a brief individual session with each newcomer soon after this group meeting was over.

By their very nature, most inmates resent being forced to do anything. I knew that reaching them required more than the mere handing out of an outline of the available religious programs and my work schedule. I was aware, too, that inmates' first impression of me might determine whether they would become involved in the rehabilitative potential of the camp's religious programs. I tried to be upbeat and friendly during the two-hour orientation session. During each of my lectures, I would come face-to-face with men who were depressed, guilty, fearful of the unknown, and angry at the judicial system, themselves, and just people in general. At times, I got the brunt of the men's frustration and pain.

Each group received the same opening statement:

Gentlemen, you are in the Chapel for orientation to the Religious Department. I know that some of you wouldn't be here if it were not mandatory. After this orientation you have a choice whether to return to the Chapel or not. This means that the next time you come to the Chapel, it will be voluntarily. Is that clear, gentlemen?

Usually, most would answer the rhetorical question with a submissive nod; others were like the overweight, ruddy-faced inmate who bellowed: "Yes, Sir."

I would then assure them that we have something for all inmates whatever their religious affiliation: Protestants, Roman Catholics, Jews, Muslims, Jehovah's Witnesses, Mormons, Native Americans, and others.

Then, with a smile on my face and looking directly into the eyes of the men, I would say:

You'll notice that when I began talking to you I addressed you as *gentlemen*. That's because every inmate in this camp is a gentleman.

This usually resulted in many snickers. I can still remember one middle-aged, bald inmate with a weather-beaten face who nudged the fellow next to him and whispered: "There goes a crazy Chaplain." Without missing a beat I looked directly at him and continued:

If you weren't gentlemen, you wouldn't be in this camp. You're in a place without walls, fences, or barbed wire. Most of you walked into this prison by yourselves. Convicts don't walk into prison, they escape from prison. The white lines won't stop a criminal from taking off, but they will stop a gentleman.

By this time inmates were beginning to like what they were hearing. Usually their eye contacts told me that we had established rapport, and I would continue:

Now, let's look at the other side of the coin. As long as you are in prison, it hurts. It hurts whether you're in 'Holiday Inn,' as Eglin is often referred to, or in Marion Penitentiary. This can be a lonely and painful place.

God has a long history of helping people with their loneliness. If you recall, after Adam was created he became lonesome and depressed until God....

During one session, a bespectacled young inmate finished the sentence by saying, "gave him a wife." Then the youngest-looking inmate added, "God put Adam to sleep and took a rib out to make Eve his wife." With a twinkle in his clear, blue, sparkling eyes, another inmate whimsically said, "God gave me a headache who took me to the cleaners." Regardless of their answers, I knew my point was understood.

Yes, separation from 'Eve' is the primary hardship of incarceration. Your state of depression right now is normal because you have to adjust to a different environment without your loved ones. Secondly, some of you feel guilty because you know your family is now enduring hardships because of your incarceration. I know incarceration is hard on you. But it's harder on your families, the 'second victims' of your crime.

Here at Eglin all your needs will be provided — food, shelter, medication, education, religion, and recreation. But your significant other still has her own responsibilities plus yours. You need to balance your reasoning and your emotions and accept the reality that there are now some things that you can no longer control.

This is where your Chaplain can help you by providing counseling for both your present adjustment and your later release. My office is the only office that you can visit without an appointment. As long as I'm here, and the door is not shut, just walk in. *You* are my number-one priority. I'll listen to you. If you don't want to talk with me, that's fine. But talk to somebody. You need one another during these difficult times. If anyone feels that he doesn't need anyone else, his needs are greater than he realizes. Be good buddies to one another and listen to each other.

Keeping busy is the key to your adjustment. Eglin is the place to be if one has to be incarcerated. Here you have to work every day. Get involved in your work assignment. It'll enable you to forget your problems and yourself for a while. Work is therapeutic. After work, you're on your own, except for head count time.

DO NOT EVER MISS A COUNT unless you want to be listed as an escapee. You'll soon learn why inmates call count time the 'Holy Hour' because prison life comes to a halt until every inmate is accounted for. After the 4:00 p.m. head count, supper is served. After supper, get involved in a program. It's my experience that inmates who participate in religious programs are able to cope easier. Religious programs are available every evening for your spiritual growth.

I ended each session by saying, "I'll be happy to answer any questions as I talk to you individually in my office." Then I would give each inmate a copy of the religious programs schedule and emphasize that all services or group programs in the camp Chapel were open to everyone. In fact, their visitors could attend the services with them. Here's the schedule I gave them:

Protestant: Worship Service led by Chaplain Castillo at 8:45 a.m. each Sunday. During this time we provide a Sunday School for children. This is the only institution in the Bureau which has a Sunday School for them.

Roman Catholics: English Mass led by Father James Grothjan each Saturday at 9:00 a.m., followed by Spanish Mass led by Deacon J. D. Trevino at 11:00 a.m. Father Grothjan is available for confession before the 9:00 a.m. Mass.

Jewish: Sabbath eve and Oneg services are led by the

Rabbi at Eglin Air Force Base Chapel 1. I will escort you there. However, on the first and third Thursdays of the month, the Rabbi visits the camp for Jewish studies.

Muslims: Juma prayer at 11:30 a.m. on Fridays. Each Sunday services held at 2:00 p.m.

All Other Faiths: See the Chaplain for dates and times.

Unusual Counseling Session

My initial counseling session with new inmates was always brief. I used this time to allow them to share their feelings and concerns with me so that I could better minister to them in the future. We usually talked in private, but I made one exception to this rule.

Inmate Jean Paul could barely speak or understand English and needed an interpreter to talk with me. Inmate Aldo Gucci was multilingual and quickly volunteered. Seeing the two of them in my office was symbolic of the world's two primary groups, the "haves" and the "have-nots." Paul was a poor Haitian turned drug dealer; Aldo Gucci was a billionaire who evaded paying taxes. *The Playground Daily News* dated October 17, 1986, printed: "Aldo Gucci admitted evading more than $7 million in taxes."

Gucci was a kind, elderly, active participant in the 4:30 Prayer Group, Bible Studies, both Roman Catholic Masses, and Protestant Services. Later Jean Paul became involved in the religious programs too. Although their social standings might have prevented them from speaking to each other on the streets, they bonded in my office and became good friends. Prison uniforms have a tendency to eliminate the social barriers that keep people apart on the outside.

Jean Paul not only had adjustment problems, but he was also depressed about economic hardships his family was suffering in Miami. His income had been the "big bucks" he earned from dealing large quantities of drugs. Now with him in prison, his wife had been left penniless and pregnant, with two small children to care for.

One day Gucci asked, "Chaplain, can I send Jean Paul's wife

some money?"

"No," I responded. "It's against policy for any inmate to give another inmate or his family anything."

His face dropped in disappointment. Then I continued, "However, since your wife isn't in prison or under the control of the Federal Bureau of Prisons, she is free to help anyone she wishes." Relief brightened Gucci's face when he heard that. It was easy to see why he was missed when he left on March 30, 1987.

The "Salt" of the Prison Camp

Just as on the outside, our programs had two types of congregants: the faithful, who attended regularly, and the inactives, who usually showed up only when their affairs got out of hand or they wanted God to get them out of a mess they had created. The faithful members were the better-adjusted ones; they kept the peace and generally coped well. On the other hand, the inactives usually kept things stirred up within themselves and in their dealings with others.

Even though many of the staff members were unaware of the good these men did, the faithful were the "salt" of the institution. Many took seriously the words of Jesus in Matthew 5:9, "Blessed are the peacemakers for they shall be called the children of God." In many instances, the "salt" kept down dissension and were a strong positive influence, contributing to the orderly running of the institution. They helped my other congregants, the inactive ones and the ones who did not cope well and needed frequent counseling.

Children's Church School Begins

Experience has shown that a strong correlation exists between the strength of the family and the extent to which inmates are successful in re-entering society. Families building their lives on faith in God are the building blocks of society. Under Mike Quinlan's administration, Eglin Prison Camp was able to help families in a meaningful way by starting a church school for children related to inmates.

Martha Tidwell visited her husband Lewie each week and they often noticed restless children in the visiting room. Being devoted churchgoers, warm and caring people, they talked about how we were missing a chance to minister to the children. They proposed that we start a Sunday School. "Chaplain, a children's church school could serve two purposes. It would give parents privacy to talk, and at the same time it would teach children about Jesus." The more we talked, the more convinced I became that it was a good idea. But I knew it couldn't be done without local Christian volunteers.

"Let's work and pray about it," I said, wanting to encourage Lewie and Martha. Upon his release from Eglin Prison Camp, Lewie pursued the church school idea with his Pastor, Dr. James Monroe, of the First Baptist Church of Fort Walton Beach, who agreed to help. Mrs. Alice Combs, Director of the Missionary Action Union of the Choctawhatchee Baptist Association, also liked the idea and wrote the proposal.

Since no other Federal prison facility had approved a church school for children, 1 knew that we would have to cover all the bases if we were to get this proposal approved. While Dr. Monroe, the Tidwells, and Mrs. Combs worked in the community, I sowed seeds with key camp personnel whose support I needed. All my efforts fell on dry ground, except for Ted Sheppard, Supervisor of Education. As the son of a Methodist minister, he knew the value of church school. As usual, I could count on his support of the Religious Department.

Others preferred not to rock the boat. Once a program was started, it was usually continued; the problem was getting it started. Any new venture like this one was typically met with skepticism and negativism. The reason usually given was that the concept was "too far out for a prison setting." When I presented my memo on the school for approval up the chain of command, department heads couldn't believe we wanted a church school in the camp.

Fortunately, Superintendent Quinlan was an innovative person who knew a church school would be beneficial. Therefore he gave his hearty blessing, and when he did his subordinates quickly followed his lead. Those who were previously against a church school became its chief supporters. I was overjoyed.

Former inmate Charles Colson, a prominent Watergate figure, started Prison Fellowship. Local volunteers of Prison Fellowship, First Baptist Church of Fort Walton Beach, and other area churches taught at what some informally called "Colson's Church School." However, I would have preferred to call it "Quinlan's Church School" because he cared enough to authorize the program's existence.

Church school began on Sunday, July 29, 1979, when faithful leaders Lewie and Martha Tidwell, Rachel Godwin, Julius Weichbrodt, Myra Burden, Glenda McMahan, and Dianne Kostelny taught the first class. Mrs. Kostelny worked five days a week in the education department, and returned on Sunday for church school. To this day, these volunteers are still serving God's little ones in the nation's only Federal Bureau of Prisons Church School.

About five years after the inception of the school, the ringing of the telephone woke me up from a deep afternoon sleep. I fumbled for the telephone and tried to sound alert, "This is George." I recognized Superintendent Paul Lewis's deep voice immediately. "I'm sorry to disturb you on your day off, but tomorrow morning WEAR TV wants to do a documentary on the religious programs featuring Lewie Tidwell, a former inmate. What do you know about him? I know tomorrow is your day off but could you be available at 9:30 when the camera crew is here?"

"I'll be only too glad to come in tomorrow morning. I know Lewie and his wife Martha very well. The Tidwells were faithful worshippers at the Chapel during Lewie's incarceration. Since his release, both he and Martha have diligently worked as Sunday School teachers for our church school. They are fine people and members of the Fort Walton Beach First Baptist Church."

At 8:45 a.m. the next day, while I was checking the Chapel to make sure it was ready for the scrutiny of the TV cameras, I felt good when Superintendent Lewis joined me and commented, "It looks great."

The WEAR TV crew took pictures of the Chapel and asked me to discuss Lewie and the other volunteers' activities. At the conclusion of the interview, Superintendent Lewis escorted our guests from the camp and called me immediately. "Chaplain, I'm proud of you. You did a superb job and carried out your responsibility in a professional manner." The program aired on May 1, 1985.

I was delighted that the Religious Department had been given the chance to provide a caring, safe environment where inmates' children could learn and have fun during the Sunday visitation periods.

Volunteers

Without volunteers our church school would not have been possible, nor could one Chaplain minister to the needs of the many religious groups represented inside the prison system without volunteer help.

As expected, I received calls and unexpected visits from many people offering their services. The hardest to deal with were the ones convinced that their denomination was the only one that could whip the inmates into line and change them into decent, respectable citizens. Following closely behind were the ones who felt their way was the only way to achieve salvation.

Pastor Dunlap was one such minister who talked about damnation to the inmates. "Chaplain, if they would accept my denomination's teachings, then they would be saved."

Since it was my prerogative to accept or reject volunteers, I denied him access to the prison, as well as those who I felt were overly aggressive, judgmental, and with Messianic complexes. Pastor Dunlap was furious and said demandingly, "Give me your supervisor's name and address."

I gladly complied. Days later I answered Dunlap's complaint letter for the Superintendent.

Fortunately, not all volunteers were like Dunlap. I welcomed the Rabbis who visited weekly and taught Hebrew and the Jewish tradition. And the Roman Catholic volunteers who also visited weekly. With joy and anticipation, the Catholic community looked forward to the Bishop's annual Christmas evening Mass.

The Protestant community also had several excellent volunteer groups. One was A Better Way Ministries (Formerly Freedom Prison Ministries) from Pascagoula, Mississippi. This committed prison ministry, led by Pat Garrison and her volunteers, began visiting in 1979. Their singing and preaching are inspirational. "Sister Pat" is still accepting inmates where they are and helping them to visualize a better future with God's help.

Prison Fellowship Ministries and its local director Stan Jarrett, a camp volunteer for over 25 years, and his volunteers conducted Discipleship Seminars to teach inmates basic Christianity and Christian outreach. They also sponsored Marriage Seminars, which were taught by trained former inmates and their wives. This valuable program enabled inmates to adjust to prison life and to overcome the hurdles they and their families would face upon release. Additionally, Prison Fellowship Ministries used volunteer inmate labor to refurbish homes for the elderly indigent who would live in substandard homes without the volunteers' help. Now that I am retired, I am a teacher volunteer with this fine organization.

Christmas Helps Inmates To Care

Many times innocent children are the victims of their parents' folly. We tried to ease at least part of that pain through an annual Needy Children's Christmas Party. It had become a tradition under the leadership of my predecessor, Chaplain Eugene Stump, and continued uninterruptedly until I left Eglin in 1988 for Pensacola Federal Prison Camp.

Inmates were the sole contributors, and most were willing to contribute freely for the benefit of underprivileged children. I had several inmates tell me, "Chaplain, I remember when I didn't have anything for Christmas." Some inmates provided more than others, but the maximum any one inmate could give was $100.00. At times, former inmates sent their contributions because they remembered how many children in Okaloosa County depended on this party for their only Christmas presents.

Our goal of $5,000.00 was always met, and some years the donations exceeded all our expectations. It was not unusual for some wealthy inmates to want to contribute more than the maximum. One inmate, a wealthy Miami real estate broker, put it this way: "Chaplain, the men have guilt money to get rid of. Why don't you help them ease their conscience?" His friend, Larry Shapiro, a bank embezzler, chimed in, "Can anyone give twice or three times on different forms?"

"Sorry, but I can only accept $100.00. That amount is set by policy, and we wish to keep it that way so that everyone can play a part."

Most of the children who were invited to the party were referred by the state's Department of Health and Rehabilitative

Services (HRS) and by local churches. Normally I requested one hundred children, but as word got around another dozen or so uninvited guests would generally attend. Fortunately, we made provisions for these children also. The party had become so established that parents would begin calling two months before Christmas asking that their children be invited to the party so they could receive a Christmas gift.

The Thursday before the Christmas party was shopping day. In a typical year, I selected four inmates to join workers from HRS and local churches and together we "invaded" the local TG&Y discount store in nearby Niceville. We divided the shopping lists so that the ladies and inmates could go into different parts of the store and pick toys and clothes. Each child put three wishes on a gift list and we were able to make at least one of the three wishes come true. The uninvited guests received gift certificates to purchase gifts of their choice.

The Christian community had a festive pre-party gift-wrapping celebration on Saturday afternoon before the big party. After the packages were wrapped, everyone — especially the inmate workers — felt pleased as they relaxed, talked, and enjoyed goodies with Christmas music playing in the background.

The party was always given the Sunday before Christmas. Finally, after many hours of preparation, we were all ready for the high point of the Christmas holiday. Though the party was usually scheduled for 6:00 p.m., children and parents were already waiting in the parking lot by 4:30 p.m. When the door opened at 5:30 p.m., bubbly, happy, excited, eager children rushed into the visiting room shouting, "Is Santa Claus here yet?"

Pointing to their gifts, I assured them that Santa had already arrived but was tired and resting; he would be out in just a few minutes. After I gave the welcome and prayer, the Chapel Choir sang a few Christmas carols. Then, with a hearty "HO, HO, HO," a smiling Santa and his helpers appeared and distributed the gifts. The joy on the inmates' faces eclipsed that of the children. We all laughed to see a tiny four-year-old boy waddling with his hands wrapped around a box too big for him to hold. The tiredness brought on by the long days of preparation disappeared instantly when we saw the happy faces of the boys and girls ripping open the brightly colored wrapping paper and beholding their gifts. Shouts of joy and all sorts of other gleeful sounds filled the usually quiet visiting room. The look on the faces of children who had asked for and received bicycles was worth all the money in the world. Tears of gratitude dotted many mothers' and guardians' cheeks.

An hour-and-a-half later everyone exited the visiting room to gather outdoors for the lighting ceremony. As the lights twinkled on the beautifully decorated Christmas tree, we joined in the singing of Christmas carols, which added to the beauty, dignity, and solemnity of the service. As usual, I ended the party with my five-minute sermonette, "What Christmas Means." The party concluded with "Silent Night" as the visitors walked to the parking lot with their gifts and wished each other "Merry Christmas."

Cons Will Use Anything, Even Christmas

It is always unfortunate when activities meant for good were overshadowed by negative experiences. But given the nature of prisons, unpleasant things do happen.

The editorial staff of the Fort Walton Beach *Playground Daily News* heard about our elaborate Christmas party and sent a reporter to cover it in 1981. Several inmates and I were photographed. Soon pictures were published in an article titled "Inmate Elves" and subtitled "The Night Kids and Christmas Came to Eglin Federal Prison."

Generally, taking photographs in the camp was strictly prohibited, except with permission granted under tightly controlled circumstances. Some inmates didn't want it known that they were incarcerated. Others were under the witness-protection program and were hidden by either the state or federal government for their safety.

The *Daily News* photographer was cleared and was supervised by the duty officer to make sure no one was photographed who shouldn't have been. However, without our knowledge, one inmate whose picture appeared in the paper was in the witness-protection program. It wasn't long before one of the top administrators saw the newspaper and immediately put the inmate into detention and arranged for him to be transferred for his safety. Just before he left the institution, the inmate confided in me that he had intentionally allowed his picture to be taken because he didn't want to be in the program any longer.

In 1987, an opportunistic, gregarious, former banker, inmate Tony Braggart, approached me with a request: "Chaplain, I want to be chairman of the fund-raising committee." When I asked him why, he replied: "Chaplain, I've been in this institution longer than most, and I know these guys. They will give a good donation if I ask them. Some are good for big bucks but don't give the maximum. A lot of these guys are getting big and fat and sloppy while some children out there won't have any Christmas."

"That sounds reasonable, Tony. You're now the chairman."

Indeed, Tony was an effective chairman because we raised $9,100 that year, a big jump from the $5,500 we had raised in 1986. I wondered how that happened. I knew the population had grown, but I asked myself, *Was that enough to account for the big increase? Did Tony bring some banking skills to this task?*

The answers came quickly when several inmates told me, "Chaplain, Tony has promised new guys that he'll use his influence to get them an early release date if they make the maximum contribution to the Christmas party." Of course, when I confronted Tony, he denied it.

Before the party, I showed Mike Pugh, the Assistant Superintendent, all the gifts. They included six adult-sized bicycles, 30 tricycles, hundreds of small packages, and several large ones. He spotted the name Cynthia P on a large package. Surprised, he said, "George, your chairman asked me my daughter's name, and there's a gift tagged with the same name. Find out if that gift is intended for my daughter. If it is, I don't want it."

"I'll find out, and I'll take care of it," I promised.

This time Tony admitted that he had prepared a gift for the Assistant Superintendent's daughter. Then he had the audacity to prepare a letter for my signature requesting that he be given additional time in a halfway house for the good work he did for the needy children.

Confident of his success, and without realizing that I had discovered his "con game," he waited a few days and came to my office. Jubilantly he said, "Chaplain, after the holidays I'll make collections for the Inmate Emergency Fund. Did you sign my letter yet and give it to the Superintendent?"

"No, Tony I did not, nor am I going to. I don't appreciate the fact that you had an ulterior motive in being chairman. You also tried to get Mr. Pugh into trouble. You know he can't accept gifts from inmates. You came here to cash in. We're not paying. Here's your letter. The administration already knows about it." Tony stomped out of my office, angrily insisting that he was not playing a game.

Although the children's parties were discontinued after I left Eglin, the joy and happiness the parties brought to the children, their families, and the inmates were etched in my mind and heart. Therefore, when I got to Pensacola Federal Prison Camp, I enlisted the aid of Hospital Administrator Gerald Payne to have the same program instituted there. Because our Superintendent, Mark Henry, was open to our suggestion, Pensacola's first party was held in 1989 under my sponsorship and supervision.

Chapter 9

Balancing Family And Prison Life

W e loved Florida. By now, everything in our lives was going well. Our daughter Marcelle was a parents' dream. Almost overnight she had changed from a little girl into a beautiful, loving, young lady who was studious, and well liked by her teachers and peers. Muriel was also achieving her own dreams. On June 15, 1980, she graduated from the University of West Florida with a Master's Degree in Public Administration. Before graduation she accepted a job offer as a Presidential Management Intern with the U. S. General Accounting Office. She decided to rest and regroup before beginning her new job. Therefore, she and Marcelle didn't join me on the trip to my family reunion in Brooklyn.

Saturday June 21 was a memorable date for the Castillo clan. It was the first time in over 40 years all seven of us were together. First came the pleasure of celebrating with my brother Jimmy as his daughter Gloria graduated as a medical doctor and his son Dennis graduated as a physician's assistant. Then we held a memorial service for our mother at Epworth United Methodist Church in Woodhaven, New York. I conducted the service with my six siblings, most of our mother's 36 grandchildren and 17 great-grandchildren, and other relatives and friends in attendance. Our oldest sister Ernesta (Yaya) had travelled from Dangriga, Belize, to be present. I asked her to delay her return trip so that she and I could go to Dangriga together for the Carib Settlement Day celebration on November 19. She agreed and continued to enjoy her vacation in New York.

Our time of joy suddenly ended on Monday, August 25, when

Forty-year reunion of siblings.
Back row, left to right: Roberto, Jimmy, and Ernesta.
Front row, left to right: Simeona, George, Alex, and Charles

Muriel received a call from my nephew, Cecil, that Yaya had died unexpectedly. Muriel immediately rushed to the prison camp to break the news face-to-face as gently as she could: "...death came to Yaya as she and your sister Simeona were climbing steps to a friend's apartment. She had a fatal heart attack and was dead on arrival at the hospital...."

I was stunned. When the reality sank in, Muriel and I reflected on the emotional changes that life presents. "Two months ago it was all laughter and joy. Today, it's tears and grief. Truly, "There is a time and season for everything," I said with a burdened heart.

Muriel added, ""Her sudden death is so hard to take, but we have to be thankful that she was with us for awhile and enjoyed the family gathering. She was blessed to leave without suffering."

My trip to Belize was painful. Instead of our going home together, I went alone to attend my beloved sister's funeral. The Reverend Charles Goff, one of my elementary school teachers, officiated at the funeral service held at the Dangriga Methodist Church. Mr. Goff suggested I conduct parts of the service, but I knew that my heavy heart would not allow me to do so.

Following the church service, the congregation proceeded to the cemetery. In Belize, store owners still show their respect by closing their doors during a procession. People pause along the street holding their hats over their hearts. The band plays religious hymns from the church to the cemetery. I walked beside the Reverend Charles Goff at the front of Yaya's hearse. After the committal service, her body was lowered into the ground as immediate family members were handed shovels to throw dirt on the coffin. The mourners sang religious hymns until the grave was covered, and they concluded with the hymn, "God Be With You Till We Meet Again."

In my culture, our final farewell to a loved one — watching the coffin being lowered and throwing dirt on it — represents closure. Some things have changed in Belize, but this ritual remains constant. Seven years later, my family and the community repeated this tradition when my niece Lorraine was buried.

While in Belize City, on my way back home, I was hungry and depressed. I decided to wait by the main bridge near the market and invite the first passerby I knew to have lunch with me. The adage, "Be careful what you ask for because you may get it," held true. Within a few minutes I recognized Helena. But she was someone I wouldn't have spoken to earlier in my life as she was Dangriga's well-known prostitute. I kept my promise and invited her and the man she was with to lunch. Her facial expression showed surprise for she knew that 30 years ago we wouldn't have had anything to do with each other. She accepted, and introduced me to her husband, Carlos.

Time had brought changes into our lives. As we ate and talked, I realized that I couldn't have found a better person to lift my spirits. Helena was no longer the bold, brash, flashy, loud, flirtatious, hip-swinging young woman who freely sold her body. She was mature, heavier, and sedate-looking with mixed grey hair, and she exuded a pleasant demeanor. She had softened, and it was obvious she was no stranger to tears.

"George, we lost our daughter thirteen months ago," she said sadly and quietly.

We exchanged condolences. Helena's experiences made her a practical, down-to-earth counselor. She ended our conversation by saying, "I understand your pain, George. Time is a great healer. Please give your sisters and brothers my sympathy. I'll keep you all in my prayers, and please remember us in yours."

"I will. Thanks for sharing." I felt so much better as I left the restaurant, grateful that our paths had crossed.

Complexities of the Chaplaincy

Multiple problems face the lone Chaplain in a Federal prison camp. In fact, more religious programs are available in a camp than in a higher level institution that has two or more Chaplains. In addition, much of my day was consumed by constantly juggling my priorities among counseling inmates, visiting those in the hospital and in segregation, representing inmates at Institution Disciplinary Committee hearings, checking and answering mail, preparing memos, consulting with department heads, and obtaining signatures from the Chief Correctional Supervisor, the Assistant Superintendent, and the Superintendent to coordinate activities. In my "spare time," I completed paperwork which had to be turned in during the hours the administrative offices were open and the other department heads were available.

Like all Chaplains, I was expected to work late one evening a week to be available for inmates during their off-time. However, I worked two late evenings in order to be available to the over-500 inmates at Eglin.

In addition to running my department, I was duty officer every three months. Policy requires the institution duty officer to be on call for any incident that may occur during other than regular working hours. That sometimes led to problems because some security staff members resented a "preacher" telling them what to do.

On two weekends while I performed the duty officer's responsibility, touchy incidents happened. The first occurred one Saturday morning during a heavy summer rainstorm, which is common for Florida. I felt sorry for the long line of drenched folks waiting to be admitted into the visiting room. I was disturbed by our unkindness to each other and asked myself: *Why do we treat one another this way? Why can't we be more considerate during ordinary circumstances? During a disaster, our differences are eliminated and we rush to each other's assistance. We need to always treat others as we want to be treated.* Suddenly realizing that I was the duty officer, I decided to do something about it. Wet and angry, as soon as I arrived in my office I picked up the phone and told Ben Stevens, the acting Lieutenant, "Visitors are outside getting soaked. Please get them all inside the building."

"Chaplain, there are only a few more left in the line, and they will be inside shortly."

I responded, "Get those who are still outside, in — now!"

"Yes Sir," snapped Ben sarcastically, as if he were called to attention.

Needless to say, my action was talked about in the institution. Inmates, and even some staff members, saw me as a hero. But other staff members, like Tom Hawkins, Jim Hall, and Buddy White, saw me as an outsider, and they were surprised that I would stand up for inmates' families. They couldn't believe that "one of us" would go against staff for "some of them." However, the criticism didn't bother me because I saw a duty and responsibility and I did it. After all, some inmates and staff said, "It was the Christian thing to do."

The next day, at the conclusion of Worship Service, I shook Mrs. Moore's hand. She said to me, "Thank you for getting me out of the rain yesterday. God bless you, Chaplain, I really appreciate it."

"You are welcome, Mrs. Moore," I responded, pleased that I had helped.

I knew I had some fences to mend quickly. When I got to work Monday, I reported the incident to Superintendent Calvin Edwards. "Cal, I'm sure you have heard what happened on Saturday. From my point of view, it was an inhumane situation, and I told the Lieutenant to bring the people out of the rain."

"Chaplain, you're a man of God. I didn't like your interference with the running of the institution. But I know where you're coming from. If I were in your shoes, I probably would have done the same thing."

I thanked him and left. But there was still another fence to mend: Yancey, the Chief Correctional Officer. As I expected, he was uncompromising in his support of his Lieutenant. He asked, "Do you want to run the institution? What do you know about running an institution?"

I responded, "I don't. All I know is we have to be kind to one another. I saw a cold and impersonal situation, and I took care of it since I was the duty officer. If I were not the duty officer, I would have called the duty officer's attention to it."

"Humanity does not run this institution. If you ran this institution, you would let all the prisoners go home," he said. With a smile, I replied, "You know better than that." When he returned the smile, I knew everything was going to be all right. And it was for the next several months, until I was duty officer again one Sunday morning.

The phone rang. It was Lieutenant Lawton. "Chaplain, please come to my office immediately. You have to make a duty officer's decision."

What an inopportune time, I thought. *Visitors are entering, getting seated, and waiting for the service to begin.*

He continued: "A woman came to see inmate Larry Thomas. She is listed as his sister. As soon as she entered the visiting room, Larry's wife saw her and yelled, 'Get that bitch outa here.' I checked and found that Larry's 'sister' is really his girl friend."

"I can't come now. I have visitors in the Chapel and you know I can't leave them unsupervised. You'll have to make the decision, Lawton."

"You're the duty officer, aren't you?"

"I am."

With irritation coming through clearly, he said, "Then you belong here."

"No, I don't. I can't be in two places at the same time. If you can't make the decision now, ask Thomas's 'sister' to wait in your office. After service I will come and talk with all of them."

"Doesn't your duty officer's responsibility come first?"

"It all depends, but right now it doesn't. Visitors are here and my service is about to begin. I just can't leave."

Immediately after service I went to the Lieutenant's office, but he had already resolved the situation by refusing admission to the pretender and giving the inmate a shot (disciplinary action) for lying. The inmate's punishment was extra work duty to be done after normal working hours.

Chaplains acting as duty officers face conflicts when they are required to perform several functions at the same time. Father Richard Houlahan, Administrator of Chaplaincy Services, recognized this and issued a "White Paper" on November 19, 1980, which applied to institutions like Eglin, now housing over 700 inmates.

The performance, coordination, direction, and presentation of worship services form only a small portion of the chaplaincy/clergy function. Whether in ministry to free society, or in ministry to an imprisoned community, the vast majority of clergy time, skill, and energy is expended in sustaining people during times of trauma and stressful situations, in strengthening spiritual and human relationships, and in facilitating spiritual and emotional growth.

PASTORAL CARE is the most important function of the chaplain. It is the vehicle through which the church — the caring community of believers of every religious discipline — represents and reinforces the concept that all persons are important individuals with inherent value and dignity and thus are worthy of love, concern and attention, even though such persons may be physically separated from the community at large. Prisoners generally have a poor self-image, ongoing guilt feelings, and more often than not suffer from the corrosive effects of incarceration (loss of autonomy, loss of security, loss of legitimate social purposes, loss of sensory and emotional stimulus, loss of privacy, and loss of identity). Chaplaincy personnel have as their major role the task of assisting prisoners in sustaining themselves emotionally and spiritually so a successful return to the free world is facilitated.

Chaplaincy personnel help diffuse the anxieties, frustrations and anger felt by prisoners during incarceration. Inmates routinely seek out the chaplains as persons who, although part of the staff, are by profession 'sensitive' to human suffering and personal needs. It is common for an inmate to 'storm' into the chaplain's office venting extensive anger or frustration concerning an institutional matter, and after constant counseling, leave the office calmer and better able to cope with the particular situation; e.g. problems of prisoner with prisoner, prisoner with staff, prisoner with family/friends. This type of 'therapy' traditionally offered by chaplains is quite beneficial to the orderly operation of institutions. Where there is only one chaplain in the institution, the overall pastoral care is grossly inadequate. One chaplain cannot physically and emotionally offer quality pastoral care continuously in an institution of 400-500 inmates.

Contract clergy and religious volunteers usually visit our institutions in one-to-two hour weekly sessions. They *do not* provide pastoral care. Their visits are brief, their contacts with inmates limited to the specific groups to whom they minister, and their understanding and sensitivity to the total institution structure are minimal. They offer worship services, lead seminars, conduct programs, etc.

Only staff chaplaincy personnel are available for pastoral care at *all times*. They are known and recognized by all prisoners, the 'churched' as well as the 'unchurched.' Chaplains understand the institutional structure and are sensitive to the dynamics of ministry within it. They have access to every portion of the institution at all times.

Without staff chaplaincy personnel there *cannot be ongoing pastoral care!"*

I was delighted when Superintendent Calvin Edwards complimented me on operating the Religious Department in an outstanding manner and relieved me of the duty officer responsibility. He showed confidence in my abilities and referred a number of inmates to me for counseling

Our Great Choir Opened Doors

I became well-known as a Chaplain in the Fort Walton Beach area and was frequently asked to preach in its churches and bring the prison choir with me. The choir's diligence, and the community's realization that we had one of the best choirs in the area, increased the demand for our appearances.

Our choir was blessed with two outstanding leaders. Our organist, Dr. Allen Belcher, had been a chiropractor and a professional organist before his incarceration. Our choir director, Mark Carpenter, another inmate, was an accomplished singer who was a former Minister of Music in one of the largest Baptist churches in Mobile. Their love for music made choir rehearsals no-nonsense sessions. A few inmates — Chester Wright, Larry Smith, and Jeff Salster — left the choir because of the stringent demands, but their replacements were serious, dependable, and very good singers. The choir's rewards for all their hard work were the realization that they were always well received for their exceptional singing ability and had the opportunity to give their testimonies at community churches.

Among the choir members were ordained inmate ministers, who occasionally would deliver the message. (Yes, we do have ministers in prison. Clerical-collar crime exists as well as white-collar crime.) Their message brought home the fact that ministers are not immune to sin and crime, and that we serve a God who not only forgives but still uses the fallen "saints."

A choir trip meant at least a fourteen-hour day for me because the trips were in the evening after my workday was completed. However, I didn't mind because I viewed the trips as beneficial rehabilitative therapy which brought about positive behavioral changes in the participants. To go on a trip, choir members had to be in good standing and without any institution infraction. Additionally, they must have attended every service and choir rehearsal.

Sometimes I accepted speaking invitations without taking the choir with me. At one such engagement, a luncheon given by a church woman's organization in Fort Walton Beach, I said, "The inmates at Eglin are nonviolent. Most of them are first-time offenders who did not physically harm their victims. Their crimes fall in the category of "white collar" crimes, such as income-tax evasion, mail fraud, counterfeiting, bank embezzling, securities fraud and, most recently, drug dealing. Drug-related crimes are on the increase. We were recently told by Superintendent Calvin Edwards that approximately 69 percent of the inmates are incarcerated for drug-related crimes."

During the question-and-answer portion, a saintly looking, frail lady who seemed to be about 80 years old raised her hand for recognition and said, "Chaplain Castillo, I don't know what you mean by nonviolent crimes. To me all crimes are violent. When a man makes drugs available to anyone, including those in elementary schools, that is violent. If one's life savings are stolen through fraud, that is violent. They should all be locked up and the keys thrown away."

I looked at her kindly face and replied, "Ma'am, I heartily agree with you, except for your last statement. It has always been my belief that we as a nation must find alternative solutions to incarceration. We just can't lock up everyone indefinitely. Many learn their lesson from the first imprisonment and won't ever be back in prison. Yes, there are scoundrels in prison who belong there. But even they won't be incarcerated forever. We just can't throw the key away. We have to find ways to rehabilitate inmates, even the violent ones, so that they can do positive things and become productive citizens."

Our discussion reminded me of two villains I counseled, Harold Turner and Daryl Waterman. Harold Turner admitted that he had fraudulently sold $165,000.00 in maternity insurance, disguised as health insurance, to ladies over 65-years old. Daryl Waterman was a drug dealer. When the tide turned on him, he cried bitterly in my office. His former wife told him that their 15-year old son was strung out on drugs. Daryl held on to me for emotional support as he cried and talked. "Chaplain, I was selling drugs out there and making good money, but I never thought that one day my son or any of my other children would be involved."

Indeed, these were violent acts that they had committed. My hope is that people like Harold and Daryl will become rehabilitated in prison.

My Pastoral Outlets and Outreach

Counseling with men like Harold and Daryl was emotionally draining. Like other pastors I needed an outlet to get away from the emotional and physical demands of the ministry. One of my pressure-release valves was the Greater Fort Walton Beach Ministerial Association's monthly meetings. I also enjoyed weekly Wednesday-morning breakfasts with the Gulf Breeze Ministerial Association. The fellowship in Gulf Breeze was worth the 80-mile round-trip drive. After breakfast, my pastor and friend, Chaplain Thaine Ford, U.S. Navy Retired, and I usually went fishing in his boat. Most of the time we caught nothing, but the relaxation was therapeutic. Eventually, we bought a net and cast it at schools of mullet since the other fish wouldn't bite.

On my days off, I found a meaningful outlet and fellowship in local congregations' midweek services, Bible study, and prayer groups, as well as in community activities. The Reverend Theodore Andrews, Pastor of Gregg Chapel African Methodist Episcopal Church, recommended me as a representative of the black community on the Okaloosa County Human Relations Council. I enjoyed the role as an agent of reconciliation to bring the community together. Muriel and I also tutored youngsters and devoted much time to the National Association for the Advancement of Colored People. We are life members, and I was local treasurer for five years. In addition, I still serve on the Board of Directors of the Mental Health Association of Okaloosa and Walton Counties.

In 1986, I was honored to be asked to give the morning message for the first Dr. Martin Luther King Jr.'s birthday celebration held at Beulah First Baptist Church, Fort Walton Beach. As I drove to the church, I thanked God for the Saints who marched with Dr. King and sacrificed their time, bodies, and even their lives. I thought *How wonderful it would have been if those Saints could have lived to celebrate his birthday as a national holiday! Those who lived must feel vindicated to realize that their leader is now venerated.* For me it was an emotional day, a spiritual reawakening.

When I gave the message, I called the congregation's attention to the significance of this day.

> Today, America is celebrating the birthday of a black person who has changed lives and the course of American history....Our God is a Father who acts. At times He comes to us plainly yet mysteriously. Who but God could have brought Rosa Parks and Dr. King together for social and religious changes?
>
> We know from where we've come. Our parents and grandparents told of their trials and tribulations. As slaves they were segregated as they listened to the Gospel of Love and Justice. Saint Paul said, "There is neither slave nor free, there is neither male nor female; for you are all one in Christ Jesus." These words were far from their experience. However, God mysteriously gave our parents another message, a message of hope and freedom. They never gave up hope and faith that the future would be better.
>
> Today, we are still heading toward total freedom. But with our advancements come responsibilities. We need to vote and prepare our children for the challenges ahead. We need to serve our communities through organizations and our churches. The better Christians we are, the better citizens we'll be, for we'll bring our teachings of love, forgiveness, joy, and hope to the world...."

The congregation enthusiastically responded with several "Amens and Praise Gods."

Muriel and I also attended the evening commemorative service held at Beulah First Baptist Church for those unable to attend the morning service. But we left before that service was over to join inmate members of the Association of Black Awareness at the prison camp. My heart swelled with joy as black and white inmates celebrated Dr. King's birthday and stood together to sing the black national anthem, "Lift Every Voice and Sing."

Arriving home at 10:00 p.m., Muriel and I talked about the importance of the day until about midnight, when I could no longer keep my eyes open. Lacking my ear, she wrote a letter to our children expressing the joy we felt. This letter was later published in "The Prince Hall Sentinel," the University of Louisville "Minority Voices," and Volume III of *When Black Folks Was Colored*.

January 20, 1986

Dearest Children,

History was made today. National history was made because for the first time in the history of the United States, a day was set aside to honor a black man, Doctor Martin Luther King, Jr. Not only was national history made, but personal history was made in our family as well.

Daddy and I have always been grateful for the sacrifices made by those black people who were in the forefront of fighting against segregation in our country. In the 1960s, we too did everything that we could to join the struggle. We were instrumental in forming the first NAACP Chapter in Bangor, Maine. We made speeches throughout the state of Maine awakening people's consciousness to the injustices and asking them to join the fight against discrimination in Maine and everywhere. Our involvement was so great that Marcelle's birth came just a few hours after one of our long, hard NAACP sessions.

In the 1980s, we realize that true equality, in this our beloved United States, is not yet a reality. Therefore, we continue to work toward eradicating inequality and instilling parity in every situation we become involved in. You need to know that racial-injustice has been so ingrained in our society that constant vigilance is a must. We must always be aware, alert, and ready to make a contribution to keep the consciousness of our fellow

Americans raised.

And raise the consciousness of our community, Fort Walton Beach, Florida, is exactly what your father, the Reverend George R. Castillo did. He was concerned that Dr. King's first birthday celebration was going to go unnoticed in the black community. So he did something about it. He issued a call to the local ministers to observe the day, for he strongly believes that Dr. King's birthday is a Holy day. (He eloquently explained this in his sermon so I won't go into it.) As a result of his efforts, the Reverend Thigpen of Beulah First Baptist Church, opened his church for two services: one at 11:00 a.m. and the other at 6:00 p.m. Both services were exceptional. Your father spoke at the 11:00 a.m. service.

I mentioned earlier that personal history was made this day, and it was for two reasons. Number 1, your father rallied the community into action and as a result black ministers, white ministers, city officials, black entrepreneurs, and the black community got together for an eventful ceremony to honor Doctor King's achievements and to remember that his dream for our race has not yet been realized even though progress has been made. Our coming together made it evident that economic parity is yet to be realized. The second reason this day will always stand out in our minds is that your father preached as he had never preached before. His sermon reached the pinnacle. Thank God it is recorded for posterity. During the sermon, a Lt. Aaron Jones slipped me this note:

'He is really imbued with the "SOURCE." Great wisdom comes thru this man. How lucky we are on this level of consciousness.'

At our third service for the day at the Eglin Federal Prison Camp, your father said, "I am so happy for this day that if there were a fourth service I would attend that too."

We can all be proud and continue to seek the best that is in us so that we too can be a contributor to history. We love you and salute the potential within you. Each in your own way – keep the dream alive and may you and your children live to enjoy the good that generations before you have sought after — God bless you.

Love, Mom (Muriel J. Castillo)

"When the work is done, the work has just begun" holds true for caring people. I was off for Labor Day and looked forward to a relaxing schedule without commitments or deadlines. This all changed with an urgent, solemn phone call from USAF Captain David Sanford. "Chaplain Castillo, can you please come to Humana Hospital to see my sister-in-law Linda Prewitt, who is dying?

I answered, "We'll be right there."

Muriel and I immediately went to the Coronary Care Unit, where Dr. Roger Riggenbach was talking to the family. In a gentle, sympathetic voice, he told them, "There is no hope for Linda."

As soon as he left the room, I put my hand on Linda's shoulder, repeated the 23rd Psalm and reassured her that Jesus was waiting for her. "Go home in peace, Linda. All is well."

I didn't know the exact moment when Linda was born into Eternal Life, but I was still softly speaking to her when Dr. Riggenbach, who had been getting information from a remote cardiac monitor, reentered the room and said, "Linda just died."

Mrs. Charles Mercer was visiting her husband, who was also in CCU. Despite Mrs. Mercer's own concerns, she set aside her pain and comforted Linda's family. As we all rallied around in support of the bereaved, the strength of the human spirit surfaced.

Security Needs Change the Institution

The rapidly increasing prison population caused security to be tightened. Previously, inmates were allowed to go home without an escort for extreme emergencies such as death. But now inmates could not leave unless a staff member accompanied them. Inmate Clarence Hall was the first to face this new rule when his father died. Hall was unable to find an officer to escort him to

Second Baptist Church in Jacksonville, Florida, for his father's funeral. So I volunteered my services on my day off. We left at 6:30 a.m. on the Air New Orleans flight and returned at 10:00 p.m. Although it was a long day, I felt rewarded seeing the fruit of my ministry in the former inmates who attended the funeral. It was like old-home week.

The Reverend Doctor J. C. Sams, President of the Progressive Baptist State Convention and former President of the National Baptist Convention, conducted the funeral service, and I read the Scripture Lesson. Derrick Small, one of my 4:30 p.m. prayer group participants, was the undertaker in charge of the funeral arrangements. Sonny Longsworth, another former 4:30 p.m. prayer group member, continued his spiritual walk and was now the ailing Doctor Sams' aide. Sonny said, "I wish you could return for my ordination in January 1985." After the funeral service, another former member of the 4:30 prayer group welcomed me and thanked me for helping him turn his life around.

I left Jacksonville feeling good emotionally, but as soon as I reported to the Control Center reality hit me. Lieutenant James motioned me to his office. There he said, "Chaplain, one of your former 4:30 prayer group members just returned for parole violation."

I learned a long time ago that one does not give up on human beings. We just keep trying and continue to work with the persons who need help, for no one knows when a turnaround may come. Therefore, the inmate's return didn't bother me. I was just curious to know who he was as I told James, "I'll work with him again."

A Good Report for Our 25th Anniversary

Regional Chaplain Charles Riggs conducted a compliance audit from January 29 through February 2, 1982, to see if our programs were in compliance with applicable law and policies. Chaplain Riggs found that I was functioning extremely well in spite of the very limited and inadequate physical facilities available for religious programs at the institution. His evaluation complimented me on maintaining an excellent and visible pastoral role with both staff and inmates and on my gaining wide community acceptance and respect. The evaluation noted that I was recently appointed by the Commissioners of Okaloosa County to serve on the Community Human Relations Council. Chaplain Riggs further stated:

The religious programming is very adequate with major faith groups provided with ample opportunity and leadership for the practice of their chosen faith. The interaction of the Jewish inmates with Air Force Chapel #1 congregation is a healthy and normalizing worship experience. The freedom of inmate visitors and guests to participate in worship in the inmate Chapel is additionally an excellent and positive experience. The Chapel was well attended for all services observed. There is a good balance of contract Clergy to provide for the needs of both Catholic and Islamic inmates. The provision of children's Church School is an excellent worship supplement to the overall Chaplaincy program.

Evaluations are always a stressful time and getting a good one was a perfect gift for our 25th wedding anniversary. Since our thoughts at the time were concentrated on our vacation to West Africa and the renewal of our vows on June 26th, we were unprepared for the surprise anniversary party Marcelle and our good friends Major George and Zara Brown gave us on our anniversary date, March 23rd.

As June 26th approached, Muriel and I wrote our covenant and order of service for the celebration. With great joy and anticipation, we looked forward to returning to Janes United Methodist Church, where our wedding was performed 25 years earlier. The present pastor, the Reverend Robert Simpson, conducted the ceremony, which included our three children. We were delighted that so many guests and our organist were again in attendance to hear us repeat our vows, which were so much more meaningful this time. Twenty-five years had passed quickly, and the beauty and solemnity of the ceremony, coupled with the love we shared, made the occasion a moving and memorable experience.

After the reception, my brothers and their families joined us at Kennedy International Airport Lounge before our takeoff to West Africa. Our festivities continued until we, along with Joe and Marcelle, boarded Air Afrique's aircraft at midnight for

Dakar, Senegal.

The eight-hour flight was absolutely delightful, and the service offered by the crew was superb. Our emotions were overwhelmed during our trip to Goree Island as we realized that this was where 40 million slaves had passed through the hands of traders. We wept when we saw the slave houses, dungeons, and prisons. It felt as if we had been there before. It was a weird feeling déjà vu.

In The Gambia, children were studying and doing their home lessons on the sidewalks near the Continental Hotel. Three students that we befriended allowed us to tutor them for a few minutes. We wished we could have spent more time with them because they were very friendly, eager to learn, and so thankful for the little attention. After returning home, we communicated with them and sent books. However, over time the communication ceased.

In Juffure we visited the historical village of Kunta Kinte, the ancestral home of Alex Haley. His book and the movie *Roots* have made Juffure one of the most-visited villages in Africa. The visitors' log which we signed had names of people from all over the world, including Mrs. Lillian Carter, President Jimmy Carter's mother. The matriarch of the village offered Muriel a two-year-old child to take home as our own.

Freetown, Sierra Leone, a former British Colony, reminded me of the country of my birth. As we worshiped at the Charles Street Methodist Church that July 4th, my mind raced back to Belize as I heard the Canticles and the Psalms and the congregation singing "Te Deum Laudamus," "Venite," "Exultemus Domino," and the "Jubilate." Even the English Methodist hymnals were the same as those used in Belize. Still dressed in the garb similar to that worn during the King Henry VIII era, the twenty-voice all male choir reminded me of a Church of England (Anglican) choir located in London, England.

At the conclusion of the service, we were heartily welcomed by the congregation into the churchyard overlooking the beautiful mountains of the area. The elementary school attached to the church was just like the Dangriga Methodist School I had attended.

During our drive to Cotonou, Benin, we asked our driver to stop near some men pulling their fishing nets to shore. It reminded me of Jesus saying to the fishermen, "Follow me." We watched the fishermen sing to the tempo of a teenager's drum. Working in unison made their task seem effortless. I felt quite at home walking over, pulling, and swaying in rhythm as I helped bring in the heavy fish-filled net.

Our trip was wonderful, filled with memories and emotions that will last a lifetime. But after being away from home three weeks, it was nice to be back in Shalimar, Florida, to rest.

A few months after my return, Chaplain Riggs conducted another audit of the Religious Department. It was essentially the same as the previous year's audit except that this time Riggs suggested that the prison camp study the feasibility of constructing a weather canopy for visitors being processed into the visiting room so they would no longer get drenched while waiting. Eglin Federal Prison Camp complied and now has an attractive canopy in place. This humane action was even more gratifying than Chaplain Riggs' favorable evaluation.

Visiting room with canopy

Riggs also suggested that we begin recognizing the many volunteers and acknowledging their contributions to the institution's religious programs. Thus began our annual volunteers
luncheon in the camp's cafeteria. Volunteers and inmates looked
forward to this affair, where they could enjoy each other's comradeship in a relaxed atmosphere. The inmates proudly worked
hard in the kitchen and dining room to prepare and serve this
special lunch to the visitors. Effective volunteers are so important in prison, and with the luncheons I could say with more
than words: "We appreciate your time and effort in making the
Religious Department programs more viable." And it provided
the Superintendent the opportunity to join me in saying, "Thank
you" to the faithful, dedicated, community supporters who gave
of themselves to help others.

Shadow of Death

Life can change so quickly. Easter weekend was here, and I
was full of anticipation in sharing the significance of the Resur-
rection. I awoke early Saturday morning, ready to put in a full
day's work and to continue preparing for Easter services. Muriel
called me downstairs to breakfast. Suddenly, as I lifted my leg to
pull up my socks, I was shocked and frightened to realize that I
had no control of my left hand. As I walked downstairs, my
speech became slurred as my tongue grew heavy. I was fully con-
scious, but fearful. I knew that we had to get to the hospital fast.

Muriel was frightened as she heard my slurred speech and
saw that my mouth was twisted slightly. "George, are you all
right?" she asked apprehensively as she dialed our doctor's office.
Doctor Michael McCoy's answering service put us through to the
physician on duty, Doctor William Haik, who said, "I'll get your
records and meet you at the emergency room of Humana immediately."

Before I left for the hospital, I made a quick call to the camp.
Lieutenant Russell Willis was on duty. "Willis, I'm having a
stroke and I'm going to the hospital. I won't be in today."

"George, are you kidding?"

"No," I responded — eager to get off the phone.

"Who is going to supervise the service?" he asked.

"The Lieutenant will," I replied as I hung up.

Muriel drove to the hospital in record time. On the way, I thought of how quickly things happen. Just the day before I was preparing for Easter services, wanting to make them very special because they usually bring worshipers out who have missed most of the year's other services. My internal chatter repeated: *What a time to get sick — on one of my busiest weekends — Holy Saturday, when the Roman Catholics will be celebrating with English and Spanish Masses—then there's Easter Sunday, and I'm supposed to conduct a Sunrise Service at 5:30 a.m., followed by the Protestant Service at 8:45.*

My mind was brought back to reality as Dr. Haik arrived and silently compared the current reading of my EKG with one he brought from the office. In a few seconds, I saw relief on his face which told me that I was going to be okay. "Mr. Castillo, there hasn't been any change in your EKG. The only sign of a stroke I detected is a clot in your right eye. It's so small I would not have attributed it to a stroke had you not shared your symptoms with me. What you had is a mini-stroke, which we refer to as a Transient Ischemic Attack." I spent the next twenty-four hours in the CCU, where I slept almost around the clock. Then I was moved to another room in the hospital.

Muriel immediately notified the Reverend S. L. Thigpen and Doctor James Monroe, who volunteered to send one of his co-pastors to take my place at the camp on Sunday. Muriel then called my siblings. Although Muriel assured my sisters Alex and Simeona that their trip wouldn't be necessary, they still came from Brooklyn to see me for themselves.

Word spread rapidly throughout the community, and soon so many visitors flooded my room that on several occasions the nurses asked them to leave. Rest was almost impossible, with flower deliveries and frequent local and long-distance telephone calls. I saw God's people, Christians and Jews, black and white, reach out in love during my brief hospital stay.

I was quite fortunate that the mild stroke hadn't left me with aftereffects. My recovery went well, so I was discharged from the hospital on Friday, April 8. I returned to the camp the following Monday and Larry Cox, my immediate supervisor, looked at me with his usual happy smile and said, "Chaplain, I'm glad to see you back."

"Thank you, I'm glad to be back."

"Tell me something. Was it the thought of Horn's coming that caused your stroke?" We both laughed. Then I shook my head and said, "Larry, you may be right. I never thought about it that way. But you may have hit the nail on the head." He tapped me on the shoulder and added reassuringly, "You've been doing a good job. Just continue to do what you have been doing. You'll be all right."

For a few minutes, I thought about the implications of my former supervisor, the one who recommended my discipline and transfer, coming as Eglin's next Superintendent. Then I said to myself: *Oh well, I can't worry about that. I have too much work to do to get caught up.* Besides, my Department's mailbox was overflowing with mail that had not been answered since I left. I knew that very soon I would have things under control if I stuck with my motto: Leave not for tomorrow things you can do today, for no one knows what tomorrow may bring.

Before tackling the pile of mail, I took time to go within and prayed: "Father, give me the strength to do what needs to be done and face whatever challenges are ahead. Amen."

Chapter 10
Letting God Fight The Battles

About two weeks after my return to work, Chief Correctional Supervisor Harrison Yancey introduced me to our new Superintendent, Bob Horn. Horn inquired about my health and talked about his past assignments. All three of us knew what was on the others' minds, but no one mentioned Ashland.

At our second staff meeting, I made two announcements: (1) the Protestant Women of the Chapel from Hurlburt Field Air Force Base would lead the Mother's Day Service in the Chapel next Sunday morning during their second annual visit to the camp, and (2) Dr. James L. Monroe, Pastor of First Baptist Church of Fort Walton Beach, would conduct Spring Revival Services in the Chapel from Monday, May 8, through May 12.

Mr. Horn wanted to know more about Doctor Monroe. Before I could answer he said, "I'm skeptical about revivals. At one institution, during a revival, an evangelist exhorted the inmates: 'If one eye offends thee, pluck it out.' That night an inmate tried to pluck his eye out."

Everyone except me laughed at the Superintendent's "joke." I didn't think it was funny and I felt that some staff joined in the laughter either out of embarrassment or to be in Horn's good favor. Of course, if the "joke" were true, then that inmate should have been in the prison's psychiatric institution.

When Horn met Doctor Monroe, the Superintendent again told his plucking-out-the-eye joke. Doctor Monroe retorted, "That's not Christianity at all! If you want to know what Christianity is, come to the Revival Services to see and to hear for yourself." This subdued the Superintendent.

Doctor Monroe continued: "George has been here for five years. He's doing a very good job. Go to services with him sometime and hear what Christianity is. He has a lot to offer. My church is supportive of his ministry." As we quietly walked to the parking lot, Doctor Monroe said, "Brother George, you have a problem, but it's going to be our problem. If that's what your Superintendent thinks about religion, the programs you have built are going to be destroyed. But I know that God won't let it. Let God fight the battle, and it will be won." I knew he was right.

Protestant Women's Visit

Regardless of denomination, Mother's Day is always special. The Protestant Women of the Chapel at Hurlburt Field arrived early on Mother's Day 1983. Those ladies did such an excellent job conducting the service the year before, and were so well received, that they and the inmates looked forward to the visit.

While on a brief tour of the institution, the ladies met Mr. Horn, and he thanked them for coming. Then he added, "I'm sure you would rather be anywhere else but here."

"Quite the contrary," Mrs. Coleman responded. "We volunteered to come because, as mothers, we know what this day means, especially to those separated from their mothers."

As soon as Mr. Horn was out of hearing, a member of the group asked, "Is he a religious person?"

I dodged the question and responded, "He just arrived."

Father Can't Teach Without Students

The next day I met with Superintendent Horn regarding extension of Roman Catholic services and programs. I invited the Assistant Superintendent, Larry Cox, and the Chief Correctional Supervisor, Harrison Yancey, to the meeting since their departments were going to be involved. I told them that Father Oscar Sarmiento (who was providing religious leadership to the Spanish Roman Catholic inmates on Saturdays) wanted to volunteer on Wednesday evenings from 6:00 to 8:00 to counsel, hear confessions, and teach catechism.

Horn fired a barrage of questions at me regarding Father Sarmiento's request. "Why does he want to come here on Wednesdays?"

"With the increase in Spanish inmates, he doesn't have

enough time on Saturdays to visit them all," I responded.

"Are you coming in on your days off to supervise him?"

"No. Father Sarmiento is already a part-time employee who has access to the camp so he doesn't need my supervision."

He continued, "There is only one office in the Chapel and no rooms. Where are you going to put him?"

"Since I'm not going to be there, he can use my office," I responded.

"If he uses the Chaplain's office, will he be authorized to use the phone?"

"I see no reason why he should need to use the phone."

"If we make an exception for him to use the Chaplain's office, who will open the office for him?"

"The correctional officer on yard duty," I answered, but thought: *Why is he asking that? The correctional officer is the only logical person to open the office.*

"Can he have the Chaplain's office key?"

"If the correctional officer lets him in, he won't need a key."

He added a few more circuitous questions. It was obvious from these questions that the Superintendent was setting up another roadblock. Finally, he said, "Let him come on Wednesday afternoons from 1:00 to 3:00."

Sadly, I told Father Sarmiento about Horn's decision, knowing that it was useless to come in the afternoons because the majority of inmates were either working on the base or were in school. His response was equally short: "Tell your bosses to jump in the lake." I was again caught in the middle. The Wednesday visits never materialized.

Do the Jews Go or Do They Stay?

One late afternoon, a phone call from Horn's office made me realize that my day was far from being over. Horn wanted to meet the volunteer Rabbi as soon as possible. I informed Horn that Air Force Chaplain Rabbi David Feld was on annual leave, and I volunteered to answer questions about his service. Horn then wanted to know, "Why are the Jews being escorted to Chapel One on base for religious services when no other group is going outside the prison for services?"

I responded with the same answer I had given repeatedly:

"Jewish inmates held services at the camp when a Rabbi wasn't available. However, when Rabbi Marvin Labinger, the Air Force Chaplain, arrived he asked Mr. Quinlan if the Jewish inmates could be allowed to attend services with the Jewish community on the base. Mr. Quinlan and the Base Commander agreed, provided the men would be properly supervised. From then on, Jewish inmates, under my escort, attended weekly services along with Jewish military and civilian worshipers at Eglin Air Force Base Chapel One. If I were unable to supervise them, the duty officer did."

"Duty officer?" he asked in disbelief.

"That's right," I reaffirmed.

"Thank you, George," he said and hung up.

Instinctively, I knew he was unhappy about the arrangement, but I also knew that if he tried to revert to the old way, the Jewish inmates would not easily give up what they had become accustomed to and would resist the changes.

The High Holy Days, Rosh Hashanah (New Year's Day) and Yom Kippur (the Day of Atonement), meant additional visits to the Chapel. Both come in the early fall, within ten days of each other. In order for inmates to attend these services, they needed to be away from the camp two extra days. Horn wanted to know why the Jews received two holidays off when the policy called for one. I explained that the High Holy Days are two distinct holidays although they are close to each other. "It's like Christmas and New Year's Day." This explanation did not satisfy Horn, and the approval memo that required his signature to allow the Jews worship days were delayed.

When the eve of Rosh Hashanah had arrived, it was a toss-up whether the Jews would be allowed to attend their services. At the eleventh hour, Horn signed the memo permitting me to escort the Jews to the Base Chapel.

Jewish inmates continued to attend weekly services without further question until Superintendent Paul Lewis arrived in 1984. Then he, too, asked me to justify taking the Jews to services on the base. I began my explanation again as I did in the previous years. He voiced no objection to my explanation so I expected that when I arrived at 7:00 p.m. on the eve of Rosh Hashanah, the inmates and I would be able to leave to attend services on the base. But the memo of authorization could not be located. I called the Assistant Superintendent's home. The baby sitter said, "I don't know where Mr. Williams can be reached."

Aw, he must be at the Officers' Club for the going-away party for Lieutenant Charles Phillips, Food Service Administrator James Cooper, and Supervisor of Education Ted Sheppard, I figured. I was right. I reached Williams at the Officers' Club and asked him for the memo of authorization to take the inmates to their service. He didn't know where it was.

"Hold on," he said, "I'll be back in a minute."

When Williams returned to the phone he said, "George, the memo is locked in the Superintendent's desk. Go ahead and take the inmates to service."

The next morning, Rosh Hashanah, I arrived at the camp an hour early, not knowing the status of the memo. Williams greeted me by saying, "The memo was signed and distributed." In the nick of time, the Jewish inmates and I left for their service.

Roadblocks Cannot Stop God's Work

During one of the Superintendent's "Early Recall" meetings with those staff members who could be released from work, I received my Ten-Year service pin on June 15, 1983. With my mouth I thanked Horn, and with my heart I thanked God for bringing me through the bureaucratic snarls. I silently prayed: "Lord, keep me in your light. Guide and strengthen me to continue working for your Kingdom and Glory."

Throughout history, roadblocks have only temporarily slowed God's work. The same was happening here. It seemed that the more roadblocks Horn created, the more our religious programs flourished. I worked well with other religious leaders, and they expressed their appreciation for my helpfulness to their programs and the community. The Eglin Air Force Base Senior Protestant Chaplain sent a letter to Horn, and Chaplain Rabbi David Feld wrote to the Bureau's Director, Norman Carlson.

Horn usually received favorable letters from pastors and congregants after each choir trip. A highlight came in August 1983, when Loyal Phillips wrote an article in *The Playground Daily News,* entitled "Eglin Prison Choir Receives an Ovation," about the choir's visit to the First Baptist Church of Fort Walton Beach. I didn't know that the article was sent to the Southeast

Regional office in Atlanta until I received an appreciation letter from Bryn Carlson, Regional Chaplain.

Custody is the number-one priority of institutions. It protects society by confining offenders. Victims of crime and their sympathizers rightfully want criminals securely locked up. I understand and accept that. It shouldn't be any other way. However, for most inmates, prison sentences do end one day. Thus, a secondary goal of the Bureau of Prisons is to help inmates learn how to end their criminal careers. The Bureau's mission statement reads: "It is the mission of the Bureau to confine offenders in facilities that provide work and other self-improvement opportunities for offenders to become law-abiding citizens."

I saw my mission as upholding the Bureau's mission, doing everything possible to help the incarcerated accept society's morals and values in order to become law-abiding, contributing members of society when released. I kept praying for the day when I could again attempt to meet that goal unhindered because I know that religion offers an opportunity for everyone, including inmates, to grow spiritually. Religion also teaches us how to be good people and have a relationship with a power higher than ourselves which offers hope, love, peace, and understanding.

A New Administration Arrives

By August 1984, Horn was transferred and replaced by Superintendent Paul Lewis. Mike Williams was his Assistant Superintendent. I hoped that their administration would look favorably on my department. However, this was not always the reality.

At the beginning of the fiscal year, my department had adequate funding for contract services, including a music director's and organist's salaries. However, I was unable to find anyone to fill those positions. Rather than let the money go unused, I returned $4,600.00 to the institution. Later on in the year, when I was able to hire Mr. and Mrs. Luther Armstrong as choir director and organist, I needed $1,000.00 to pay their salaries for the final month remaining in the fiscal year. I felt certain that I would be able to "withdraw" that amount from the "bank." Instead, Assistant Superintendent Williams told me, "George, that's your problem. There's no money. Why don't you call the Regional Chaplain and see what he can do for you."

Chaplain Bryn Carlson, although sympathetic to my need, didn't have any money either. Like me, he found it hard to believe that the camp couldn't find $1,000.00 for my department after I returned over four times that amount a few months earlier.

When I later told Williams that Chaplain Carlson's office didn't have any money either, he simply shrugged his shoulders and dismissed the topic without any regard for how part-time workers' salaries would be paid. Not wanting the subject to drop, I said, "Chapel attendance suffers when we don't have good music. The quality of service isn't the same. It's important that I have the good, qualified musical leadership which our part-time employees provide. After months of searching I've found a capable couple willing to take the positions. Isn't there any way I can get the $1,000.00 needed to pay for their services?"

Unfortunately, when he declined I retorted in anger, "Where your treasure is, there will your heart be also. Religion has a very low priority in this institution."

I then told the Armstrongs, members of Abundant Life Church, "Your services are invaluable, and I want to retain you, but my department does not have the money. I really don't want to impose upon you, but if you could possibly take the month of September off, then we can begin paying you in October, the beginning of the new fiscal year."

"Chaplain," Mr. Armstrong responded, "We need the money, but serving God is more important. We'll continue." I was so grateful, that at the end of the month I gave them a letter of thanks for the $1,000.00 in services they had given the government.

I had become adept at handling the paperwork which saddled all departments. Preparing a memorandum for authorization had become routine. To gain approval, I simply had the previous memo retyped with appropriate changes in personnel and dates. For years, I used a long-standing goal as justification for our programs: *"To enhance spiritual growth among the inmates and to provide positive interaction between the inmates and the community for normalizing worship experience."*

But our new administration felt that the memos were too short and wanted more detailed information about the exact purpose of the meetings and the goals we hoped to achieve. Additionally, I learned from Williams: "George, this is a brand new ball game. Just because it has happened before doesn't mean it's going to happen again. Memos of a major project need to be in my office thirty days in advance."

Prison Fellowship Marriage Seminar

It is actually possible to teach inmates how to improve their family relationships while they are separated. As an aid to helping them attain better marital relationship both during and after incarceration, Prison Fellowship sponsored a Marriage Enrichment Seminar for inmates and their wives during the 1984 Labor Day weekend. This first annual Marriage Enrichment Seminar lasted for six hours on both Saturday and Sunday, and was held under the auspices of the Religious Department in the visiting room.

Saturday's seminar went well until the 8:00 p.m. ten-minute break. Most participants happily chatted and drank coffee inside while smokers stepped outside with my permission. Custodial officer Jake Taylor came into the visiting room, passed less than three feet away from me, got some candy from the machine, and left. A few minutes later, the Evening Watch, Lieutenant Carr, asked me to please step outside: "Chaplain, I want to talk with you."

"Sure. What's it?"

"Officer Taylor said that he saw inmates and wives smoking outside. They seemed to be standing extra close to each other."

Disappointed, but not surprised, I responded, "Lieutenant, I wasn't outside with the smokers so I can't confirm or deny that. But, Lieutenant, are you saying that Taylor saw something wrong without correcting it and telling me, the responsible official? What kind of officer is he? What's his motivation? Is he a team player or is he snitching to you for a favorable evaluation?" I asked in disgust. "They should have been confronted so we could handle the situation properly."

He didn't respond to my questions. However, we reached a compromise the next afternoon. The smokers were allowed to smoke under an outdoor light where they could be easily observed.

Fortunately, this incident did not detract from the effectiveness of the seminar. I often wished that inmates could somehow see how much their lives could be improved if they would only practice impulse control.

Bulging at the Seams

Every minister's dream is to have a full church for services. Our dream was becoming a nightmare as people started to recognize religion's place in prison life. We had long since grown past being crowded; we were packed like sardines. The Chapel that had been built to accommodate a population of 350 inmates was now serving 709 in 1984. Most Sunday services were late starting because we had to wait for people to be seated. Every Sunday, Chapel was packed, but it was even worse on three-day weekends, when extra visitors attended services.

The Spanish Roman Catholic Mass was the most crowded. What a paradox, I thought: *People here are being turned away from hearing the Word of God:* Duty Officer Peter Allen reported in the staff meeting: "During our three-day weekend, I opened the Chapel door and some Cubans almost fell out on me."

At least this Superintendent and his assistant recognized the problem and wanted to find a solution. Unfortunately, their idea of adding another Mass or moving the worship services to another building with more space was just as impractical now as it had been a few years earlier. We had tried that approach, and it didn't work. For one thing, the Priest had no time for an extra Mass. Besides, the largest classroom in the Education building was smaller than the Chapel.

Space had been a problem for years. My predecessor, Chaplain Eugene Stump, had submitted "Repair and Improvement" requests for the renovation and expansion of the Chapel every year. I did the same from 1978 until 1984, at which time I didn't submit a request because the Religious and Medical Departments were to share a new Inmate Services building. Unfortunately, the plans changed after the building was completed. Instead of relocating, the Chapel was slightly expanded. But the extension still didn't provide enough room to accommodate the increased number of worshipers. Each Sunday we had to borrow chairs from the reading room and the law library. This arrangement continued until August 20, 1992. On that date I was a happy, proud, and thankful Chaplain when I attended the dedication of the camp's new Chapel. It is an absolutely beautiful, spiritually conducive place of worship, with more than enough space to accommodate worshipers and with extra rooms for programs.

Volunteers' Luncheon

As our programs grew, so did the number of volunteers. In gratitude I wanted to enlarge the volunteers appreciation luncheon by inviting their spouses and paying for the spouses' $1.25 meal tickets out of my own pocket. But my suggestion was denied. Nevertheless, the attendees were happy to meet again. During lunch I said, "I'm grateful to you for making my work easier. All of you deserve accolades for your faithfulness."

When the meal was over, Mr. Lewis commended the volunteers and thanked them for showing the inmates that people in the free world do care about them. "We couldn't function nearly as well without your efforts. With a growing trend in the Bureau for one Chaplain in an institution, we will continue to need your services."

After his talk, Superintendent Lewis opened the floor for a question-and-answer session. Mrs. Strauss asked, "Will the monthly choir visits to area churches continue?"

Lewis responded, "As long as Chaplain Castillo can escort them. However, the population is increasing daily, causing more demands on his time. He may have to cut back on the visits."

Harry Jenkins asked abruptly, "How come the Chaplain finds time to take the Jews to their service every week? How about the others?"

Lewis shot back, "The Religious Department is unable to get a Rabbi to come to the institution for Sabbath services. So the Jewish inmates go to Chapel One on the base where the Rabbi's services are held. Inmates work on the base, every day, and since we're located on the base it's not considered a community visit. For the other religions, we have contract workers and volunteers who come to the camp. There are two contract Roman Catholic Priests and four Roman Catholic volunteers; one Imam; several Protestant volunteers; and one full-time Chaplain who works about 50 to 60 hours weekly to make sure all denominations' needs are served."

The luncheon ended, but not my appreciation for Lewis' understanding of the work done in the Religious Department.

Rest and a Trip Result in Investigation

Belize's Carib Settlement Day celebrations were approaching and Muriel and I wanted to attend. But a "hot" General Accounting Office congressional audit required her to stay on the job. I accepted her suggestion that I make the trip alone.

A few days later I drove 255 miles to New Orleans International Airport and boarded a Taca Airlines non-stop flight to Belize. I arrived to familiar sights, sounds, and smells. The rich aroma of plantains, fish, cassava, hot peppers, rice, and beans made me hungry for the tropical dishes. I saw smiling young faces and gaunt older faces, worn by the hot sun and years of deprivation from living in a third-world country.

That evening I stayed at the home of Justice of the Peace Daisie Hornby. "Mother Hornby," had been my elementary school teacher and considered my siblings and me as some of her many "children."

The following day, I boarded a bus and headed south to Dangriga. As the bus pulled into the town, we could tell from the sounds of the drums that the week-long celebrations had already begun. Although the town looked more modern, there were many things that had remained the same. Just as in my youth, older folks had their young audiences spellbound under the old tamarind tree with their Carib Anancy Stories — allegories that teach morals and values using animal characters. The teenagers entertained themselves with Punta Rock dancing until the early morning.

Elders of my home church, Dangriga Methodist, asked me to give the Sunday evening message. I wasn't told until the last minute that the audience expected me to deliver my message in my native Carib tongue. I couldn't do it.

"Brother Cayetano, I'm truly sorry for not being able to speak articulately in Carib. I lost my ability after spending 32 years in the United States."

Brother Arthurs, who was nearby, said, "Reverend George,

you can deliver the sermon in any language as long as we hear from you."

I gave the sermon in English.

Monday, November 19, was the climax of the celebrations. The day began with the mock enactment of the Caribs' arrival in paddled canoes at the Stann Creek river. They were met by drummers, who led the parade to the Roman Catholic Church, where they were met by a Carib Priest, who then led the procession into the church. The entire Mass was sung and recited in Carib under the leadership of Bishop Osborne Martin, thought to be the first Carib Bishop in the history of the Roman Catholic Church.

The congregation, along with hundreds who were unable to get into the church, paraded to Princess Margaret Park, where I asked God's guidance on the nation. Prime Minister George Price started the speeches with political promises. He was followed by other political and community leaders, who reflected on the past and visualized a bright future.

I saw many positive changes since I had first left. Among them were radios, telephones, TV, a huge American-style supermarket, and a central reservoir bringing running water to homes and yards. I never thought that I would see such changes in my lifetime. When I was growing up, Mr. Edgar Pascascio had the only radio in my neighborhood. It was our communal contact with the rest of the world. Mr. Pascascio put it by his window and turned it up really loud so that the whole community could hear music or news.

The morning after Joe Louis' heavyweight championship fight, however, the neighborhood was quiet. When neighbors asked what had happened to our morning music, Edgar said, "Man, I can't get a thing this morning. The battery ran down after last night's fight."

Mr. Pascascio's communal radio was replaced by another type of communal radio — boom boxes that carried youngsters' music all through the neighborhood. The music coming from the boom boxes in Belize was no different from what I heard when I arrived in Pensacola, Florida, a week later.

Going "home" to Belize was nice, but it was good to be back to my other world which had become home. I returned in time to enjoy a sumptuous meal at our tenth annual Thanksgiving family reunion at Mrs. Lydia Wilson's home in Atlanta.

I had been back in my office for less than an hour when Mrs. Rhonda Armstrong, the Chapel pianist, walked into my office in tears. She put a small package on my desk and told me, "Chaplain, I received this through the mail. It contains a pair of earrings, a gold necklace, and a cross from choir member Howard Mann." Still upset, she continued: "Chaplain, I come here to play the piano and worship. I'm not looking for an affair. I have a family and I love them. In the past I have found flowers on the piano, but I didn't think anything about it. Now I get these through the mail. Am I in trouble?"

"No, Mrs. Armstrong, you are not in trouble. Your action is appropriate. I'll take care of it. Now, let's go to the service; we are running late."

Relief washed over her face immediately. After service, while shaking other congregants' hands, I shook hers and whispered, "Don't worry."

I knew Howard Mann well since his arrival at the camp in May 1984. Having heard that I was a Belizean by birth, like him, he visited my office quite frequently to brag about his accomplishments and his material gains since coming to America. At the camp he was ridiculed and referred to as "Prime Minister." He repeated to anyone who listened that he was going to follow George Price as the next Prime Minister. It was alleged that for a fee, he offered to sell several inmates land in Belize and public-office positions in his administration. His economic plan was to give each of the 140,000 Belizeans $1,000.00 to raise their standard of living.

In one conversation he said, "Chaplain, I know that as one Belizean to another, you'll do me a favor. I heard that you can take inmates to the community for female companionship and that you've done it before. I'm ready to go."

"Howard, that is definitely not true. Where did you get that erroneous information?"

He replied cockily, "From a good source."

I emphasized that his information was incorrect. "I have never, ever taken anyone out of the institution for other than religious purposes. Mann, I don't intend to fulfill your fantasies."

I knew that a staff member had been caught doing precisely what Mann wanted me to do. This staff member took an inmate to town on official business, added some sexual business to the transaction, and detoured to a motel. When the inmate entered the room to meet a woman, the female awaiting him was an FBI agent from Miami. After trial, the inmate was transferred from Eglin and the staff member incarcerated at a maximum security prison.

For two days I deliberated on the best course of action to take regarding Mrs. Armstrong's uninvited attention. Situations like this are never easy because there is no simple solution. Should I talk to Howard or take the matter directly to the Chief Correctional Officer Tony Martinez? As a Chaplain, I always tried to help inmates keep out of trouble or keep them from getting into trouble. Now I was faced with "what ifs." If I took the package to Martinez, the Belizean could be shipped from the institution. If I didn't tell the administration and they found out about it, then I could be in hot water. But if I just talked to Mann, his behavior might not change because he was erratic.

Then there was the security consideration. The items Mrs. Armstrong received were contraband. *How did Mann get those articles into the camp and mail them to Mrs. Armstrong?* I wondered.

In the end, I decided to report the incident and turn over the package to the chief correctional officer. Surprisingly, he took Mann's actions lightly. In fact, no action was taken other than to order Mann not to visit the Chapel when Mrs. Armstrong was there. He stopped coming to the Chapel altogether. I didn't mind because Mann had become a pain in the neck. We really didn't need inmates in the religious program whose motivation was other than spiritual growth or contribution to the worshipping community.

Christmas was coming and Mann applied for a furlough. Not surprisingly, when his furlough was denied, he asked me to intervene on his behalf. I agreed to try to find out why his request had been denied. When I asked Bob DeChene, his unit manager, and Tony Martinez, his detail supervisor, DeChene answered, "Chaplain, his furlough was denied because his Pre-Sentencing Investigation stated that a gun was found in his desk at the time of his arrest. That's serious stuff. Besides, he messed up recently by missing count."

I added, "I can certainly understand why he wasn't granted a furlough."

When I told Mann what I had learned, he claimed, "It wasn't my gun. It belonged to my wife." After that meeting he stopped coming to see me. About six weeks later, Superintendent Lewis told me, "Chaplain, allegations were made against you to the FBI. I wouldn't worry, but the allegations have to be followed up. One allegation is that you have been influential in securing furloughs and releases to half-way houses for inmates. The other is that you have been paying Johnny Lowe to give you trumpet lessons."

"I understand you have to investigate, but you know the allegations are not true." Almost immediately the allegations left my thoughts because they were so baseless and ridiculous. The Superintendent knew that he was the only one who could secure inmates' furloughs or releases to half-way houses, and he knew, too, that I had never attempted to influence his decisions on any inmate's behalf. As far as the trumpet lessons were concerned, the allegation was far from the truth. Johnny Lowe and I had been practicing the trumpet together to perform a duet for the Chapel's Christmas service. I did not pay him. He was only too glad to have the spotlight for performing.

Days later, the Superintendent assured me, "Chaplain, nothing was found to be valid. However, your judgment of playing the trumpet with an inmate was questionable since you could have eventually compromised yourself. Go and see Tony Martinez, he wants to talk to you."

"I will, thank you," I responded.

"By the way, see me before the day is over," Lewis added as I had my hand on the doorknob ready to leave.

A chill ran up my spine as I answered, "OK." But I wondered *What's next?*

My next stop was Tony Martinez's office, where he read my rights and the charges against me. To my surprise two new charges had been added which I was completely unaware of. I was shocked to say the least.

One charge was that inmates sent money to my relatives in Belize in care of Justice of the Peace Daisie Hornby, my former teacher. The second was that inmates Arthur Freeman, Robert Edwards, and Richard Edwards paid for my vacation to Belize.

I was the victim of another attempted "set-up" given in

retaliation for not giving an inmate his way. I realized quickly that Mann was the culprit. "Mann told those lies," I told Tony. "Because he and I are from Belize, he expected privileges from me which I could not or would not give him or anyone. I counseled with him on a weekly basis, and the more I counseled with him the more I realized that no behavioral changes were taking place. He was always asking for favors which were unreasonable and against policy. At one time he asked that I go to Miami to talk with his wife about her financial hardships. Then I would be able to convince the Superintendent to let him go home. Mann became angry because I refused to entertain such a ludicrous request. Then he really was furious when I gave you the package he sent to the Chapel organist."

Tony said, "Chaplain, you're not telling me anything that I haven't already proven because I have turned every stone. You're clean. However, the allegation regarding the trumpet playing is debatable. You'll have to answer all the allegations immediately."

"Tony, there's no way I can answer them today. It's already 3:00 o'clock, and I haven't picked up mail or reached my office since I came in two hours ago. But I'll have the answers in your box before I leave for the Chaplaincy Conference on Sunday."

When I finally reached my office, inmates had been waiting two hours to see me. Apologetically, I told them, "Sorry fellows, I can't see you until tomorrow." Frustrated and annoyed, I looked at my watch and mumbled to myself: *Time is flying, and the duty officer hasn't been briefed about supervising the religious programs during my absence. The long-range plan is due today, but I didn't have time to complete it. The roster for the Jewish inmates has to be duplicated and distributed, and I have a 3:50 appointment with Lewis.*

Seconds before my appointed time, feeling like a child who has been sent to the principal's office, I entered the Superintendent's office and closed the door behind me.

"Chaplain," he said, "Martinez couldn't come up with anything about you except the trumpet allegation, which is borderline. You did not compromise yourself, but you could have."

"Paul, you know I have always used the inmates' talents in the Chapel programs. Lowe is a good trumpet player. I thought our duet would make the Christmas program better, so we practiced together. But we stopped practicing immediately after we performed at the Christmas program, and I have not played with him since," I explained.

I didn't fully realize how serious things were until the Superintendent said, "I received a call from the Bureau's Office of Special Investigations. Their investigators have instructed Captain Martinez to conduct a thorough investigation because your Ashland incident indicates this is a pattern of your behavior."

When the words *Ashland incident* were mentioned, I became furious and Paul recognized it. "How long is that incident going to be held against me?" How long must I remain in the PENALTY BOX?" I asked.

The Superintendent knew he had touched a raw nerve, and he listened attentively as I retold the Ashland incident as if it had happened yesterday. He knew that I was hurt about the circumstances surrounding it, and the fact that my career would be tainted forever.

When I had finished, Lewis continued, "What about this lady Hornby? Tell me about her."

"She was my elementary school teacher from Belize. Last year she spent the month of July with my family. While here, she visited the prison, met your predecessor, had lunch at the cafeteria, and read the Scripture lesson during one of the worship services. She later talked with Howard Mann briefly in my office since both of them are from Belize City and know several people in common. If you want her address, it's on my desk."

"No, it won't be necessary. Tell me about Mann. What did he want you to do for him?"

I repeated what I had told Martinez earlier.

"Chaplain, there's one thing you failed to do. You should have given that inmate a shot (ed note: disciplinary report). Consider yourself verbally reprimanded. Have a safe trip and a good conference."

"Thanks, Paul," I said without bothering to mention that although it's true I could have given Mann a shot, Martinez could have punished him, but did not.

Months earlier, I wouldn't have dreamt that a trip to Belize could have resulted in such trying circumstances. I felt badly about the entire situation as I left Paul's office, and wished that it hadn't happened. But since I couldn't undo it, I asked God for the strength to complete the work that needed attention before I left for the conference.

I spent Saturday answering the allegations, preparing my sermon for Sunday, and running an errand to secure a check to purchase an inmate's plane ticket for an emergency trip home. After making several stops to get the check, I rushed back to work to continue plans and preparations for the following week.

Mann apparently never changed his ways. In 1992, I saw an article in the Belizean newspaper *Amandale* which stated he was in trouble with the law there for some shaky business deals.

God Provides Healing, Again

It was still dark on Sunday morning, February 10, 1985, when I arrived at the camp. I immediately went to work making copies of my answers to the allegations. I put them into Martinez's mail box long before my workday began. As I reviewed my sermon, *JESUS OFFERS US FRIENDSHIP*, my love for my calling overcame my recent negative experiences. My words to others became a relevant personal testimony for me. I re-acquainted myself with my friend Jesus. My closeness to Him offered me an assurance that "All is well." This enabled me to put aside hurt feelings and ask myself, *What can I learn from this experience?*

As soon as the prison service was over, I hurried to Eglin Air Force Base Chapel One to give the 11:00 a.m. sermon. Immediately afterwards, Muriel and I grabbed a quick lunch and drove to Okaloosa County Air Terminal for my Chaplaincy Conference in Memphis. Before the flight attendant completed her instructions, I was sound asleep. My tiring and harrowing week left me exhausted. When I awoke and looked through the window, I saw the majesty of God's creations: a lovely blue sky with the mountains of white clouds creating a peaceful, harmonious picture.

I knew again who was in control, and it wasn't me.

Chapter 11

Each Day Presents New Challenges

U ntil budget cuts curtailed travel, one of the highlights of each year was attending the Chaplaincy Conference. These conferences had always been a pleasant retreat and a time for us to "recharge our batteries." They brought home the fact that we all faced similar struggles and successes. The days were filled with the inspiration and support that true comradeship brings. This year's opening message by Chaplain Glenn Crook gave the homily about Jesus' experience in the Garden of Gethsemane, where He let go of weak friends and held onto God, who is our strength and fortress when friends, coworkers, loved ones, and all else fail. Glenn's sermon spoke to my heart.

After the devotion, the Chaplains sat in a circle and shared our high and low points for the past year. When my turn came, it wasn't difficult for me to share my emotional roller coaster.

There were smiles as I described my trip home to Belize for the Carib Settlement Day Celebration, and the joy I felt preaching one of my "best sermons" at my home church. I felt proud bragging about how well my daughter Marcelle was doing in her pre-law classes, and how our children had sent us to Jamaica for my 54th birthday and our 28th wedding anniversary. From this mountain top, I descended into the valley at work. I told them how an inmate brought allegations against me which were investigated by the Bureau.

At day's end, I met with Charles Riggs, the Chief Chaplain, and Bryn Carlson, from the Southeast Region. Bryn said, "The Regional Director, Mr. McCune, mentioned the recent allegations about you and emphasized *it was only allegations.*"

Riggs added, "I know it's upsetting, George, but try to forget about it. Accusations like these are one of the unpleasant parts of working with inmates. All I ask is that you continue doing as good a job as you have been doing." Comforted, I left wishing that I felt as calm as they did about the incident.

My internal fears surfaced the following day. As usual, I checked my messages after lunch. I felt shaky when I saw my telephone message light flashing as I entered my room. The operator said, "Call Mrs. Linda Paulk at your office." Fearing the worst, I wondered, My God what could it be? I whispered a prayer while dialing the camp's number. Mrs. Paulk answered the phone pleasantly and I realized that my worry was in vain. "Chaplain, I'm working on your time and attendance report, and I want to know what your schedule was last week and what's next weekend's schedule?" I exhaled with a sense of relief before giving her the information.

My relief didn't last long, though, because she added, "Mr. Williams wants to speak with you." As I waited for the transfer to go through, my anxiety returned.

Williams got on the line. "George, how's it going?"

"Great so far," I answered nervously.

"I want to be sure that you'll be working on Monday and Tuesday, February 25 and 26, when the American Correctional Association will be here to re-accredit the institution. I need you to work late both evenings."

"I'll be there. You can count on me," I answered with relief.

The call was routine, but I found myself shaking after I hung up the phone. *Why am I shaking?* I felt insecure and almost paranoid while resenting what was happening to me. In anguish I threw myself across the bed and wondered: *Is it worth it? Is it time to go?* But I kept talking to the Lord: "Lord, you have called me to minister to inmates and I intend to do Thy will as long as You give me the strength. Help me, Father. I can't do it without You."

The comradeship and support at the conference provided strength and allowed the dreams to continue. I listened intently as the various speakers shared useful ideas about ways to implement and improve programs at our respective institutions. Many of the speakers had truly forward-looking ideas that would help both the religious community and the prison system as a whole. But I felt somewhat discouraged because I knew that many of these ideas would never be executed at the institution level. On the other hand, much practical help was given, such as providing resources where Spanish and Muslim literature was available.

As I bade my fellow Chaplains goodbye, I knew that God had answered my prayers. I resolved to remain a prison Chaplain, knowing that with God's help I could continue to work within the system to bring light to the incarcerated.

Christianity Is Not the Only Religion

At the staff meeting following my return, I reported on the conference and paraphrased the Bureau's broader definition of religion:

> Religion is a body of beliefs and moral codes giving purpose and meaning to life. It is also the practice of religious beliefs. Religion shares common societal activity to demonstrate a relationship to the Supreme Being.

I explained to the staff that the new, encompassing definition now allowed groups previously unrecognized by the Bureau to be classified as religions. "We also learned that the Bureau is about to recognize Santeria as a religion. It's a synchronism of Roman Catholicism with African and West Indian voodoo. Chaplain Riggs told me that an inmate, Justine Rayes, is having problems at Eglin because he belongs to Santeria. You may get a call because his wife called the Director saying Justine can't get his religious articles into the institution."

We were already familiar with this problem because a few weeks earlier a receiving and discharge officer found beads, feathers, artificial flowers, and a drinking glass among Justine's personal property. When the officer asked me if these items had any religious significance, I told him, "They do for Native Americans." Now I know that some of these items also have religious meaning for Santeria participants.

Later that afternoon, about eighteen inmates were waiting for me. Each had some problem that "only" I could solve. I handled the routine problems first. The first one was easy. Three Jewish inmates wanted to be added to the Sabbath worship service and kosher rosters. The more complicated problems followed. The last seven inmates were members of the Indian

Council with a problem that I did not have the power to resolve. Some weeks before, they had requested permission to attend a Pow Wow in Atmore, Alabama, approximately 100 miles away, and they wanted to know if their request had been approved. Diplomatically, I told them, "As you know, I just got back, and I need a few more days to work on it." Actually I needed more time to talk to Williams about his notation on the memo which was waiting for me when I returned from Conference. It read: "Where did you get these Indians from? The Sentry System says we have no Indians!"

The Sentry was the computer database containing information on each inmate. It was common knowledge that inmates' religious preferences were no longer noted in the Sentry, but we all knew that Indians were in the camp and had been meeting for several months. I felt that Williams knew Indians were at the camp, but that his question was a way of procrastinating to avoid making a decision. However, I met with Williams and assured him that Indians had been meeting in the Chapel for months. He countered, "Are you looking at Indians as a religion or a race?"

"Both," I responded.

"Can I practice the Indian religion if I want to?" Williams returned.

"According to Bureau policy, you may. Anyone may change his religious belief or accept one." As he walked away, he said, "Let me talk to Paul. I'll get back to you."

Days passed and no answer. The Indian Council was getting tired of waiting. At lunch about a week later, Counselor Ernie Dube gave me a heads up: "Chap, the Indian Council wants action. I gave them a BP 9 (official Inmate Complaint Form) this morning, and they're ready to go. Be prepared when you meet with them this afternoon."

I was grateful for the information, which prepared me when the Indian spokesman, John Broadwater, said, "If other inmates can go out of the institution on seminars and other related religious programs, why can't we go to our Pow Wow?"

"If anyone is to blame, gentlemen, it's this department. You know that I'm a one-man department and that I was gone for a while. I wasn't here to answer Mr. Williams' questions." I tried to take the blame, but knowing how cooperative I'd been with them, they told me with their body language that my explanation didn't fly.

Inmate Raintree shot back, "You of all people, Chaplain, should understand discrimination."

Yes, I understood their frustration, dissatisfaction, and disappointment. Native Americans had been waiting over a month for the administration to make a decision on a reasonable request. The lack of a decision put me in a bind because I had recommended that the Native Americans be permitted to attend their Pow Wow, and my recommendation was being ignored. Yet I was put in the position of having to make excuses for the administration's inaction. The council members were still in my office when the 4:00 p.m. head count forced them to leave. They were furious about having to return to their dorms without a decision. There was nothing any of us could do but wait.

The waiting ended a few days later when the memo was returned: "POW WOW denied."

The inmates' response was immediate. The completed BP 9 form was submitted to the Superintendent, the first step in a complaint process that could escalate to the Federal courts. The Native Americans had done their homework and had carefully documented the times other groups had been given permission to attend outside religious functions. Seeing their resolve, and knowing that their position would be hard to defend against in court, the Superintendent changed his mind and authorized three Native Americans to attend the Pow Wow.

Over the years, as the Native American population grew, they requested a Sweat Lodge and permission to wear beads and headbands in the Camp. Almost immediately they were allowed to wear their religious paraphernalia, but their request for a Sweat Lodge required a long study before it was approved. Lodges were already provided by the Bureau in Western states where large Native American populations exist.

Ours Is the Only Way!

My ecumenical background, my love of people, and our Creator prepared me for the Chaplaincy and for accepting those who don't believe or share my worship experiences. As I stated earlier, I was baptized Roman Catholic, grew up in the English Methodist Church, and was ordained a United Church of Christ

Minister. To my way of thinking, religious people are known by their behavior: Matthew 7:16, "You will know them by their fruits."

I made sure that the Chapel at Eglin was an ecumenical place and a place of solace where anyone could find comfort. Christians, Jews, and Muslims could worship in their own traditions without hindrance. Then after each of the services, I returned the Bible to the altar, placed it between two candles, and opened it to the 23rd Psalm.

Unfortunately, some religious leaders felt that their way was the only way to God and that it was their job to change everyone else. Jerry Walton, leader of the Jehovah's Witnesses volunteers was one of these. He faithfully met inmates every Saturday afternoon for Bible Study. However, he was not satisfied just to teach. He passed out literature to inmates whether they were receptive or not, and even tried to convert me to "The True Fellowship."

I kindly told him, "Mr. Walton, I appreciate the service you are rendering, but I'm not interested in being converted."

This response gave him an opportunity to comment negatively about other denominations. "Anybody who doesn't worship Jehovah is not a true believer.... Jehovah's Witnesses is the only true congregation of Jesus Christ." He opened his Bible, pointed to Psalm 93:18, and condescendingly told me to read it for myself as he began reading from the King James Version: "That men may know that thou, whose name is JE-HO-VAH, art the most high over all the earth."

I then asked him, "Is that the only name God called himself in the Old Testament?"

He didn't respond. I continued. "Brother Walton, your exclusiveness gives the impression that yours is the only church. Everybody who isn't in your tradition is branded as wrong. Does it mean that I am going to hell because I call our Father, God and Lord?"

"No, even JW's are going to hell too," he responded.

"We have to come to an understanding. Will you please stop forcing your religion on me and those inmates who are not interested?"

"I feel called upon to save those who don't know Jehovah," he said proudly and adamantly.

"Whether you call our Father Jehovah, Yahweh, I Am,

Elohim, or Allah doesn't bother me, but it bothers me when you force your religion on others. In the past, you have made remarks and innuendos that any religion other than yours is wrong. You consistently give me articles to read which support your position. We need to agree that as Christian brothers we are here to reach inmates and help make them better people. I see us as being in the same boat. Though we have some differences, there's enough room for both of us to serve in God's Kingdom. With cooperation, we can have unity without uniformity."

A moment of silence, then Walton looked seriously at me and responded, "George, I'm so eager to share the Gospel that I sometimes get carried away."

"I can understand how you feel, for I, too, have heard and preached the Gospel. But please don't get carried away with me or with those who do not want to accept your way of thinking," I emphasized.

We walked silently toward the Control Center, but I knew that his unresponsiveness wasn't acceptance of my way of thinking. Later, Walton kept trying to proselytize, but at least he checked himself when he became too pushy. I reminded myself of Dr. Andrew Banning's words during a lecture on Sects and Cults at Bangor Theological Seminary: "You have to learn to accept them. As long as your kind is around, they will be too."

My exchange with Walton reminded me, too, about the time my credentials were questioned. Terry Harlings, a staff who was a believer in the JW religion, wrote a six-sentence paragraph about Jesus for inmate Ed, who was hungering and searching for the Word. Not knowing how to interpret the paragraph, Ed asked, "Chaplain, what does this mean?" I read it, but couldn't understand the message; it was words strung together without meaning. While I was trying to interpret the paragraph, Terry entered the room. I said, "Terry, I'm reading your discourse, but I have a question pertaining to the first sentence. Can you explain it to me?"

"Where did you go to school?" she asked sarcastically.

"Bangor Theological Seminary, Bangor, Maine," I responded, and in turn asked, "Where did you go?"

"I didn't," she said, and walked out without further explanation.

Ed shrugged his shoulders, rolled his eyes, and said, "I'm

confused."

"Come to my office after count and let's talk." After a few sessions, he began to attend Bible Study, the 4:30 prayer group, and Sunday religious services on a regular basis. I saw growth and positive changes in this young man's life.

Some months later, during Oneg (the serving of light food after the Jewish Sabbath evening service), a wonderful friend, Mrs. Etta Stack, mentioned that persistent Jehovah's Witnesses had been calling on her recently. "This afternoon I told one, 'You can't tell me anything about Jesus for he was a Jew and, therefore, my brother.' My startled visitors left. Hopefully, that'll be the end of my conversion," she said.

Thank God all people are not the same. Our next-door neighbor and family friend is a practicing Jehovah's Witness. Mrs. Lorene "Rene" McLaurin lives her religion without proselytizing us. She is a loving, caring, nurturing person who is known by her good fruits. While participating at her father-in-law's funeral service in Mary Grove Baptist Church, McGee, Mississippi, I noticed how she consoled her husband. Unlike some Witnesses, she attended a church service to be with and comfort her family.

When religion was mentioned between us, it was I who introduced the subject. I asked for information to help me better serve the Jehovah's Witnesses inmates, as I always sought ways to provide a spiritual dimension to those I served.

A Muslim Leader

Muslims, like other groups, were allowed the freedom to meet. However, they were inactive for several months until Doctor Charles Ray Muhammad arrived. Instead of watching television or playing cards, he spent his time either studying or worshipping. Religion played an important role in his life, and I gladly provided a space in the Chapel for his daily prayers and Friday afternoon Juma prayer. For weeks he faithfully worshipped alone. He was so interested in religion that he even attended the Protestant Chapel services every Sunday. Many Sundays, his family joined him. We got along well.

Doctor Muhammad was always clean-cut, decent, and respectful; I'm sure that his demeanor brought men to the faith. Before his arrival, the Muslim religious community was small and inactive, but it quickly grew to 50. Followers admired and tried to emulate the discipline he exemplified. However, knowing inmates, I believed some of the new converts were probably motivated by the 11:00 a.m. release from work on Fridays to attend Juma prayer. This early release gave them a four-and-a-half day workweek instead of the usual five.

The calming effect that Muhammad had over the inmates left with him. Unfortunately, he chose authoritarian Attorney Malcolm Toner, a convert to the Muslim religion, as his replacement. Under Toner's leadership, the group became two — the Sunnis and the Nation of Islam. Tension rose between the two groups, and they paid allegiance to different leaders. The Sunnis followed Minister Wallace D. Muhammad, while the Nation of Islam followed Minister Louis Farrakhan. I used my mediation skills to alleviate the tension between them and bring peace. To help avoid conflicts, I gave them separate rooms and times for their worship and study.

Institution Disciplinary Committee

Muriel was performing a government audit away from home the morning I woke up with chills, cold sweat, and a general malaise. I knew that I needed medical attention and tried to locate my doctor, but he wasn't in and I couldn't wait. I dressed quickly and drove to the local hospital's emergency room. While my X-rays were being developed, I felt worse. The doctor appeared and said directly, "Sir, you have pneumonia and must start on antibiotics immediately. You need to take all of them and remain home for at least a week."

"Pneumonia?" I asked weakly. My thoughts raced to my father, who had died of pneumonia in 1938, and the suffering he must have endured without antibiotics! I hated to be away from work, knowing that during my absences my department virtually shut down.

After a week of antibiotics, prayers, and rest, I was glad to be back to work, even though it meant facing a backlog. During my absence, the inmates' religious needs were not met and three large boxes of mail were awaiting my return! Through a fortunate coincidence, inmate Mark Coleman was near the administration building when I collected the mail. I enlisted his help to carry the boxes to my office. That suited Mark because he would be first in line to talk with me.

Mark had come within a week of being released to a halfway house when he received a "shot," a disciplinary report that required him to appear before the institution's court, the Institution Disciplinary Committee (IDC). He wanted me to represent him during his hearing, scheduled for the next day. Mark was frustrated and depressed because he knew that the IDC's ruling would determine whether he would be released as scheduled, remain at the camp, or be transferred to a higher level institution.

Mark was nervously waiting for me as I entered the Chapel the next morning. "Chaplain, we only have less than an hour before my IDC hearing, and I'm scared." I put my hand on his shoulder and said, "Okay, Mark. We'll go over your case and plan a defense."

From what Mark had already told me, I knew he was guilty of an infraction. I also knew that 99% of inmates going before the IDC were found guilty. (Of course, I didn't share that knowledge with him.) The best we could hope for was to soften the blow. I hoped we could achieve this because Mark had been a good inmate.

As we began planning his defense, Mark placed several sheets of paper on my desk. His release authorization to the halfway house was on top of the pile. As I checked his clearance papers, I said to myself: *These are his best defense.* His other papers listed the three charges against him, (1) lying to a staff member; (2) absence without permission; (3) disobeying an order.

"Chaplain," he cried, "I screwed up. I was scheduled to be at the hospital. I reported and signed in and then left to make a telephone call to my girl friend to have her pick me up at the bus station. While I was gone my name was called. Minutes later, the staff in charge saw me sitting in the waiting area. When she confronted me about my whereabouts, I said, 'I was sitting here all the time.'"

"Mark, how do you plan to plead to the charges?"

"What do you suggest?"

"Tell them the truth. The truth is always the best defense. It's my experience that the IDC is more lenient if you tell them you are guilty and apologize."

"I see what you mean," he said, as he nodded his head.

"Have you cleared the camp?" I inquired.

"No, I have about three more stops." With apprehension he asked, "Do you think I'll be leaving tomorrow?"

"Mark, I can't predict what is going to happen. I can only emphasize, TELL THE TRUTH. I'll be there for support."

On our way to the IDC, I met Bill Applegate, Supervisor of Education, who was one of the three IDC members. All department heads served on the committee on a rotating basis except the Chaplain. Since I didn't serve on the IDC team, I was glad Bill was one of its members, for he was a reasonable person.

After reading Mark his rights and the charges against him, Chief Correctional Officer Martinez, IDC chairperson, asked Mark how he pleaded.

"Guilty with an explanation," said Mark.

"What's your explanation?"

Mark slowly, nervously, and in a thoroughly frightened manner, explained the situation and said over and over, "I am sorry. I was so excited about leaving that I wanted to be sure my girl would be waiting for me."

Then I was asked if I had anything to say. "Yes," I responded. "As you know, Mark has pleaded guilty because he knows that he had made a mistake. Under the circumstances, I'm asking for leniency. He's been in prison for almost three years and has done well. The last four days have been torturous for him. He has been sick with worry, not knowing if this incident will prevent him from leaving. As we sit here, we are giving him a double signal. On the one hand, he is in possession of his papers to clear the camp. On the other hand, he doesn't know if he is going to leave tomorrow."

"Chaplain, you're not contributing anything to the issue," Martinez responded.

"I thought I was," I retorted.

"No, you're not," Robert Miller, a case management coordinator and the third member of the committee, added emphatically.

It was obvious to me that they had already made their decision. My suggestion of leniency was upsetting their plans. For a few minutes, I was tempted to walk out of the room, but I knew it would reflect negatively on the IDC. Moreover, it wouldn't be team play and it might give Mark a basis for appeal. A number of inmates had filed administrative appeals of IDC decisions to the camp Superintendent, the Regional Office, and the Federal Bureau of Prisons. When their rulings were unsatisfactory to the inmates, the next step was to seek remedy in the Federal courts. Some inmates had successfully appealed their transfers to other institutions, and had been returned to Eglin when IDC's rulings were overturned.

Instead of walking out, I said, "I'm sorry. I made a mistake. Like Mark, I make mistakes too. I have nothing more to say."

Mark and I were asked to leave the room while the members of the committee deliberated. He paced the hallway. After about five minutes, which probably felt like fifty to him, Mark asked, "What's taking them so long, Chaplain?"

"I don't know. Relax, Mark. It has been less than ten minutes."

I motioned to Mark to walk ahead of me when we were called in for the verdict. Upon reentering the room, we were asked, "Is there anything else you have to say?"

Mark responded, "No, Sir."

"Chaplain?"

"No."

The verdict was issued, but it contained so much double-talk that it was hard to interpret. However, it was clear that the charge of disobeying an order had been dropped, and that the sentence was suspended for lying to the officer. But the ruling on the charge of absence without permission was so ambiguous that we didn't know whether Mark would be released. All it said was: "Your sentence has nothing to do with your leaving for the half-way house."

The committee dismissed us, and we left without knowing the actual verdict. Mark asked me, "What does all that mean? Am I going home?"

"I don't know." Trying to hide my confusion, I added, "Wait until your records reach your team and ask your case manager to interpret it for you."

I made it a point to have lunch with Bill Applegate that afternoon. Bill smiled at me as I pulled my chair out and placed my tray on the table. He exclaimed, "Champion of the oppressed." We both chuckled.

"Bill, is Mark going home tomorrow?"

"I don't know," said Bill.

Immediately after lunch, I conducted the Admissions and Orientation lecture at the Chapel. As soon as it was over, Mark, with sadness written all over his face, shared his news. Thirty-five-year-old Mark seemed to have aged ten years.

"Chaplain, I have to stay here another sixty days. Thank you very much for your help and concern."

Although I was getting ready to go home, I took time to counsel with Mark and encouraged him to do what was right for his remaining sixty days. In my own mind I wondered: *What is he going to learn in the camp for another sixty days which he hasn't learned already in thirty-eight months?*

The verdict was still bothering me a week later as I sat through the staff meeting. When it was over, I asked Assistant Superintendent Williams if I could speak to him privately about Mark's verdict. "Mike, I don't believe Mark had a fair verdict from the IDC last week. As you know, he lost sixty days."

"Yes, I know."

I continued, "Mark's infraction wasn't great enough to secure him in detention. Nor did his action warrant a transfer from the camp. However, a day before he was to leave, he received the maximum punishment — release denied. On top of that he lost sixty days' good time. The worst thing that can happen to an inmate is to lose his date to leave the institution."

"I see what you mean. But the boss and I reviewed the case, and we both agreed with the IDC's decision," answered Williams.

"Is his case closed?" I asked.

"Yes."

"Okay. Let's look at something else. It's my understanding that Officer Terry Harlings wrote five shots that day. Isn't that excessive?"

"Not if the inmates were wrong."

"What about counseling with an inmate? Couldn't that be just as effective?" I pleaded.

"It all depends on the circumstances," he shot back.

"True, but I feel we can accomplish more through counseling than throwing the book at an inmate who has been well-behaved." The conversation ended — no change.

I walked to the Chapel more convinced than ever that there is more than one way to change behavior. From the administration's point of view, Mark became an example to other inmates: "DON'T MESS UP." However, although harsh action might be a temporary deterrent, giving someone a chance to make inner changes could well have longer-lasting effects, and I considered that a better alternative. I was grateful to note that the Chaplain wasn't the only one to feel this way. I overhead Lieutenant Russell Willis say to an inmate who could have received a shot for an infraction, "Buddy, this one is on me. The next is going to be on you. Don't do it again."

I feel that the fair and reasonable approach Willis took and my recommendation for Mark are effective for minor infractions. In retrospect, many of my conflicts with the administration stemmed from my standing up for this approach, which was an important part of my belief system. I prefer to deal with people from a position of principle rather than power.

Inmates' Fight Ends with Two Winners

Fights are common in prison, but this fight ended differently. One Saturday afternoon, every seat in the television room was taken as inmates waited with anticipation for a championship boxing match to start. As the fight time approached, one tall, slender inmate left his chair for a few minutes to use the rest room. Upon his return, he found his chair occupied by a small, boisterous inmate who refused to give up his newly-acquired seat. They exchanged words, pushed a little, and then the loud one invited the other to step outside to prove who was more macho.

As they stepped outside, I was right behind them. "Continue walking to my office," I said sternly. When we got there, I admonished them and pointed out that neither would win a fight. With the first blow, the staff would require all the inmates to return to their dorms. "Do you really want all those guys angry with you? Then you both would probably be shipped from Eglin for fighting, regardless of who was wrong. Gentlemen, you're not teenagers any more. You are men. And it takes a man, particularly a gentleman, to walk away from a fight. You're in one of the best institutions, so don't do anything foolish to jeopardize your stay here. If you get transferred, you'll lose. You'll be sorry. Think and act like mature men. Do you understand?" Sheepishly, both nodded.

"Any questions or comments?" I asked before dismissing them.

"No, Sir," they replied in unison.

"Let's shake hands and get back to the fight. We have only missed about three rounds."

The three of us shook hands with one another and walked back to the television room. When we arrived, somebody shouted to me: "Chaplain, did you knock them out?"

Some of the inmates laughed aloud when I responded, "Yes, I did, and in the first round!"

The following day, I recognized the tall, slender inmate in the morning service. On Monday, the other one came to my office. "Chaplain, thanks for saving me from getting into trouble."

The Chaplain's office provided a win-win situation for both men in that instance. It remained a place for inmates to work out problems; unburden anxieties, guilt, or concerns; and discuss their difficulties in making adjustments.

Never a Dull Moment

In some situations, the Chaplain had to intervene with the inmates and their families because incarceration caused so much anxiety. Sometimes all it took to send some inmates into a frenzy was an unanswered phone call. In situations like this, I was frequently called upon to act as a link between the men and their families.

Tim Duncan was typical of inmates who always expected the worst when they called collect and no one answered their calls. Tim said, nervously, when he came to see me, "My wife was always home at this time of the day." I asked, "Tim, could she be out doing some of the things you previously did for the family?" That was a possibility; and I also knew that sometimes wives refused to accept collect calls because the family's budget couldn't handle the added financial strain. Tim, like other inmates, had the option of writing letters, but this means of communication was too slow for anxious men used to instant gratification.

I agreed to help Tim by finding out if there were any problems at his home. When I finally got through to Mrs. Duncan, she put it this way, "I don't have time to write after standing on my feet all day, rushing to day care to pick up the children, cooking, putting them to bed, and washing my uniform for the next day. Writing isn't on my mind. But Tim doesn't have to worry. I'll be here waiting for him."

All the problems weren't that simple. At the conclusion of my service on the 3rd of January, wiry Billy Jenkins said, almost in a hushed, nervous whisper, "Chaplain, I have to talk to you very badly." Normally I would have asked him to wait for me until I returned from escorting visitors to the visiting room. That morning, though, I only had 45 minutes left before a speaking engagement at the First Christian Church, Disciples of Christ, in Fort Walton Beach. Therefore, I said, "Billy, I want to talk with you, but I'm in a rush to get downtown for a preaching engagement. Come back at 2:00 p.m."

Unlike some inmates who don't keep their appointments, Billy was in my office promptly at 2:00. He stated, "I have something confidential to tell you. Two Spanish inmates sexually assaulted me a few nights ago. I can't identify them. Even if I could, I'd be afraid to do so. They might kill me."

As we talked, I knew this information could not stay in my office. This was serious and required more than counseling. Yet I could not violate his trust.

"Billy, you have to talk with the duty Lieutenant now." At first he refused, saying that he didn't want anyone apart from me to know about the incident. With a little persuasion, reasoning, and the assurance that I would go with him to the Lieutenant's office, he agreed to talk to the Lieutenant.

I called the Lieutenant immediately. Dodge said, "Come on over."

Billy repeated his story to Lieutenant Dodge. The officer questioned him, and Billy responded comfortably. After about fifteen minutes, I left them, relieved that Billy had someone who could help him. I counseled with him, but custody could take appropriate action. Before leaving for the day, I checked with Dodge about the disposition of Billy's case.

Dodge said, "We put Billy in detention for his safety until our investigation is completed."

I felt proud of the sensitive way the incident had been handled. To my dismay when I returned to work the following afternoon, the camp was ablaze with a rumor: "DON'T TALK TO THE CHAPLAIN BECAUSE YOU'LL END UP IN THE HOLE."

I soon discovered that Billy got the rumor started. It's natural for inmates to ask other inmates, "What got you here?" Instead of saying he was there for protective custody, Billy had responded, "I didn't do nothing. I just talked to the Chaplain and all of a sudden I found myself here."

Fortunately, this rumor died as quickly as it had spread because my credibility was high among the inmates. Soon the prison administration began to wonder if Billy had had a hidden agenda in making the report. Our suspicions were confirmed about two weeks later when an article entitled "Prison Rape" appeared on page 2 of a local newspaper, *The Destin Log*, dated Wednesday, January 15, 1986.

> FBI officials and authorities at the Federal Prison Camp at Eglin Air Force Base are investigating an alleged rape of one male inmate by another two inmates which occurred about two weeks ago at the camp.
>
> According to FBI Special Agent Mike Dill, no suspects have been arrested. He said the bureau is determining the validity of the allegation.
>
> "We expect to make a determination within about 30 days following the completion of our investigation," said Dill. "There has been an allegation and we're working on it."
>
> Michael Cooksey, prison camp superintendent, said an internal investigation into the complaint is also taking place, however identification of the suspects and the date of the alleged crime was not made available...."

I thought it strange to see the report because I knew that this type of incident was not one that staff would "leak" to the press. Therefore I wasn't surprised to learn that the investigations proved that Billy's allegations were false. Like so many, Billy had lied in an attempt to gain what he hoped would be conditions more favorable to himself. It didn't work. The two suspects that Billy had implicated were released from detention and remained at Eglin, but Billy was quietly transferred to another institution.

Saving Lives Is a Part of the Job

People's behavior in confinement mirrors what happens in the larger society — attempted suicides included.

The Sunday service was over and the Chapel empty. I was thankful for the quiet and seized the opportunity to work on my report for the region uninterruptedly. Just when I was making progress, a member of the 4:30 prayer group knocked on the door and said, "Chaplain Castillo, I see that you're busy, but I have to share something important with you."

I was reluctant to stop, but responded, "Okay, Derrick, what is it?"

"My 'homey' Pete Carragan is acting funny in his cubicle. He's been asking for pills. I'm scared that he may attempt suicide. You have to see him right away."

As I picked up the phone to call the Lieutenant, Derrick pleaded, "Please don't get security involved. Pete won't talk to anybody but you."

I knew Pete. Although he had been in the camp only a month, he had become an active worshiper and Bible Study member. We also had had several counseling sessions, and I had gained his respect and trust. Problems at home were making it very difficult for him to adjust to his eighteen-months sentence. His parents were in their late 60's and ill. His wife couldn't help them as she was struggling to provide for their three children. During our last session, Pete had said that he'd just learned that conditions at home had deteriorated.

I quickly gathered my report, locked it in my desk drawer, and headed for Pete's cubicle. On the way, two more inmates called me aside and whispered, "Something's wrong with Pete."

When I got to his cubicle, Pete was weeping. His thin, brown-skinned face seemed to brighten when I said, "Pete, you seem upset. How goes it today?"

"ROUGH, Chaplain, ROUGH. I can't bear it any more," he said in a high-pitched voice.

"I understand. Pete, let's go to my office so that we can talk privately." On the way to my office, his distress was evident. He kept mumbling to himself, "Why me? Why me? My wife is catching hell. It's my fault. Mama's heart is broken. It's all my fault."

Behind closed doors, he asked, "Chaplain, what does God say about suicide?"

"Are you thinking about that?"

"Yes, sir."

"Pete, is it that bad?"

He cried so loudly that his wailing pierced the room. He screamed, "I can't take it anymore, Chaplain." Suddenly his three "homeys" from Atlanta who were waiting outside for him came rushing into my office to find out what was going on.

"It's all right. I have everything under control," I assured them, as I closed the door behind them.

For about fifteen minutes I sat quietly as Pete cried until there were no more tears. He said weakly, "I feel better now, Chaplain.

"Good," I responded, "but I don't."

"What's wrong with you?" he asked as he perked up.

"I want us to go to the infirmary."

"Is that for me or for you?'"

"For both of us," I responded.

I knew he didn't want to deal with the authorities. However, he needed medical help.

"Pete, you have to see the doctor. We have a bigger problem than you and I can handle. Trust me. I'll go with you. Will you trust me?"

"Yes, I will."

I dialed Physician Assistant Guillermo Acevedo at the infirmary and told him I had an emergency and we're on our way."

"What kind of emergency, Chaplain?"

"A big kind."

"Okay, come over," he quickly responded.

Pete and I walked slowly to the infirmary. After briefly counseling with Pete, Physician Assistant (P.A.) Acevedo concluded that indeed the matter was serious. He excused himself, went to another room, and called P.A. Doug Hartman, the infirmary's director, who was also the Duty Officer. In a few minutes Acevedo was back. "Mr. Hartman will be here in fifteen minutes."

Pete's stress level began to increase as we waited for Hartman. Acevedo and I continued our counseling session. After a few minutes, Pete said, "Chaplain, I can't sit any more. I have to walk."

"Can I walk with you?" I asked, as I assisted him to stand.

"Yes."

We walked back and forth from the administration building to the cafeteria until Hartman motioned us into the infirmary. He listened to Pete's problems and counseled with the distressed inmate. I waited quietly. Hartman said, "Pete, let's go to your quarters and get those pills." I sensed Pete's reluctance as his facial muscles tightened.

"I'll go with you, Pete," I volunteered.

"Chaplain, stay with me," Pete implored.

By the time we returned with the pills, Hartman had made the necessary arrangements for Pete's admission to Eglin Air Force Base Regional Hospital. Pete was calmer, but he refused to go to the hospital without me. When we got there, the emergency section was filled with active-duty military personnel, dependent wives and young children, and retirees waiting to see the doctors. I kept a running conversation going with Pete as we waited, while Hartman talked to the admitting personnel. Three hours later, when Pete was admitted, I was drained, but I breathed a sigh of relief and thanked God this ordeal was under control.

My concerns made me visit Pete and another inmate at the hospital the following day, even though I was off and had lots to do. I felt much better that Pete was getting in touch with reality. Upon release from the hospital, he was transferred to Butner Correctional Institution in North Carolina, which has facilities to care for inmates needing psychiatric attention.

Dealing with Death Is Never Easy

Dealing with the death of a loved one is never easy, but it is especially hard on inmates, who cannot be with the family or loved ones during the last moments. One evening, as Muriel and I were relaxing at home watching "60 Minutes," Lieutenant Strickland called: "Chaplain, can you come back to the camp and counsel with inmate Carl Higgins? His father, mother, sister, and wife were involved in an automobile accident in Pensacola on their way home from visiting Carl this afternoon. Both parents and his sister were killed instantly. Carl's wife is in the Intensive Care Unit at West Florida Hospital."

"Strickland, give me a few minutes. I'll be there."

I tried to console Carl, but I didn't know if I got through because he was uncommunicative. Only a dull stare came from his eyes. Understandably, he was in a state of shock. I was saddened; I talked little and held his hand. I really didn't know what a Chaplain could tell an inmate who was suffering under such tragic circumstances. I allowed my caring presence to do the talking.

The following day, I went to work two hours early to talk with Carl. My first stop was the Assistant Superintendent's office to discuss Carl's tragic loss. I found Superintendent Michael Cooksey, Williams, and Case Manager Coordinator Rick Harris discussing Carl's situation. They were making arrangements for Carl to visit his wife at the hospital that evening. He would need staff escort, and I quickly volunteered. I felt that Carl's Chaplain should be with him.

Immediately after the 4:00 p.m. count, Carl and I left for the hospital in Superintendent Cooksey's car. Carl was distraught, nervous, and restless. Counseling and conversation were of little help, for his mind was on his family and the accident. Guilt was now a factor.

"If I hadn't been in prison this wouldn't have happened," he constantly repeated. He wanted to get to the hospital as quickly as possible, yet he wanted to stop to smoke a cigarette. Mr. Cooksey didn't approve of smoking in his car, but I gave Carl permission. Mr. Cooksey, a reasonable person, would not have objected.

We hurried into the ICU waiting room. His three sisters tearfully brought us up to date on his wife's condition. She was unconscious. They thanked me over and over for bringing their brother to the hospital.

"The Superintendent, staff, and I want to be of help. You have our sympathy," I assured them.

As I sat in the ICU waiting room, I noticed that the surroundings hadn't changed from two years earlier, when I had spent several hours with Mrs. Mary Stevenson while her husband Steve was a patient. The Stevenson family's home was the first one that my family visited in this area. Steve and I had become very good friends immediately. We shared a love for fishing, and he patiently taught me how to fish with a rod and reel, which was different from Belize, where I fished by holding a line in my hand. When the bright, hot tropical sun made me tired, I tied the line to my toe, leaned back, and put my hat over my face for shelter. Steve was so kind and humble that I visualize him helping the Father as much as he helped His children in this community.

Carl cried as he watched his young, helpless, bandaged wife with tubes everywhere. Upon leaving, we entered the elevator along with other visitors. One turned to the other and said, "Did you hear about that terrible accident last night? Another drunk killed innocent people."

The other responded, "Yes, it was just awful. I couldn't even look at the scene on television last night."

Carl and I looked at one another, but we didn't say anything. At the newspaper dispenser, *The Pensacola News Journal* headline on Monday, June 3, 1986, read, "Five Die in Wrong-Way Accident." Although distressed, Carl was beginning to talk a little during our hour-and-a-half ride. Just before 11:00 p.m, we arrived at camp.

The following day at 7:30 a.m., I informed the Superintendent about the hospital visit. In a sorrowful voice he said, "Chaplain, thanks for your commitment."

A few days later, I purchased Carl's ticket to return home for the funerals. After the funeral services, he went back to court and didn't return to Eglin. Carl, who was in for stealing credit cards, was put on probation. The judge justified his action by saying: "He has suffered enough. His tragedy will remain with him for the rest of his life."

Not long after that, I was supervising an evening Revival Mass for the Spanish-speaking inmates, when a correctional officer slipped into the service. "Chaplain," he whispered, "I'm here to relieve you. You need to report to the Lieutenant's office immediately."

The call to the Lieutenant's office made me feel uncomfortable as Lieutenants are responsible for the institution's security. As I rushed to the office, I asked myself, *What could it be now? Have I been involved in any breach of security.* As I reached the office, Lieutenant Pickett, the duty officer, Case Manager Chuck Harris, and a P. A. were waiting for my input on the easiest way to break the news to inmate Tony that his wife had died that afternoon in childbirth. Our concern for Tony brought us together. As we discussed Tony's situation, staff was empathetic. Such shocking, unexpected news is traumatic for the strongest of us. But for Tony it could be devastating. We knew that he would be very upset to put it mildly. His grief would be compounded because he had spoken to his wife that morning as she was getting ready to go to the hospital to deliver their child.

Tony was a large, emotional man who weighed at least 300 pounds. His beet-red face and his huge stomach hanging over his belt made him impossible to miss. And if you did, he probably would make himself known. During his first week he had contacted various department heads to ask for their assistance in getting a transfer back to Terminal Island Prison in California. I remember Tony's saying to me, "Chaplain, my family was only twenty minutes from Terminal Island. Now I'm 3,000 miles away. I want to get back. Please help me."

I talked to his case manager, but there was nothing we could do to effect his transfer. Like most expectant fathers, he was somewhat apprehensive because he didn't know what to expect and wasn't with his wife to give her emotional support. However, his unit team leader assured Tony that childbirth is a normal process and nothing to worry about.

After a lengthy discussion, we decided that we'd have Pastor Romero in his hometown break the news when he called back at 8:30 p.m. We would stand by for support. When Pastor Romero called, Tony was paged. He reported to the case manager's office within seconds. As he walked in, I told Pastor Romero, "Tony is here. Please hold on for a minute."

"What's the problem?" Tony asked.

"Tony, brace yourself. Your Pastor wants to talk to you," I responded.

I gave Tony my seat. The staffs' concern, sympathy, and empathy filled the office as Tony clutched the phone and cried bitterly as his Pastor talked to him. The phone conversation lasted almost an hour. When it was over, the staff consoled and counseled Tony. We answered his rapidly fired questions:

"When can I leave on an emergency furlough?"

"Once I'm in California, can I stay there to finish my sentence?"

"She died at 1 p.m. California time. Why wasn't I told earlier?"

"Why did it happen?"

"What went wrong?"

"Who will pay for my plane fare?"

"When can I get my ticket?"

While we cooperatively and sympathetically answered all his questions, Tony was in no mood to accept or hear our answers. Shock had taken over. He kept asking the same questions which had already been answered. Then it was my turn to talk to him calmly and reassuringly.

"Tony, we're here because we're concerned for you. We are on your side and not against you. However, there is nothing else that can be done until Superintendent Cooksey comes in tomorrow morning. Case Manager Harris will work on your furlough the first thing tomorrow morning."

At 4:37 p.m. Friday, November 14, Tony flew to Los Angeles with our prayers. A Federal judge ordered his sentence to be completed in California.

Distressing news seemed to come in bunches. Shortly after Tony left, another inmate suffered the loss of his mother. Gloom and despondency were heavy in the air as Victor and several of his friends waited for me at the Chapel. Deep depression was written on Victor's wrinkled face.

One friend spoke up: "Victor just got word his mother died."

I shook my head. I knew Victor. He was a "hard luck" inmate. Just eight months earlier, a judge had delayed his reporting date to Eglin so he could attend his father's funeral. Now his mother had died.

Victor said chokingly, "Chaplain, the Superintendent won't let me go home unescorted. I want to say goodbye...." He couldn't even finish his sentence. When he regained his composure, he blurted out. "Chaplain, you're my last hope. I can't afford to take an officer with me."

On an escorted trip, Victor would be responsible for paying both his and the staff's costs for transportation and meals. In addition, he would be responsible for the staff's wages after the first eight hours. Being his last hope made me uncomfortable. I thought: *What if I cannot convince Superintendent Cooksey to let Victor go without an escort?* Prayerfully, I said to myself, *I have to try.*

"Victor, I'm sorry. We'll pray for your strength and God's blessings on your mother's soul. I can't promise you anything, but I'll talk with Mr. Cooksey."

Mr. Cooksey was sympathetic to my plea as I asked him to please reconsider his decision pertaining to Victor's furlough.

"Chaplain, I would like to have a Pastor like you. Tell the unit manager to bring Victor's records back to me."

"Thank you Mr. C, I appreciate your concern," I responded as I almost flew out of his office headed for the Chapel, where the men waited.

When I got there, everyone's eyes were on me, anxiously waiting to find out what news I brought from Mr. Cooksey. I called Victor into my office, "Victor, Mr. Cooksey is willing to reconsider his decision. Hear me carefully, Victor. Mr. Cooksey *did not say that he'll let you go home unescorted.*"

"Thank you, Chaplain, at least there's hope."

"Yes, there is," I responded.

As Victor listened, I called Unit Manager Bobby Finch to have him carry Victor's records immediately to the Superintendent's office. "George, are you sure he told you that? I just left there about a half hour ago with Victor's records, and he turned down his furlough."

"Yes, he's going to reconsider; he's waiting for you."

"Okay, I'm on my way," Finch responded.

"Thank you, Bob. I appreciate you."

Mr. Cooksey granted Victor an unescorted furlough with two days to travel to and from Louisiana and one day at home for the funeral.

In a matter of minutes the camp knew that Victor was going home unescorted. Inmates walked over to shake my hand. "You're a good man, Chaplain. We're proud of you." I reminded them that it was Mr. Cooksey who had taken the action.

Seven months later, the sickly, older-looking, 49-year old Victor died of a heart attack in prison. The Chapel was filled with bereaved staff and inmates at his memorial service.

One of my difficult tasks is to notify immediate family about emergencies and an inmate's death. I made a call on July 23, 1987, to Kevin Woods' family to tell them that he had died at Eglin Air Force Base Regional Hospital. Kevin's family was very poor. They were upset because he had died, but also because they couldn't afford to pay for his funeral. His brother and Kevin's girlfriend had exhausted their funds visiting him a few weeks earlier. In a situation like Kevin's, the Federal Bureau of Prisons is responsible for getting an inmate's body to the airport closest to the next of kin's residence. Then the family is financially responsible for other arrangements. Since no one in Kevin's family had the financial means to accept his body, the Bureau of Prisons would have to pay for his funeral. Some institutions have their own burial grounds, but not Eglin. This meant burial at a local cemetery, without a service or headstone.

We planned a memorial service for Kevin at the camp Chapel, as we did for every inmate who died while incarcerated. As time for Kevin's memorial service approached, word spread quickly about the situation. A few inmates said, "Chaplain, there has to be somebody or some organization out there who can pay for a decent funeral for Kevin." A staff member investigated and found that Kevin was a veteran and was entitled to be buried at Barrancas National Cemetery in Pensacola. As the business office finalized burial plans, I asked the newly arrived Superintendent, George E. Killinger, and his Assistant, Michael Pugh, if I could take six inmate pallbearers to the graveside service. They were agreeable to the idea, but were concerned that the media would hear about it, attend, and possibly take pictures. Assistant Superintendent Pugh said, "It would make a good human-interest story, but I'm not in favor of the press being involved."

"There's no guarantee, but I don't know how the media would learn about it," I responded. They consented, so I went about finding the deceased's best friends to be pallbearers. Suddenly about 50 "best friends" showed up to volunteer. It was surprising how a trip to the outside can turn acquaintances into friends. They looked surprised when I asked them why, if he had been such a good friend, they hadn't attended his memorial service. I chose six inmates who had attended the service to accompany me as I performed my first Committal Service in a United States National Cemetery.

Prayer Changes Lives

Prayer is the mainstay of my faith. It works. Former inmate Harold Ford knew this. Therefore, he didn't hesitate to call me at home about 7:00 a.m. on Sunday, June 22.

"Chaplain, I'm sorry to call you this early, but I've been up all night worrying. My twin brother recently died of cancer. I hadn't been feeling well myself before he passed. I thought about you and how helpful you were to me at Eglin, and just needed to talk with you."

Despite the anxiety in his voice, I recognized Harold.

"Harold, don't worry about getting me up. Feel free to call me at any time. I'm sorry to learn of your brother's death. Things must have been very rough on you!"

"Yes. I haven't been able to eat or sleep. My blood pressure is high and my heart problem is getting worse. My doctor wants to operate, but I won't let him. What do you think?"

"I would get a second and a third opinion. Ask for Divine Guidance, and then decide which way to go."

"Chaplain, will you please pray with me."

I prayed with my brother as he sobbed painfully into my ear. I concluded by saying, "I wish that I could be with you, but since I can't, I'll hold you up in prayer. Keep praying because prayer lifts us to a higher plane of consciousness where we can communicate with God and receive guidance. Keep the faith; God is able."

Harold's distress stayed with me the rest of the day as I prayed and sent positive thoughts his way. I shared his prayer need with his former prayer partners at the 4:30 prayer group. We all lifted him up in prayer. Whenever he crossed my mind, I prayed for him. Three years later, he called again just to say, "Hello. I'm doing well....Thank you."

Discrimination Dilemma

I was available not only for tragedies but also for whatever problems inmates needed to talk about. Sometimes, however, problems were so obvious that even I missed them. Federal prisons are full of highly-educated people who held responsible positions before becoming involved in crime. I hadn't realized that black inmates had not been assigned to office positions at Eglin until four black professional inmates who felt they were being treated unfairly confronted me about job discrimination.

One evening, Tom Seymour, a lawyer; Daniel Thomas, a Ph.D. professor; Joe Jones, a certified public accountant; and Dean Greene, a high school teacher, shared their concerns about discrimination in assignments. Joe said, "Black inmates have been excluded from working in any office in the camp. Not even a janitor is working in the administration building."

I thought a minute about their charge and had to admit, "You're right."

Dan interjected, "Normally, white inmates get jobs in their related fields. Look at the white lawyers. They work in the law library here or on the base. Seymour is a lawyer like the rest of them, but he's working in the laundry. I'm a Ph.D. and I pick up cigarette butts. Less-qualified white inmates are working in education, but Dean has his master's in education and he and Joe are working on the roads and grounds crew."

Seymour added, "I don't mind working, but I have an ailing back. Although my doctor limited my lifting to no more than 25 pounds, my warehouse supervisor required me to lift heavier loads. When I protested, I was fired. Then I was reassigned to the base laundry which, everybody knows, is the worst assignment and usually reserved unofficially for punishment. Prior to that, I had applied for a law library assignment as the law library was in the process of relocating. I thought the job would be mine because Mrs. Gooden, the Supervisor of Education at Miami Correctional Center, gave me a good recommendation. However, a white U.S. Congressman who arrived later was assigned to the legal job."

Dan asked, "Chaplain, would you talk to the administration and ask for some fairness in our situation?"

"Thanks for talking with me. I have to admit that I wasn't aware of the situation. Your discussion helps me see things from your viewpoint. I'm going to talk to them."

The following day, I made an appointment with Mr. Cooksey and Mr. Williams. I said, "Yesterday, I received a complaint from four inmates that I need to bring to your attention. There aren't any black inmates working as clerks anywhere at the camp, nor have I seen a black inmate working in the administration building."

"George, I never thought about it," said Mr. Cooksey.

"I didn't either until it was brought to my attention. Will you do something?"

Mr. Cooksey was noncommittal; Mr. Williams was quiet. Some "progress" was made, however. About six months later, a black former law-enforcement officer from South Carolina became a janitor in the administration building. But the camp still had no black office workers.

Then an opportunity presented itself in the Religious Department. I would need a clerk, as Steve was scheduled to leave shortly. The job required the usual typing and clerical skills plus another important criterion: PARTICIPATION IN THE RELIGIOUS PROGRAMS. The participation requirement was important because I couldn't attend all the 4:30 prayer group meetings and other religious programs. My clerk needed to take information from me to the groups and also inform me of happenings during my absence.

Unfortunately, my goal of changing the racial situation was not to be reached. The only two inmates who applied were white, and I eventually chose a banker from North Carolina. This troubled me greatly. At the same time as I was so keenly aware that we didn't have even one black clerk working in the prison camp, I had been placed in the position of having to hire a white clerk.

It was no surprise to me when one evening the four angry black inmates came back to my office. "You had a chance to hire the first black inmate clerk. Why didn't you hire one?" Dean asked.

I understood their anger and felt uncomfortable about my decision. However, I too had a problem. "Gentlemen, I know what you're talking about, and I am sympathetic. I wanted to hire a black clerk. We do need black clerks in the camp, and we do have qualified men to fill many posts. However, my conscience would have bothered me to fill my clerk's position with a black clerk who was not active in the religious programs. I expect my clerk to make announcements at the 4:30 prayer group and keep me aware of that group's concerns as well as what is going on in other religious programs. Yes, we have a few black brothers in the prayer group, but you know as well as I do that not one of them is qualified. I don't have time to teach typing, office procedure, English usage, etc."

"Did any blacks apply?" one of the inmates asked.

"No. Not one. I received applications from two white Christian brothers who were qualified and members of the religious community. I chose one over the other because I know the quality of his work. There's a lot of paperwork to be done in this

office. He voluntarily did some work for me while Steve was at
Prison Fellowship Seminar in Washington, D.C. "

It was obvious that my reasoning was unacceptable to them.
They concluded that I did not understand, for I think white. Besides I am a foreigner. They walked out of my office still angry. I
was saddened by their anger. My whole life had been based on
helping people of all races achieve their goals. Now I had to face
a sad fact: A black Chaplain who sought equal treatment for
black inmates could not hire one for his own department.

The following morning, I shared my experience with Mr.
Cooksey and explained how and why I arrived at my decision.
His agreeing with me didn't make me feel any better about the
situation. As I left his office, I again reminded him that the institution's discriminatory inmate-assignment problem still existed
and needed to be corrected.

When my banker clerk left ten months later, there was still
not a black clerk in the institution. As the banker was about to
leave, three applications were submitted for his job: one from a
white lawyer, another from a white state politician, and the third
from a black businessman with a master's degree. All three men
were qualified in office skills and active participants in the religious programs and the Christian community. This gave me an
opportunity to choose a qualified black clerk, Al Robinson. Al was
not only Eglin's first black clerk, but he was still the only one
when I left for Pensacola Prison Camp in 1988, ten years after I
arrived.

As soon as Al became the clerk, his desk and filing cabinet
were ransacked. Not to give the perpetrator(s) a victory or publicity, Al and I decided not to tell anyone about the incident. Without explaining why, I requested security measures from Kaj Ste-
fansen, Chief of Mechanical Services. Al did an exceptional job;
in time he was no longer harassed and was accepted by the inmates.

A white woman who was a frequent visitor to the camp demanded to know why I chose Al, a black man, over the white
state politician, Jimmy. I told her, "It's true both men were qualified. However, I offered Al the only opportunity he had to become
a clerk. Jimmy had other options. In fact, shortly after I made
my selection he was hired to teach in education."

Chapter 12

Onward, Christian Soldier

August 16, 1988, was a milestone in my career. It marked my tenth anniversary at Eglin Federal Prison Camp. It came quietly. No bands played, nor were there any celebrations. Instead, I just spent a few extra minutes of thankful, prayerful reflection in the quietness of the Chapel.

During these years, I had changed, as had the camp's composition. When I had arrived, the inmate population was only 350; now it was 870. Then, most inmates were highly educated professionals who held influential business or government positions. No more. By 1988, about 90% were incarcerated for drug-related crimes. Many were functionally illiterate or non-English speaking and had fewer coping skills than the inmates of earlier years. The demands on my time kept escalating greatly as the population increased.

It became almost impossible for me to provide quality pastoral care to over 800 inmates with assorted religious beliefs and varied personal and family problems. The lines outside my office seemed to get longer each day. Someone always wanted something. Consequently, I spent more hours at the camp, and then brought home administrative tasks which I previously had completed at work. Additionally, I made telephone calls from home to volunteers, and took care of other camp-related matters in off-hours because of constant interruption at the office. I'm fortunate that Muriel felt herself part of my team and didn't complain when I started doing most of my paperwork at home.

My evaluation indicated my efforts did not go unnoticed:

Despite his increased workload, George's overall performance was excellent as noted on his last Employee Performance Appraisal. His excellent performance was also noted by the Religious Services audit team during their May 1988 visit. Their report stated, "A second staff chaplain's position would be very desirable at Eglin." Although George remains a one-man department, the audit team concluded, "Eglin Religious Services has continued to expand a noteworthy innovative program that I have not seen elsewhere in the Bureau of Prisons. Approximately four or five dedicated volunteers teach a children's Sunday School class for the children of inmates on Sunday mornings while the parents are able to attend worship services.

Even though I loved working at Eglin, I began to realize that my time there might be growing short. Crime was on the increase and the prison population was exploding. The astounding growth required new prisons. In Northwest Florida alone, three Federal prison facilities were opened in 1988. I knew that before long I'd have to leave Eglin because the Bureau liked their senior Chaplains to initiate programs in new institutions, and I would likely be one of those targeted for this purpose. So I took the initiative and called Regional Chaplain Bryn Carlson to ask him to seriously consider me for a transfer to the new Federal Prison Camp in Pensacola. I wouldn't mind this transfer, and I was willing to endure a three-hour commute each day to spare my family another move. Besides, the Bureau would not have to pay my moving expenses.

Carlson agreed: "I think you've made a good decision, George. Pensacola is going to be just like Eglin, a minimum security camp."

Superintendent George Killinger and his new Assistant Superintendent, Willis Gibson, understood my wanting to transfer and were supportive of my decision, but they didn't want me to leave. Mr. Killinger, recognizing my ability to go beyond the Chaplaincy, spoke to me about assuming additional administrative duties for career advancement. I thanked him for his support and for the quality step increase in pay I was awarded. I gratefully said, "Thank you. I appreciate your thoughtfulness and concern, but I love the Chaplaincy and feel called to that minis-try, and I wish to continue ministering."

I then spoke to Mark Henry, Pensacola Federal Prison Camp's first Superintendent, and expressed my desire to work at his pris-on. He made no promises but said, "Chaplain, you will be given serious consideration. I have heard about the work you're doing at Eglin. You're one of the best."

I vowed to continue doing my best, just as I had always done. I found myself thanking God for the opportunity to do what 1 love — helping others.

Leaving It in God's Hands, Literally

I didn't know where I would be working in the future, and all I could do was wait. The timing was perfect for the vacation to China, Hong Kong, and Japan which Muriel and I had been plan-ning. Now we would leave and allow the bureaucrats and God to worry about where I should serve. By the time we joined our Inter Pacific tour group at Tokyo-Narita airport, I had moved any thoughts of my impending transfer to the deepest recesses of my mind. I felt peace as the wheels of our giant aircraft touched down in Shanghai, China, where the tour actually began.

The next morning we fully appreciated the accommodations in our five-star hotel. We relaxed in our luxurious room as we watched a CNN news broadcast in English. However, outside the hotel the clock turned back. Old ladies wearing coolie hats swept the streets with handmade frond brooms. People on bicycles were everywhere. We had never seen that many people or bicycles in our lives. Crossing the street required us to maneuver among the bicycles, not unlike the adventure of crossing New York's 42nd Street between fast-moving cars and taxis during rush hour. Mu-riel summarized China as "a country where antiquity and the 21st Century come together."

At the Great Wall of China, I had a dramatic religious experi-ence. I was too ill with an excruciating stomach pain to get off the bus and join the group as they walked the Wall. *"What a terrible time to be ill,"* I whispered as I sat there alone. Suddenly the pain was so intense that tears fell involuntarily on my cheeks. Alone and afraid, I turned to God. *"Father, I am sick. I need your help."*

Instantly and miraculously, the pain left. I have heard of other people receiving instant answers, but never in my life had I received an immediate answer to my petition. "For I will restore health unto thee, and I will heal thee of thy wounds said the Lord...." (Jeremiah 30:17).

We were mesmerized during our tours of Beijing, Xian, and Guilin, where our educational and informative tour of China ended. Then we spent more fascinating days in Hong Kong and Japan. After 19 days of exhausting, but happy, travel, we returned home. I took a few days off to get my biological clock in sync.

A few months later, while relaxing at home one afternoon, Superintendent Killinger called: "George, congratulations! You have been chosen to be the first Chaplain at Pensacola Federal Prison Camp. You did a good job here. It'll be their gain."

I was overjoyed, and could hardly wait to share my good news with Muriel. I immediately called her at work and jubilantly announced, "You are now speaking to Pensacola's first Chaplain, who will be reporting around November."

Passing the Torch

The date was set for my transfer to Pensacola when I received my 15-year Bureau of Prisons service pin. I was eager to begin my new assignment and was excited about ministering to fewer than 300 inmates, a bonus which would give me more time to provide pastoral care and start religious programs.

The time was fast approaching for me to pass the torch. In mid-October 1988, I met and welcomed my successor, Stephen Johnson, who transferred to Eglin from Pennsylvania. I was happy to meet the warm, middle-aged, medium-built, white male Chaplain, and I immediately invited him to join me at the Tuesday morning Superintendent's staff meeting. Then I gave him an abbreviated tour of the camp and highlighted the religious programs. When he reported for duty on Sunday, November 13, 1988, my dream of having two Chaplains at Eglin was fulfilled, even if it was for only a few days.

I invited Steve to preach, but he said he would rather see how I had been conducting the services. I based my sermon, "The Winning Team," on the life of Joseph. At the altar call, two converts committed themselves to Christ in front of a packed Chapel

LDS HOSPITAL

Eighth Avenue and C Street, Salt Lake City, Utah 84143,
801-321-1075

DEPARTMENT OF INTERNAL MEDICINE
G. Michael Vincent, M.D., Chairman

Associate Professor of Medicine,
University of Utah School of Medicine

May 31, 1988

George and Muriel Castillo
Federal Prison Camp
Elgin Air Force Base, Florida 32542

Dear Mr. and Mrs. Castillo,

It was certainly a pleasure to meet you in Xian, China. I wanted to thank you again for the materials that you left with me to distribute. I did arrange for them to be distributed, and they were received with considerable thanks and appreciation. Your warmth and generosity are excellent examples of the Christian spirit.

I certainly enjoyed visiting with you, and I wish you the best of success in all of your endeavors and in your future travels.

Sincerely,

G. Michael Vincent, M.D.

Muriel with Chinese girl in Shanghai

Chinese children playing games in Shanghai

of enthusiastic and responsive congregants. I then asked the congregation to stand and repeat after me:

> We the members and friends of Eglin Prison Camp Christian Community, gladly receive the Reverend Stephen Johnson to be our Chaplain. We covenant to hear the Word of God from his lips with humility and love; to pray for him at all times; to encourage and support him when he is right; and to patiently and lovingly talk to him behind closed doors when there are differences. We further covenant to walk with him as a faithful people of God in this place, as Christ shall be our helper. AMEN.

As the congregation stood, I turned to my successor and said, "Chaplain Stephen Johnson, I present to you some members of your winning team." We then walked outside the Chapel, where I baptized eight inmates.

The transition was completed. Johnson and I worked together until I officially started as Chaplain of Pensacola Federal Prison Camp on Sunday, December 4, 1988.

My transfer did not go unnoticed in the local community or in the prison camp. Loyal Phillips, a noted columnist with the *Northwest Florida Daily News,* acknowledged my ten-year ministry at the camp with an article entitled, "Inmates' Religious Needs Well Served at Eglin." Shortly after the article appeared, inmate Fredrico Hernandez casually asked, "Chaplain, are you going to be at this afternoon's 4:30 prayer group meeting?"

"Why, of course. My calendar is clear for this afternoon." As I entered the Chapel that afternoon, I was totally surprised to find it full. In a quick glance, I noticed the regulars as well as Jews, Roman Catholics, Muslims, blacks, whites, Native Americans, and members of various secular organizations. As usual, the service coordinator began with the opening hymn and prayer, but instead of a Bible topic discussion, representatives of various groups presented me with Certificates of Appreciation. As they left, most of the inmates formed a line to shake my hand and say, "Thank you, Chaplain...."

I knew then that my work at Eglin had not been in vain. My heart was full of gratitude as I witnessed a microcosm of the world's people united in working, praying, and praising together. I prayerfully hoped that one day a fellowship like this would

Inmates' baptism

become a reality among God's children.

Penscola, Here I Come

Pensacola Prison Camp is located on Saufley Field Navy Base.

To help make it fully operational as a camp, 65 inmates had been detailed there to get it ready. By March 1989, the population had grown to 257 men, and I was able to provide pastoral care to my satisfaction. My lessened workload enabled me to visit inmates at their work centers and throughout the institution. Inmates weren't used to this. One day as I walked through the carpentry shop, Jonathan Yates, a young forger and drug dealer, was surprised that I took an interest in the men. He asked suspiciously, "Why are you visiting us?"

"Because I didn't see you in service last Sunday. I decided to look for you and find out how things are going."

His young, distrustful, hardened face, softened enough for a faint smile to show through. Five of the six inmates in his carpentry shop came to service the next Sunday.

The prison camp at Saufley Field drew the public's attention. As the word spread, so did offers from Christians who wanted to volunteer their services. In less than four months, I had enough volunteers from several denominations who had successfully completed the approval process to get our programs off the ground and running efficiently. Regional Chaplain Bryn Carlson was thrilled to hear the news. During our conservation, Bryn mentioned that Chaplain Arthur Becton was chosen to fill Eglin's training slot. He was a well-thought-of young black man whose home church was Beulah First Baptist Church of Fort Walton Beach. I thought: *How great for Steve. I wanted and needed additional help for the last seven of the ten years I was at Eglin, but only three months after I left it became a reality!*

A Chance To Tell My Story

In many prisons there is an attitude of "us" against "them" that permeates the relationship between correctional personnel and other staff members. Chaplains are viewed as being primarily interested in conducting their worship services and Bible classes and not particularly interested in security. Being a new facility, many of the correctional officers were straight out of higher-level institutions; some others were rookies. The experienced ones were the hardest to convince that Chaplains are, in fact, a very important part of the correctional team. Therefore, I welcomed the opportunity — my first in 16 years — and found it therapeutic, to explain "The Role of the Chaplain in an Institutional Setting" at Pensacola Federal Prison Camp's first annual training session.

I assured staff that Chaplains are also staff, and share the same institutional concerns they have. I pointed out that Chaplains act as liaison between inmates and inmates, inmates and staff, and inmates and their families. I further explained that our duties and responsibilities require us to spend much time counseling, building self-worth, mediating disputes, reconciling differences and reducing stress and frustrations of both inmates and staff. I also made it clear that most inmates see the Chaplain as their last resort, and added that I was available to help staff members with their frustrations caused by constantly working with inmates. I emphasized that one of the important goals of the Chaplains is to assist in the orderly running of the institution.

All Dressed Up and No Place To Go

While part of the Navy base was being renovated to accommodate Pensacola Prison Camp, all departments were short of space. The Religious Department didn't have a Chapel so we held services and masses in the cafeteria, the visiting room, and then the conference room. By March 1989, my congregation had outgrown these facilities. Anticipating even more worshippers at Easter services, I discussed holding Easter sunrise service outdoors with the Chief Correctional Supervisor (CCS), Harold Mays. His acid response to this suggestion was, "This is the most asinine and ridiculous suggestion I have ever heard in all my career."

With a surprised look on my face, I responded, "Outdoor sunrise services are quite common. Many churches even hold them on the beach. I held outdoor sunrise services at Eglin for the past ten years." This caused him to reconsider, and we toured the camp and agreed on a convenient spot for the service. As Mays gave his approval, I thanked God that He rolled away the stone before Easter Sunday morning this year. My suggestion also received the approval of Superintendent Mark Henry and his assistant, Donna

Stratman. In fact, Mrs. Stratman asked if I would be amenable to having services outdoors after Easter. "I would love to do it, but you'll have to work it out with the CCS," I advised.

In subsequent years, we continued to have our outdoor worship services, except when the weather was inclement. Then the services were conducted in the Naval Reserve auditorium. When reservists were on duty and we had to be indoors, we moved the worship services to the gym.

Despite the inconveniences of working in an unfinished prison camp, I enjoyed every day because each one offered different challenges for spiritual growth.

Great Things He Has Done

Commuting can be both a pain and an opportunity. The time it took to drive the 120-mile-round-trip commute gave me an opportunity to plan, reflect, meditate, and think of creative ways to implement my ministry. I always thanked God for bringing me a mighty long way. Who else could have made all this possible but God.

To God be the glory, I reflected frequently as I drove, thinking back on the great things He had done and was doing for our family. Muriel and the children were doing very well in their careers. Our granddaughters, Tiffany and Erica, were excellent students, and our grandson, Erick Jr., was a healthy one-year-old.

Thank God, Marcelle, like me, had proved that limiting labels placed by so-called "authorities" can be very wrong. An uncaring second-grade teacher had told us that Marcelle wasn't college material and that she didn't have the ability to be a Cornell University student like her brother Joe. Doctor Stanley Evans' words came to mind: "George, we have always been told that we can't learn." Muriel and I both knew that Marcelle, like many others who have been mislabeled, was a good, bright, highly motivated student. She proved her case as she received her Juris Doctor degree on May 7, 1989, from Georgia State University College of Law.

Ecclesiastes 3:1 reads, "To every thing there is a season, and a time to every purpose under the heaven." Indeed, this was a good time for me to rejoice in God's goodness.

*Marcelle with brothers at her Law School
graduation. Erick on left. Joe on right*

*Grandfather with grandchildren.
Left to right: Erica, Ricky and Tiffany*

*Mother, father and Marcelle at her Law School
graduation, 1989*

Seasons Change and Storms Come

Florida is known for its sudden storms, but not all of them come out of the sky. One "storm" came in May 1990 about five months after Joe Peters took over the reins as the new Superintendent and just before I was scheduled to attend the June 1990 Chaplaincy Conference in Phoenix, Arizona. He was at Eglin in 1978 when I arrived and, of course, knew about the Aiken/ Ashland fiasco. I was thankful that all appeared to have been forgotten as he and I discussed the status of the Religious Department, which was operating without any problems. I knew that I had grown and the inmates were responding to my leadership.

Knowing that, without special permission, staff is prohibited from having contact with former inmates until two years after their parole has ended, I requested permission from Superintendent Peters to see a former inmate who lived in Phoenix but who did not meet the two-year criterion. Requests to see a former inmate still on parole had routinely been approved so I felt no need to worry about receiving approval to see Dennis Ferguson, one of my former inmate clerks. I handed Peters a memo stating Dennis had sent me a birthday card and that I would like to visit him and his new family while at the Chaplains' conference. I explained: "I spent several months counseling with Dennis while he was my clerk, and also with his fiancée during visits. I'm eager to see how well he has adjusted to being a free man again."

Fury replaced Peters' calm demeanor as he shouted, "Chaplain, what bothers me is that you have been in contact with a former inmate without letting me know about it. You could be fired for this. If I were to send your memo to the Regional Legal Department you could be in big trouble, subject to dismissal."

His unjustifiable outburst signaled, "I gotcha." Stunned, I couldn't believe that I was still firmly within the grips of the *Penalty Box* after all these years. With fire breathing from his mouth, Peters ordered: "Bring me the card immediately. And while you're at your office, check the policy and then call the Regional Chaplain for a reading of the situation.."

Flabbergasted, I retreated from his office and went to get Dennis's greeting card and call the Regional Chaplain, as he had ordered. The Chaplain wasn't in so I left a message on his answering machine to call me as soon as possible. Then I called Chaplains Riggs and Schulze in Washington. The only response was the repeated ring of their phones.

I immediately went back to Peters' office. "Mr. Peters, it's 5:05 p.m. Eastern time, and I couldn't reach any of the Chaplains."

His anger faded when he saw Dennis's card, which read: "TO A SPECIAL PASTOR ON YOUR BIRTHDAY." The handwritten message stated:

> To a very special messenger of the Lord. God bless you and your family on this joyous and blessed day. Happy Birthday, Dennis and Debbie. (Hebrews 13: 3)

Printed below: "It is God who arms me with strength and makes my way perfect. II Samuel 22:23."

As Peters read the card, his face flushed! He appeared humiliated by his unjustified outburst. Tossing the card aside, he said almost apologetically, "Forget about it."

Still stunned, I responded, "Chaplain Carlson will call back. I left a message on his answering machine."

With an embarrassed laugh, he said, "Call him back and tell him that *Father* Peters took care of it!"

My response, "I will," reflected the defeat I felt for having been treated so shabbily when I had followed policy by letting Peters know of my proposed visit. If a staff member could be fired for receiving a greeting card from a former inmate, Federal Prisons would be emptied of employees overnight. There is hardly a staff member who, at one time or another, has not received correspondence from a former inmate who appreciated some kindness extended during his stay.

However, to reassure myself, I reread the policy in "Standards of Employee Conduct and Responsibility," which states in part F, Personal Conduct 2A,

"NEITHER SHALL AN EMPLOYEE ACCEPT ANY GIFT, PERSONAL SERVICE OR FAVOR FROM AN INMATE OR FORMER INMATE, OR FROM ANYONE KNOWN TO BE ASSOCIATED WITH OR RELATED TO AN INMATE OR FORMER INMATE."

TO A SPECIAL

Pastor

ON YOUR BIRTHDAY

*M*ay there be light
on every path you follow...
Wisdom to guide
your every step...
Peace to confirm
your every decision...
the Father's joy in all you do.

Happy Birthday

to a very special messenger
of the Lord. God bless you
and your family on this
joyous and blessed day.
Happy Birthday,

Debbie and Dennis
Ferguson

Hebrews.
13:3

"It is God who arms me with strength
and makes my way perfect."
II SAMUEL 22:33 NIV

You, the reader, be the judge. Does a greeting card fit that prohibition?

During my ride home, the day's events replayed in my head, and I was reminded that although Aiken had died two months ago he was still alive in Peters. I thought about the Biblical parable of the Priest and a Levite who were so steeped in regulations and traditions that they forgot acts of kindness. (Luke 10:30-37).

Peters was like the Priest and Levite. He had interpreted regulations so tightly that he had limited my Christian ministry to care for God's children out of prison. He was not mindful of Hebrews 13:3: "Remember them that are in bonds, as bound with them; and them which suffer adversity, as being yourselves also in the body."

I really wanted to see Dennis and his family while in Phoenix, but I didn't, even though it was completely within policy for me to do so with the Superintendent's permission. I couldn't stand the humiliation and threats that the Superintendent's policy interpretation had subjected me to when I tried to obtain that permission.

Walking on Eggshells

The change of scenery and philosophy at the Chaplaincy Conference was most welcome. As I talked with other Chaplains, it became obvious that many were struggling not just with our ministry to the inmates but also with the system's policies.

We were all pleased that Director J. Michael Quinlan had come to our conference. His being there provided us with an emotional pickup. In his speech, Mr. Quinlan reiterated his faith in the Hebrew-Christian-Muslim tradition. "There is some good in every one of us. Inmates should leave the Federal prison system a little better than when they arrived. We should help to motivate them so that they can help themselves." Being a realist, he added, "It'll take many years for this philosophy to filter down to the institution level."

Chaplains were excited about his talk; most of the 130 heads nodded in agreement. As I looked at the Chaplains and saw approximately 40 minorities, including blacks and females, among them, I was mindful of what great changes the Lord had wrought!

The newest minorities, black and female Chaplains, were well represented in numbers, but they were still far behind in equal treatment. For the first time, individual Chaplains were recognized for achievements and given awards by their Regional Chaplains. White Regional Chaplains gave awards exclusively to white Chaplains. However, Matthew Hamidullah, the only black Regional Chaplain, gave awards to both a white and a black Chaplain, the only black to get recognition at the conference. Some black Chaplains voiced their anger about the fact that only one black received any recognition. I remained quiet, but I was inwardly pleased to see that the younger generation was not going to face the paradox of Christian injustice without protest.

The Chaplains who received awards didn't do anything extraordinary or different from what other Chaplains had accomplished. In fact, when Chaplain Carlson read Chaplain Ames' accomplishments, I silently said, *Oh, he's describing me*. I guess the tie-breaker was, "He prayed with the Chamber of Commerce." I did this, too, in Ashland, but not last year.

Before the conference ended, Bryn Carlson asked me about my cancelled call last week. I briefed him. He said, "George, this seems to be a leftover from Ashland. Just drop it. My advice is to continue letting Peters know what you're doing."

On my return home, a former inmate, whom I didn't immediately recognize, approached me at Okaloosa County Air Terminal and asked, "Are you the Chaplain at Pensacola?" We engaged in small talk about his adjustment since his release. Although this encounter was brief and without significance, I let the Superintendent know about it.

As things come in bunches, so did another inmate contact. I received a letter from my former clerk "JJ," who had been transferred from the Pensacola camp to Jesup, Georgia, Federal Prison Camp. Rather than risk another "chastising and threat of firing," I asked Peters how he wanted me to handle JJ's letter.

"George, open it and give it to me."

As I watched him read the letter before I had a chance to do so myself, I FELT MY ECCLESIASTICAL CALLING AND MY WORTH AS AN INTELLIGENT HUMAN BEING COMPROMISED.

When Peters handed me the letter, he said, "I don't need to see your response." This was one of those times in my career when I felt despondent and vowed that before going through this "exercise" again, I would not accept any correspondence from former inmates or those currently incarcerated. This became my unwilling policy: Return letters to the U. S. Post Office marked, "REFUSED, RETURN TO SENDER."

Working in prisons is difficult enough without working for a boss who doesn't trust his employees to make intelligent decisions. Unfortunately for me, Mr. Peters' example was followed by his newly-assigned assistant, Marjorie Thompson, who became my supervisor. I expected a knowledgeable supervisor to at least find out what was going on in the various departments before making radical changes. I hoped in vain that she would trust a Chaplain with over eighteen years' experience to run his department efficiently. But not Ms. Thompson. She didn't have a clue about the Religious Department's functions, and she wasn't interested in learning before giving orders.

Bureau regulations, backed by court decisions, require that all religious groups be offered a minimum number of programs. Even with the population increase, we had been able to achieve this goal. Without examining anything or even talking with me, Ms. Thompson ordered: "Cut programs!!!"

Afterwards, she steadfastly refused to discuss which programs she wanted cut, or even offer any suggestions. Without follow-up, that order and another to change my work schedule died a natural death from her inaction. However, she continued to micro-manage all my activities.

The Jewish Holidays were approaching and, knowing her style, I would not make any arrangements without her approval. Last year we had no Rabbi or Jewish volunteers at the camp to lead Rosh Hashanah (New Year) and Yom Kippur (Day of Atonement) worship services. Consequently, the inmates were allowed to go, under supervision, to the temple in town to celebrate.

Well in advance of these holidays, I provided Ms. Thompson a "heads-up" memo stating our usual practice: (1) Jewish inmates would be released from work for the two Jewish High Holy Days: Rosh Hashanah and Yom Kippur; (2) Eligible inmates would be escorted to the temple for celebration of the holidays; (3) The Chapel would be reserved during those days so that Jewish inmates unable to leave the camp could use it for meditation and prayer.

Days later, she told me, "Chaplain, I don't want the Jewish inmates to go to the synagogue in the city for their holidays."

Knowing the implications of this, I offered a compromise: "I'll work without compensation to escort them to the synagogue."

"It won't be necessary to do that. They are *not* going," she said firmly. "I spoke to Region, and was given an okay."

I knew that the Jewish inmates would be unhappy. I also wanted to create an alternative without showing any conflict with the administration. So I scheduled the Chapel for the Jewish inmates' exclusive use and began securing the religious books necessary for the ceremonies. As I anticipated, the Jewish inmates didn't find this acceptable. They wanted to go to Temple Bethel for their services as they had the previous year. Phone lines began humming constantly with collect calls to families, institutions, and Congressional representatives.

Action was swift. Early Saturday morning, Regional Chaplain Bryn Carlson called me at home. "George, why aren't the Jews being escorted to town for the High Holy Days?"

"Bryn, Ms. Thompson has issued an order saying they must worship here at the camp. She told me that she got the okay from Region."

"I don't know who she spoke to. But I need some answers quickly for the Regional Director and some Congressmen."

As I arrived at the camp for Sunday services, I left another memo for the Superintendent and his assistant outlining my conversation with Chaplain Carlson and telling them to expect a call from him tomorrow.

I don't know what transpired during that call from Carlson, but an about-face came at 4:00 p.m. Monday. Although I had tried to avert the situation, Superintendent Peters shouted at me when I entered his office: "What the hell are you doing getting me into trouble with Region?" Before I could answer, he shoved the paperwork at me which I needed to escort the eligible Jewish inmates to their celebration. His behavior was entirely unjustified. I had done everything in my power to avert the situation, but still I had no choice but to comply with my supervisor's edict. His rage should have been directed at his assistant, who gave the order, not at me. His ranting made me painfully aware that my words had fallen on deaf ears. To him, I was solely responsible for the "trouble." I left his office feeling as if I had been the victim of a severe beating. I found out later that the staff was still answering Congressional inquiries three weeks after the Jewish holidays had passed.

Death, Hope, and Stress

My pain was further deepened when Jim Pease, Chief of Mechanical Services, met me as I left the Superintendent's office. He gave me the news that staff member Donald Pacheco had died that morning. I had known Don from Eglin camp, and we both had transferred to Saufley Field at about the same time. Staff and inmates would miss Don's friendliness and outgoing manner. That Thursday, September 19, 1991, I conducted Don's funeral service at Faith Chapel Funeral Home in Pensacola. After his interment at Barrancas National Cemetery, I visited Don's family. Before leaving for home, I called on an inmate at the hospital. I was fatigued as I started on my 60-mile journey home.

I was thankful for having the next day off. After a day's rest and meditation, I felt better and I had reaffirmed my belief that there is a time and season for everything (Ecclesiastes 3:1), even my ups and downs with the administration. Knowing that it, too, shall pass, I released with prayer and forgiveness other annoyances and frustrations, such as Ms. Thompson's removal of my clerks and janitor without my knowledge and her threat to take away the meditation room. A surprising boost came in the form of a letter that arrived on October 27 from the Regional Director, Mr. F. P. Sam Samples:

> Your years of ministry in the Bureau have contributed a great deal to the mission of the Bureau of Prisons. I do wish you the best in the remaining two years of your ministry with the Bureau. Your service and dedication to caring for people in a correctional environment is often a difficult and thankless task. I thank you for your faithfulness to that task.

It felt good to have someone say, *Thank You*, words which were rarely expressed at the institution no matter how hard one worked and tried to accomplish difficult tasks. I was uplifted and felt the still, small voice saying, "I didn't call you to this ministry to be alone. Lo, I am with you always." (Matthew 28:20). Samples' encouragement and God's words became a source of strength and hope in my time of need.

I never realized how much the strain was affecting me until Muriel again said, "George, I'm worried about you. We haven't done anything together since I retired. You fall asleep the minute you finish supper."

"You're right, Muriel. But I just can't get the energy to be involved with activities after working eight hours a day and driving three," I responded in a voice that showed my fatigue.

Then, yearningly— almost wishfully — she inserted, "Wouldn't it be wonderful if you could finish your last year back at Eglin?"

"Ain't no way! Steve Johnson will be at Eglin long after I'm retired."

We were both concerned that my health was failing. My excessive palpitations and general malaise increased. Finally, I listened to Muriel's pleadings and went to see my physician, Michael McCoy. After a battery of tests, he confirmed that all was not well, and warned, "If you don't take time off for rest and recreation, you may be headed for another stroke. Only this time you might not be as lucky as in 1983. You have got to get away from the stress of work for awhile."

Time was of the essence. Doctor McCoy immediately put me on six months' rest, exercise therapy, and medication which I must take for the rest of my life. For the first time in 18 years, I used sick leave. I had always used vacation time in the past whenever I became ill.

I felt fully refreshed when I reported back to work on Sunday, May 3, 1992. Both staff and inmates greeted me warmly. The Chapel was full. New inmates were waiting to meet me. There was so much to do, I hardly knew where to begin. However, my priority was set for me, as members of the Christian community angrily demanded that I tell them why programs were cancelled TWO DAYS before I returned to work. Then they showed me a copy of a memo which Ms. Thompson had posted on the Chapel door. I was as dismayed as they were, and thought how helpful it would have been if my supervisor had informed me instead of posting a memo on the Chapel door which read:

There will be no worship services, scriptural studies or organized theological discussions held in the Chapel area without the presence of certified religious volunteers, contractors or chaplain. Only those activities outlined in the schedule will be sanctioned by the Religious Department of FPC Pensacola. Although all inmates are encouraged to attend these activities, no inmates will be allowed to lead worship services, scriptural studies or organized theological discussions within the confines of the Chapel or surrounding areas, such as visiting room.

I knew that unless there had been a change while I was out sick, Ms. Thompson's directive was in violation of Bureau policies. I also knew that the timing of her posting was to let me know who the boss was. However, it was most important at that point for me to calm the rough waters and pacify the angry voices.

Inmate Pete LaMar said, "Chaplain, why can other inmates meet and play cards without any supervision in the visiting room, which is in the same building as the Chapel, while we Christians can't meet on our own?"

"Chaplain, why are they picking on us?" inmate Dixon asked.

Tom Harris held up his Bible. "I would like to help myself with this Book instead of gambling for cokes and candies like those guys over there," he said, pointing to the visiting room.

I didn't know what to say. It was my first day back to work and I had no idea what was behind the memo. I was caught in the middle. On the one hand, I had to give the appearance that I supported the administration. On the other hand, I felt a responsibility to challenge directives I felt were contrary to policy. I needed time. I listened to the complaints of the various inmates and promised to answer them as soon as I talked to staff. Some told me about letters they had sent to their Congressmen that week. Others preferred not to talk, but had already put their complaints in writing. They handed me their "cop-outs" (inmates' requests to staff) asking for the reinstatement of religious programs.

It didn't take long for me to discover that my supervisor's decree was contrary to current Bureau policy. I also knew that there was no way I could answer all the request forms in the required length of time and in a way that would support the staff, knowing that each answer would have to hold up under the scrutiny of the courts, if necessary. I explained this to Ms. Thompson and gave her the requests to answer. Looking at them, she blasted, "Who gave you the authority to give me work assignments?"

"I feel that your memo is against Bureau's policy, and since you issued it you should be the one to respond to the cop-outs, which must be answered within a prescribed time and prepared as if we were going to court."

It was hard to follow Thompson's "policy" laid out for me while providing rehabilitation programs, dealing with the struggle of the human spirit, and doing God's work. Each day I prayed for strength to make the most of some difficult working conditions.

God answers prayers in unusual ways. I knew that Marjorie Thompson and Joe Peters would not allow my challenge of her authority to go unanswered. I just didn't know what they would do. The answer came about a month later, when Superintendent Peters called me at home. Without the usual salutation, and in an irritated tone, he told me I was being transferred to Eglin. After a pause, he continued in a caustic tone: "I can't have someone working for me who is on the side of the inmates." I refuted his statement. "Joe, you know that isn't true. I've obeyed every directive you and Ms. Thompson have issued. But I understand your support of your assistant."

Despite its abruptness and tone, Peters' call was good news. I was grateful for the transfer, and I gave God the glory and the praise, for He protects his own. Some say good fortune opens doors, but I say God makes doors out of brick walls. God knew that, at 61, I was bone tired of dancing with bureaucracy on top of a three-hour daily commute, and that, at the end of each day, I arrived home drained and soul weary.

After I hung up the phone, I wondered if Eglin was going to have three Chaplains. That seemed unlikely. More realistically, someone would be transferred. Would it be Stephen Johnson or Arthur Becton? Normally, that's what would happen, but in this instance another intrigue was taking place. Pastor Richard Dortch, president of Jim and Tammy Bakker's PTL, was incarcerated at Eglin after being convicted of mail and wire fraud in connection with offering lifetime partnerships on television. It was alleged that he and Chaplain Stephen Johnson had

George entering "Quinlan Chapel"

George in "Quinlan Chapel"

become friendly and that Chaplain Johnson had requested gifts from him. As a result, Chaplain Johnson had to leave Eglin and he resigned from the Bureau of Prisons.

Heaven Came Early

On Sunday, June 28, 1992, I returned to one of the best Chapels in the Bureau. During my three-and-one-half-years' absence, Chaplain Arthur Becton had successfully completed his training under Chaplain Johnson, and we began working together with a secretary shared with the Psychology Department. An impossible dream had materialized!

God does work in mysterious ways. I feel strongly that God works through people, but I am convinced that He also works through all His creations. God used termites to achieve what years of audit recommendations, Chaplains' pleadings, and prayers hadn't accomplished. Not long after I had left Eglin for Saufley Field, an inspection showed that the old Chapel had become so infested with termites that it was no longer repairable. Therefore, Eglin got a new Chapel, with a large sanctuary, office space, a library, classrooms, and all the modern amenities that had been dreamed about and hoped for. My cup overflowed at its dedication on August 20, 1992.

Blessings continued to flow at Eglin. Having another Chaplain in the camp allowed me to take a three-week vacation and concentrate on matters at hand without dealing with a backlog upon my return. Chaplain Arthur Becton made this possible. My excellent relationship with Chaplain Becton and the administration allowed me to serve my final year at Eglin in as close to a stress-free and pleasant environment as is possible inside a prison. Each week, Becton and I took time to plan, enjoy our fellowship, and minister to one another. We made sure that Chaplaincy services were always available for inmates and staff. Our joint ministry and alliance demonstrated the importance — indeed, the need — for having two Chaplains.

During this time Ms. Thompson was transferred to Miami Metropolitan Community Center and Peters retired.

George and Warden Larry Cox

Chaplaincy, a Life-Saving Ministry

The Sunday after my return from vacation, inmate Robert Lasiter came to my office with a swollen red face and tear-filled eyes.

"Bob, what's the matter?" I asked anxiously.

"It's my mother, Chaplain."

Fearing that she had passed, I waited a moment until he was ready to begin talking again.

"I've been trying to call her for the last day-and-a-half, and I can't get any answer. I'm worried because she lives by herself."

"Hold on, Bob. Has she been ill?"

"Yes, she's 85 years old and a diabetic."

"Give me her number." I got the same non-response. Trying to keep calm, I then asked, "Do you have any relatives or friends who live nearby that I can call?"

"Mrs. Smith lives across the street, but I don't know her telephone number."

The information operator wouldn't provide Mrs. Smith's unlisted telephone number.

Ah, my United Church of Christ Year Book, I thought. Thumbing through the pages, I located two churches near her home. I called The Reverend Robert Hudder, Pastor of Melbourne Congregational Church, the closer one. After I identified myself and stated our concern, Mr. Hudder assured me that he would act promptly on my request to visit the senior's home.

Less than an hour after I talked with Mr. Hudder, a different Bob returned to my office. This time, with tears of joy, he told me, "Chaplain, I just talked to my mother. Church people found her in the bathtub, where she was stuck since Friday. Thank God and thank you. "She's fine. She's weak, but not as hungry as she thought she would be. She's going to be okay," he said with relief.

I was gratified that Eglin Federal Prison Camp's Religious Department, with the help of other caring people, may have saved a life.

Winding Down

By Christmas, the Okaloosa County community was aware that I had returned to Eglin. They assumed the "Needy Children's Christmas Party" would be reinstated, and I was bombarded with calls from parents and foster parents asking that their children be invited to the party. Unfortunately, for the last three years the party had been a thing of the past, and I didn't reinstate it upon my return.

As in previous years, the beginning of the new year found me in prayer, thanking God for the past, and asking for guidance to meet the future. I didn't know then how much that guidance would be needed the next month, when my eldest brother, Jimmy, had a fatal stroke.

To alleviate some of my grief, I worked in my yard as I wrestled with the meaning of life. Silently, I praised and thanked God for my brother's commitment and faithfulness to our God and his family. Questions popped into my mind. *If he hadn't sponsored me to the United States, what kind of person would I have been? What would I have been doing? Would I have become a Chaplain? Would I have met Muriel, my wife of 36 years, and become the father of attorney Marcelle Angela Castillo and the role model for our two fine sons?* Of course, I couldn't answer these questions. But I could resolve to BE MYSELF, DO GOOD TO ALL PERSONS WHO CROSS MY PATH, AND LEAVE THE REST TO GOD. LET GOD BE GOD, AND I'LL BE HIS SERVANT.

On Thursday, February 24, 1993, Jimmy's funeral service was held at Janes United Methodist Church in Brooklyn, New York. My heart hurt at my loss. The emotional pain and the emptiness were far greater than any physical pain I ever had. My only relief was the promise that we would meet again.

As life cycles change, we go from the valley to the mountaintop. Three months later, on Saturday, May 8, 1993, Peggy May, senior staff writer for the *Northwest Florida Daily News*, wrote an article about me and told about a retirement party to be held for me that evening at the First Baptist Church of Fort Walton Beach. At that time I was blessed by one of the most beautiful and meaningful events of my Chaplaincy. The retirement party was a cooperative effort sponsored by Prison Fellowship, former inmates, and volunteers. About 200 guests attended the celebration. Among them were family, pastors, staff, volunteers, and friends, including many former inmates who came with their spouses from other states. One of them, the Reverend Harold Thompson, attended with his wife Mary. In 1973, I had met them in Atlanta Federal Penitentiary, where Harold was an active member of the Christian community. He had a 105-year sentence and spent 17 years in prison. Upon his release, Campus Crusade for Christ sponsored his ministry. To this day he continues to serve as one of their ministers. Harold is a fine, decent human being whose life proves that one can live a good, useful, productive life after incarceration.

One of our biggest surprises was the presence of Dave and Gerri Jellison — the first couple I ever united in holy matrimony. They were wed at the First United Methodist Church in Brewer, Maine, in 1965. The family later honored me by asking that I perform their daughter Connie's wedding.

My family and I were touched by the tributes paid to me. My eyes and heart were full when former inmates from Eglin and Pensacola Federal Prison Camps and Atlanta Federal Penitentiary repeated over and over in their own words: *Chaplain, you had a positive effect on me. You were my teacher and inspiration. Through your encouragement, you showed me a new way of life. Thank you.*

I fought back tears as I listened to the accolades. Indeed, having loving friends is one of the rewards of the ministry. As I touched lives, my life, too, was touched and enriched. Silently, I whispered repeatedly: *To God be the Glory for the Wonderful Things He Has Done. I am truly blessed to be able to savor my roses while I yet live!*

On Saturday, June 26, 1993, my family and I were again feted at a retirement party, this one given by friends and co-workers of Eglin Federal Prison Camp. Warden John Hahn stated, "This is the largest employees' retirement party I remember."

My wife and I were given lovely gifts, the usual plaques and letters from the Bureau, and a surprise letter from President and Mrs. Bill Clinton. As my 20 years with the Bureau were coming to a close, I reflected on the good times, the not-so-good times, and the things I had tried to accomplish. I can truly say that I am grateful to the Bureau of Prisons for the opportunity it

George Castillo, Dave Jellison, Gerri Jellison, and Muriel.
The Jellisons were the first couple I joined in Holy Matrimony

George, Col. Stanley Jarrett, Ret., and Dr. James Monroe, Pas-
tor Emeritus at First Baptist Church, in Ft. Walton Beach, FL.

Guests at Retirement Party

provided me to grow and serve in the capacity I love — the Chaplaincy. In all my sermons, I had tried to lift the congregants' spirits by assuring them of their worth.

> God is counting on you to do His will, not only when you get home, but right here and right now. Some people may call your religion 'Jail House Religion' and doubt your sincerity. Others will be convinced that because you've been in prison, God will not use you. That is not so. We are here on earth for a purpose. Yes, even in prison and beyond, God uses us for His Glory and Kingdom if we remain in accordance with His will and obey His commandments.

Four days later, on June 30, 1993, I signed my retirement papers with the satisfaction that I had answered my call to the best of my ability. A short time later, Mary Lane, one of our neighbors, wrote in a letter: "I've never known more caring people than George and his wife. At the dinner, while talking to former prisoners, I learned how he helped them get through their sentences, without becoming despondent, by the faith he imparted to them. His love saved them from becoming bitter and unforgiving. He rescued them so they could start their lives anew."

THE WHITE HOUSE

WASHINGTON

June 14, 1993

Chaplain George R. Castillo
Elgin AFB, Florida

Dear Chaplain Castillo:

Congratulations on your retirement from the
Federal Bureau of Prisons.

America's tradition of hard work has made
our country strong, and you can be proud of your
contribution to that legacy. Your dedication to
the public is an inspiration to others. On behalf
of all those who have benefited from your service,
I thank you for a job well done.

Hillary and I wish you good health and every
future success.

Sincerely,

Bill Clinton

EPILOGUE

Retirement is wonderful! It gives me an opportunity to do some of the things I love, like fishing, serving our community, and fellowshiping with brothers of Prince Hall Free and Accepted Masons. Retirement also gives Muriel and me time to do more things together, like travelling to her Delta Sigma Theta's sorority conventions.

My extra time enables me to minister to shut-ins and the unchurched while maintaining my ecclesiastical standings with the United Church of Christ and Christian Church, Disciples of Christ. I'm also able to say "Yes" to most preaching invitations and actively participate in local ministerial associations. Additionally, I serve on the boards of the Mental Health Association of Okaloosa and Walton Counties and the Greater Peace Missionary Baptist Church's Community Love Center. My time also goes to the First National Bank and Trust Minority Small Business Loan Advisory Committee and the Head Start Policy Council. This Council is very important to me because I'm convinced we must give our young people a good mental, physical, and emotional start. Hopefully, if young people receive proper training, nutrition, and nurturing, our prisons will be less full. If we value our future, we'll value our children.

I haven't completely abandoned prison work. Upon request, I conduct services at the Eglin prison camp; additionally, I am a leader and teacher for Prison Fellowship Seminars. Also I volunteer as Chaplain of the National Association of Retired Federal Employees, Chapter 1428.

Being free to say "Yes" also means my being able to minister without restrictions. While a Chaplain, I performed several inmates' marriages, but I am generally opposed to men getting married while they are incarcerated. I feel if the commitment is strong enough, the parties should wait until the incarcerated is released so that husband and wife can live together. On the other hand, I realize that sometimes marriage is necessary for a family's survival. I think of an instance when a marriage certificate was required to enable children of a union to receive welfare assistance and for the wife to transact legal matters while the father/husband was incarcerated.

Since I retired, I have had the great satisfaction of performing the marriage of Richard and Sherrie Johnson. I got a surprise call from Richard one afternoon as I relaxed at home. "Chappie, I want you to know how much I appreciate what you have been to me and Sherrie during my confinement. I've done my time and I'm free now. Will you do us the honor and perform our wedding?"

"Praise God," were the most appropriate words that I could utter. After the impact of his statement sunk in, I continued: "Richard, I've been waiting for this. Yes, I'll be delighted to perform your wedding. You have a good partner." (Proverbs 18:22 - He who finds a wife, finds a good thing, and obtains favor from the Lord.)

Friends rejoiced with the happy couple on that beautiful Friday afternoon in September 1994 when I united them in Holy Matrimony. I was delighted that the past was gone and a bright future with all its possibilities lay ahead. When Richard was incarcerated at Pensacola, I had witnessed the numerous rollercoaster emotions those two people experienced. I counseled and consoled Richard through his tears, fears, hurt, and frustration when Sherrie was ill and he couldn't be there for her. As soon as she recovered, Richard got ill and was shipped temporarily to Springfield Medical Hospital in Missouri. She couldn't join him there, but their love and commitment remained strong. It never wavered during those seven years of Richard's incarceration. Sherrie is indeed a "shero" who gave up her home, job, and family security in order to be with her Richard on visiting days.

Welcome Home, Good and Faithful Servant

One of the nicest parts of being fully retired from both the military reserves and the Chaplaincy is having the freedom to continue serving God and my fellow man, and to vacation without a deadline. This freedom enabled Muriel and me to start a working vacation in Belize on September 29, 1993. I realized then that indeed my life had come full circle. I was going back home to minister.

As the plane cruised, my eyes were closed and my thoughts were filled with *Thanksgiving* to God for His Mercy and Blessings. Forty-one years ago, at age twenty-one, I left the country of my birth with the burning desire to become a Christian Minister.

With my dream realized, I was returning to conduct the Thanksgiving Harvest services in my home Methodist Circuit. *How blessed I am to have realized my goal and have an opportunity to share with my people not only material possessions but also spiritual food.*

When Muriel and I cleared customs in Belize City, we received our first surprise. My brother Charles and childhood friend Victor "Tush" Francisco were waiting to drive us "home" to Dangriga, the heart of the Carib community. Before leaving the city, I met with the Reverend Otto Wade, Chairman and General Superintendent of the Belize/Honduras District of the Methodist Church, who welcomed my services as interim minister for the month.

Our journey then took us through the new capital, Belmopan, which is lovely. But further down the road our chatter diminished with the discomfort of the bad road from Belmopan to Dangriga. As we bounced into Dangriga, I was amazed to see its growth. Former swamplands now accommodate new homes. Despite the changes and hurricane Hatti's major damage in 1961, several of my landmarks remained — such as the bridges, the hospital, and the police station, whose clock Uncle Gus, Public Works Chief Mechanic, and I set and repaired 45 years earlier. I was the only one he had entrusted with the technical knowledge needed to repair the clock. I was happy to see it still running.

Our next surprise came while viewing cable television at my sister's home. This announcement flashed on the screen: "OUR OWN CHAPLAIN GEORGE R. CASTILLO WILL BE HONORED AT A SPECIAL WELCOME HOME SERVICE ON FRIDAY OCTOBER 1, AT 7:00 P.M. AT THE METHODIST CHURCH."

The following Sunday, in Dangriga Methodist Church, three services were held for Harvest Thanksgiving. At 9:00 a.m. children marched down the aisle and placed canned goods and various fresh products, including golden plums, citrus fruits, yams, bananas, and flowers, on the altar. These gifts were an expression of thanks to God for the bountiful harvest.

At 3:00 p.m., young adults marched in procession with gifts to thank the Almighty. That evening at 7:00 p.m., the older members of the church, representing various organizations, marched. Muriel and I marched with them. Emotion nearly overcame me as the Garifuna drummers marched and sang in our native tongue. Songs which stirred my ancestors were dedicated to me, "a son who made good and returned home." The joys of my youth returned with each song. Just as I remembered, the gifts were sold to the public early next morning.

Being the district's only circuit minister, I conducted Harvest Services in the villages of Gales Point, Sittee River, and Mullins River. As a child, I had thought of these villages as distant lands; we could only reach them by dory since there were no roads. Now, I was following the footsteps of my childhood ministers by serving these same communities. I also conducted services in the Silk Grass community, which was established after hurricane Hatti. It was a humbling experience.

I enjoyed every minute of preaching, performing baptisms, and blessing homes. However, the most spiritually rewarding moments came when I visited senior citizens, the sick, and the shut-ins. As I prayed and administered the Sacrament of Holy Communion to them, I thanked God for these Saints. Directly and indirectly, some had nurtured me during the first 21 years of my life. They had provided the basic foundation for America to build upon!

Yes, one can go home again! I did, and I enjoyed advantages of Belize that I couldn't afford as a young man. For instance, Muriel and I loved snorkeling at Ambergris Cay and were fascinated with the underwater scenery of the Barrier Reef. In the evening, we relaxed in the quaint, quiet beauty of San Pedro. The mountains of Toledo District reminded me of God's creativeness. How true are the words of the Psalmist: "For a thousand years in thy sight are but yesterday when it is past, or as a watch in the night." (Psalm 90:4).

However, the trip down memory lane was bitter at times as well as sweet. In Punta Gorda, I was delighted to meet Mrs. Olympia Vernon. She remembered my Uncle Luther and grandfather Peter J. Velasquez, who almost fifty years earlier had made chairs for her family which are still being used. Muriel took a photograph of us standing between two of the chairs. It was sad, however, to become reacquainted with schoolmate Henry Genus, who was the smartest boy in our school. He was full of emotional pain and regret as he said, "George, I stayed and am still here struggling."

Harvest Thanksgiving service, Dangriga Methodist Church, October, 1993

Mullins River, Belize School/Church. Left: Angus Cayetano, Fred Francisco, and George

Mrs. Olympia Vernon, and George in Punta Gorda, Belize with chairs George's grandfather made. They are still being used after 50 years.

Yes, God has been good to me. I felt a sense of personal satisfaction and triumph for breaking from my past as I visited Alta Vista and Pomona Valley Citrus Companies, where I once worked for fifteen cents an hour. As I toured the Agricultural Station, I well remembered the hardships I had endured on my first job for a sixty-cents-a-day wage. I empathized with the misery I saw while watching agricultural workers swing their machetes to level the tall grasses in an attempt to keep Belize's lush vegetation under control. I also empathized with the men working into late evening in unbearable heat and humidity to repair the roads. I said to myself: *There was I, and there I might have remained in those jobs were it not for the Grace of God.*

Advancement and progress always carry a price. I felt mixed joy and pain as I saw what "progress" had brought to Belize. Modernization meant that students no longer had to awaken at 4:00 a.m. to perform farm chores and bring water from the river for household use before beginning school at 9:00. Unfortunately, however, their high unemployment and their rampant drug use had stolen many of the young people's gains.

Yes, going home had brought me full circle. As I looked down from the pulpit and bade so long to my people, I whispered a prayer for God's blessings on them.

Muriel and I returned to our beloved America which, indeed, to me is home, the land of opportunity. Here, also, I intend to repay my good fortune by accepting the challenges to serve and help others. That is my plan for the future.

Changes Need To Be Made

My twenty years of service with the Federal Bureau of Prisons taught me a lot, and the Bureau was good to me. I worked with very good supervisors and co-workers, and some that could be classified as tyrants. I saw inmates from all races, colors, and creeds prove that God still has the power to change the hardest heart. My philosophy in dealing with people was, and still is: "We show our divinity by our humanity in treating others with respect and dignity. Everyone is a child of God." I see the Spirit of God in every human being. When an inmate walked into my office, I did not treat him just as an inmate, but as a child of God made in God's image.

Inmates appreciated my treating them with respect and dignity. With the respect I accorded them, many decided to give God a chance. As one inmate put it, "I've tried everything. Why not try God?" My messages were based on the life and teaching of Jesus, where there are lessons for living a better life, forgiveness, salvation, hope, and eternal life. However, since guilt predominates in prison, I concentrated my counseling primarily in alleviating guilt.

My years of service would not be complete or meaningful if I did not share my strong belief that we ought to:

• Treat every person as an expression of God. In doing so, we'll treat one another with respect.

• Learn to forgive. No matter what we have done, God still loves us. We need to love and forgive each other.

• Allow non-violent first offenders to serve their communities instead of doing prison time. This would keep families together, and could save many individuals from becoming bitter and less-than-desirable citizens upon their release. As a bonus, the Federal government would save over $57.00 a day, the cost to keep each non-violent offender incarcerated.

• Require inmates to learn marketable skills that they can use to earn an honest living upon their release.

These recommendations become more important as our prison populations grow. According to the Justice Department's latest statistics, as reported in *Northwest Florida Daily News* on August 19, 1996, the number of men and women in jails and prisons more than doubled since 1985. The Federal Bureau of Prisons operated 26 percent over capacity in 1995, while state prison systems reported operating between 14 and 25 percent above capacity.

With God's Help, I Press On

My time between the cross and the bars has come to an end. I now look forward to the next chapter and what God has in store for me. As I enter the next phase of my life, I claim the challenge that Saint Paul wrote to the church of Philippi, which is recorded in Philippians 3:12-14, New Contemporary English Version:

I have not yet reached my goal, and I am not perfect. But Christ has taken hold of me. So I keep on running and struggling to take hold of the prize. My friends, I don't feel that I have already arrived. But I forget what is behind, and I struggle for what is ahead. I run toward the goal, so that I can win the prize of being called to heaven. This is the prize that God offers because of what Christ Jesus has done.

Grace and Peace

September 6, 1996

With Thanks.

From Your

FPC Eglin

Family

My Life Between

The

Cross and Bars

by

Rev. George R. Castillo

Mail to:

G. & M. Publications

PO Box 657

Shalimar, FL 32579

Please send me _____ copies at..............$21.95 each $ _____

Plus postage and handling........................3.50 each $ _____

Enclosed is check or money-order................TOTAL $ _____

Name _____

Address _____

City _____ State _____ Zip _____

Make check payable to: G. & M. Publications   850-651-3103

E-Mail: g-mpub@gnt.net

Web address: http://www.angelcities.com/members/gmpub

Mail to:

G. & M. Publications

PO Box 657

Shalimar, FL 32579

Please send me _____ copies at..............$21.95 each $ _____

Plus postage and handling........................3.50 each $ _____

Enclosed is check or money-order................TOTAL $ _____

Name _____

Address _____

City _____ State _____ Zip _____

Make check payable to: G. & M. Publications   850-651-3103

E-Mail: g-mpub@gnt.net

Web address: http://www.angelcities.com/members/gmpub

Mail to:

G. & M. Publications

PO Box 657

Shalimar, FL 32579

Please send me _____ copies at..............$21.95 each $ _____

Plus postage and handling........................3.50 each $ _____

Enclosed is check or money-order................TOTAL $ _____

Name _____

Address _____

City _____ State _____ Zip _____

Make check payable to: G. & M. Publications   850-651-3103

E-Mail: g-mpub@gnt.net

Web address: http://www.angelcities.com/members/gmpub

Mail to:

G. & M. Publications

PO Box 657

Shalimar, FL 32579

Please send me _____ copies at..............$21.95 each $ _____

Plus postage and handling........................3.50 each $ _____

Enclosed is check or money-order...............TOTAL $ _____

Name _____

Address _____

City _____ State _____ Zip _____

Make check payable to: G. & M. Publications   850-651-3103

E-Mail: g-mpub@gnt.net

Web address: http://www.angelcities.com/members/gmpub

- -

Mail to:

G. & M. Publications

PO Box 657

Shalimar, FL 32579

Please send me _____ copies at..............$21.95 each $ _____

Plus postage and handling........................3.50 each $ _____

Enclosed is check or money-order...............TOTAL $ _____

Name _____

Address _____

City _____ State _____ Zip _____

Make check payable to: G. & M. Publications   850-651-3103

E-Mail: g-mpub@gnt.net

Web address: http://www.angelcities.com/members/gmpub

- -

Mail to:

G. & M. Publications

PO Box 657

Shalimar, FL 32579

Please send me _____ copies at..............$21.95 each $ _____

Plus postage and handling........................3.50 each $ _____

Enclosed is check or money-order...............TOTAL $ _____

Name _____

Address _____

City _____ State _____ Zip _____

Make check payable to: G. & M. Publications   850-651-3103

E-Mail: g-mpub@gnt.net

Web address: http://www.angelcities.com/members/gmpub